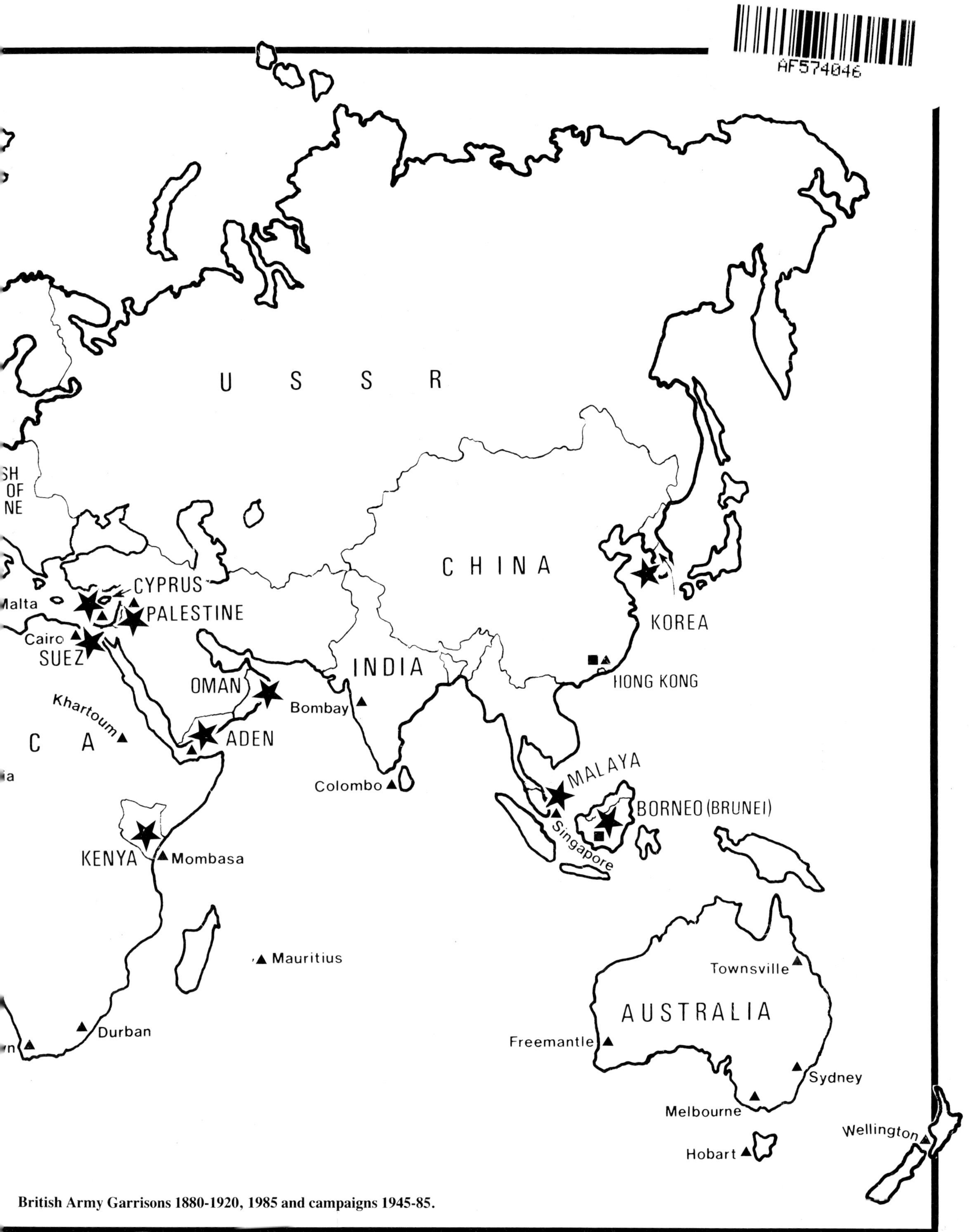

British Army Garrisons 1880-1920, 1985 and campaigns 1945-85.

The British Army in the 20th Century

1895; Cpl Long, of the 17th Lancers.

The British Army in the 20th Century
Ian V. Hogg
LONDON
IAN ALLAN LTD

First published 1985

ISBN 0 7110 1505 8

Published by Ian Allan Ltd, Shepperton, Surrey; and printed by Ian Allan Printing Ltd at their works at Coombelands in Runnymede, England

Front cover:
Chieftain. *Simon Forty*

Contents

Left:
A Sapper of the RE Electrical Engineers in 1901.

Introduction and Acknowledgements

When one contemplates the many multi-volume histories of the British Army which had appeared even prior to World War 1, or the multi-volume history of the Royal Artillery by General Headlam, it becomes obvious that attempting to deal with even a limited area of the history of the British Army in this number of pages can only result in a rather idiosyncratic overview. The aim has been to record, in a brief manner, the technological development of the Army in the years since the Industrial Revolution first began to make its mark, signposting this development at various points by reference to the general condition of the Army as a whole. Under a different hand the story could have been written totally differently, and I trust that readers will appreciate that what is seen here is simply one man's view.

In considering the technological changes which the army has seen, it is as well to begin by remembering that until 1914 (and, to some extent, until 1939) the British Army was primarily considered as a system for policing and protecting the British Empire. Thus the 1880s and 1890s saw immense technical effort put into developing coast defence artillery because the coaling stations upon which the Royal Navy (and thus the Empire's communications) depended had to be fortified against similar technical developments in warships. On the other hand the basic infantry weapon was, if not neglected, at least regarded with a less critical eye, since the likely enemy was unlikely to be very technically advanced. Against the Mahdi's legions, the heavy Maxim machine gun was perfectly adequate; against the Imperial German Army in 1914-18 it proved to be cumbersome, and led to the adoption of light machine guns, something which had been technically possible since 1903 but not, apparently, desirable.

When Mr Haldane began his celebrated reform of the Army in 1906, his brief was simply to make the army, in modern parlance, more cost-effective; indeed, to economise on defence as far as he could. But by regarding the army and its role with a fresh eye, and in the light of foreign relations as they stood at that time, he was among the first to realise that sooner or later the British Army was going to have to abandon its traditional role and prepare itself for continental warfare. And so in the course of reorganising for economy he was able to reorganise in such a manner that a coherent structure for modern warfare was realised. The army which went to war in 1914 owed its initial success to Haldane and its eventual survival depended largely upon his system being intelligently applied.

Technically, the army owed much to its own experiences in South Africa and to the reported experiences of the combatants in Manchuria in 1904. In both these wars modern armament — the machine gun, the magazine rifle and the quick-firing artillery piece — showed their capabilities and, contrary to received legend, most of the lessons were assimilated by the soldiers. As

Below:
The quick-firing 18pdr gun, standard divisional field gun, with a No 4 firing platform. The platform was introduced experimentally in 1918; it gave a firm and smooth base around which the gun could be rapidly swung to fire against moving targets such as tanks, and it became standard with the later 25pdr gun.

Above:
A typical trench scene in 1917, with the Lewis light machine gun as the focus of attention.

has always been the case, embodiment of these lessons into weapons, and embodiment of the weapons into a tactical doctrine, depended entirely upon the whims of the purse-holders, and it was finance which governed the army's emergence into modern warfare.

The outbreak of war in 1914 cut the purse-strings, but revealed the problems of harnessing the national industrial base to wartime production. Prior to 1914 the government armaments factories, assisted by a few private contractors, were capable of sustaining the limited warfare of the time. But the 'nation in arms' concept, which had never really affected Britain before, and the vast army which had to be assembled and equipped in order to fight on the continent, suddenly made the supply of armaments so demanding that industry had to be mobilised. It might be noted that this industrial mobilisation was not peculiar to Britain; the other combatants were also caught out by the enormous demands, which was perhaps just as well otherwise British industry would not have had the breathing space in which to set up tooling and begin production.

The 1914-18 war brought several new weapons into use, but the one which caught the public's fancy — and the fancy of a lot of military commentators — was the tank. Not, to be sure, a war-winning weapon — as was often said at the time — but a weapon of vast potential. Unfortunately there were several different views as to what that potential was, and the inter war years are often seen as being a long drawn-out wrangle between the tank supporters and their opponents. This did happen, but one should not lose sight of the fact that a great deal of other weapon development and tactical thinking went on at the same time, concealed from view by the smoke and flame of the tank controversy. And in spite of all the argument, the one major reform — general mechanisation of the army — went through with little opposition, with the result that in 1939 the British Army was the only completely mechanised army in the world. True, there were those who bitterly resented the passing of the horse, but they were a good deal fewer than is commonly supposed; very few of the rank and file lamented the horse's departure — they had had to feed, water and groom the wretched animals, and with that chore removed their days had far more free time than ever before and their environment smelt somewhat sweeter.

But the tank controversy brought to light one peculiar feature, which had been remarked upon the in past; that nobody had ever stood up and given an unequivocal statement of the British army's purpose in life. What was it for? Where was it to be trained to fight? *Who* was it to be trained to fight? And an army without a well-defined role is an army incapable of developing its full potential, since it cannot know what armaments it should adopt, what formations it should practise, what tasks it should train for. Fortunately for the British, the question was answered by Herr Hitler, and after 1936 there was little doubt in anyone's mind as to what the next war would entail.

However, although there was what might be called a 'grass-roots' comprehension, there was still no formal declaration, and this lack of defined purpose had its effect on the development of the tank in British service. Without a defined philosophy of warfare, without a policy statement of precisely how the army would operate, it was difficult to specify the sort of tank that would be required. The theorists had a field day, financial stringency gutted the design offices, and Britain went to war with a rag-bag of ill-conceived and poorly engineered tanks.

If this uncertainty caused damage to the armoured strength, it had far less effect, fortunately, on the other 'teeth arms'. The infantry and artillery were fairly certain that whatever role they were to be called upon to play, their tactics would be more or less the same, and they were thus able to organise, equip and train with rather more certainty. As a result these two arms were able to face the war with excellent weapons, sound doctrines and, perhaps most important of all, an adequate communications system. World War 1 was unique in one respect in that it was the one war in which the commanders had little or no communication with the commanded once the battle was joined. Prior to 1914 the battles had been small enough to permit direct voice command or, at worst, the issue of orders by runners. From 1914 to 1918 the size of the battle and the intensity of fire rendered both these expedients useless and led to the imposition of rigid timetables on the participating troops; rigid not from a mere disciplinary demand but so that the commanders would have some idea of what the troops might be doing and where they might be situated at any given time — provided they had managed to adhere to the timetable. Since they rarely managed this, the further a battle went, the less likely was it that the commanders would know what was going on and be capable of giving orders which would affect its outcome.

But by 1939 radio telephony — speech over the air — had been developed to a moderate degree of reliability and units could be commanded by radio. It took some time for this to become established; radio was considered satisfactory for emergencies but to be replaced by telephones and wire whenever possible; moreover there

Left:
Royalty on the gun position. Her Majesty Queen Elizabeth (now the Queen Mother) and Princess Elizabeth (now Queen Elizabeth II) visiting a Mixed Battery RA (male and female personnel) in 1944, during the flying bomb campaign.

was a well-founded fear of the enemy overhearing the transmission. But the rapid movements of 1940 soon showed that radio was a satisfactory day-to-day system, and with the adoption of some rudimentary codes, sufficient to delay enemy understanding until it was too late to matter, radio communication was eventually perfected into a manageable and coherent system which provided a flow of orders downwards and a flow of information upwards. By 1941 commanders could once more command, safe in the knowledge that their orders would reach their destination in time to have some effect, and safe also in knowing precisely where their forces were and what they were doing.

The aftermath of World War 2 differed from the aftermath of former wars in two major respects; firstly, after an initial feeling of freedom, it soon became apparent that there was to be no relaxing of the defences of the western nations; secondly, partly to alleviate the gradual run-down of the army, partly to meet the 'cold war' threat, conscription was retained into peacetime. Both these factors proved to have advantages when, in fairly rapid succession, minor conflicts broke out which demanded the army's presence. These ranged from terrorist campaigns in the Middle East to the full-blown war in Korea, and continued with the Malayan Emergency, the Borneo Confrontation, and similarly euphemistically-titled small wars. And, of course, in 1969 came the running sore of Northern Ireland.

Before this, though, conscription had been abandoned; for one thing it was politically unpopular, and for another the galloping expense of equipping a modern army demanded a sizeable reduction in forces so that the available finance could cover the basic requirements. There was also the unanswerable argument that whereas the army had been maintained at a level of strength sufficient to provide garrisons across the empire, once the empire vanished, as it did fairly rapidly in the 1950s, there were too few tasks for the massive army to perform. Since then the strength of the army has gradually been whittled away on one pretext or another until in 1985 it is lower than it has ever been since the outbreak of the Crimean War.

In answer to this complaint the whittlers point to the fact that the present-day army is more highly-trained, more effectively equipped, and an all-round more professional force than at any time in its history, and it is hard to argue with that after seeing the competence with which the land forces operated in the brief Falklands campaign. The other side of the coin is the staggering cost of equipping this army with the high-technology armament needed to make it effective with so few men. Whereas the infantryman's rifle of the 1890s cost about £5, today's micro-calibre automatic rifle will cost closer to £250; whereas a 10in coast artillery gun and its complicated hydropneumatic mounting cost a few shillings under £10,000 in 1899, the same sum in 1985 would fail to cover the cost of two anti-tank missiles; and the significant difference is that the 10in gun was 'capital plant' with years of service ahead, while the missiles are one-shot expendable munitions.

A notable effect of this escalating cost of weaponry is the growing adoption of artificial methods of simulating the operation of weapons. Instead of learning his trade on the actual weapon or equipment he will use in operations, today's soldier is more likely to train to some fairly high degree of competence on simulators before he is ever given the chance to fire or operate the actual equipment. Even so, these simulation devices are still expensive, and the military procurement authorities of today must do some complicated accounting before they can say where the available cash is to be spent.

The soldier, too, has changed; today's soldier is, by comparison with his 19th century forebear, a highly-educated, technically-oriented man with a mind of his own. This means that he can operate more effectively without immediate supervision, and is less likely to run out of steam in the absence of officers or NCOs to tell him what to do next. It also means that he is alert to what he considers to be fair treatment, and is prone to expect a great deal more from the army in the way of social benefits, from a play-school for his small child to a reasonable pension at the end of his service.

Countries are said to get the governments they deserve; in a similar manner, most countries seem to get the army they deserve. Some countries, and Britain is one of them, seem to get better armies than they deserve; the lack of public and political support which the British Army habitually enjoys in peacetime would ruin lesser armies, but, as the General said, 'it just shoulders its rifle and falls in on parade'.

Acknowledgements
For indirect assistance in preparing this book, in the form of reminiscences of campaigns and prewar days, I ought to thank such men as 'Old' Harry Waller, Vic Tickle, Bert Hazell, Busty Webb, Chota Chettle, Badgie Warren, Tim Hatfield, Sammy Woolmer and many more who were old soldiers when I was a young one, for in the writing I have frequently drawn on things remembered from conversations with them. More direct assistance has been rendered by the Library of the Royal United Services Institute for Defence Studies and the London Library, upon whose combined shelves surely every book ever published on the British Army is to be found. I would particularly thank Peter and Gareth Sprack and Denis Quarmby for their invaluable aid in unearthing old photographs and also Margaret Fall, whose family collection provided some unusual images.

Works of Reference

The number of books about the various aspects of the British Army which have been printed in the past century is enormous, and a complete list would be a waste of time and space, since it would be idle to suggest that every one has been studied in preparing this work. However, for those who wish to delve further into some particular aspect of the Army's development, some notes on suggested books are appended.

Information on the technical aspects of equipment and its adoption into service has largely come from *Lists of Changes in War Materiel and Stores*, a monthly official document which was issued from 1865 to 1966; copies are not easy to find, but may be available in some specialist military libraries and museums. The periodical Treatises on equipment published by the Artillery College — *Treatise on Ordnance, Treatise on Carriages, Treatise on Ammunition* — appeared at roughly 10-year intervals from about 1870 to 1936 and are valuable sources of detailed information on those three subjects. Again, they may be found through libraries, and copies occasionally appear at military book auctions, where they command high prices.

For small arms, *The Lee-Enfield Rifle* by Maj E. G. B. Reynolds (Herbert Jenkins, 1960) is the standard work on the subject. It covers the development of the Army's standard rifle from the 1850s until the late 1940s and also has useful background information on pre-Lee weapons.

Below:
General Sir Reginald Pole-Carey, commanding the 11th Division, watching the crossing of the Modder River, South Africa, 1900.

The Pictorial History of the Machine Gun (Ian Allan, 1971) and *The Pictorial History of the Submachine Gun* (Ian Allan, 1973), both by the late Maj F. W. Hobart are probably the most concise works on these two groups of weapons and the only books in which the available information has been gathered into one place. While they cover the worldwide aspects of their subjects, they have valuable sections on British developments. For postwar small arms development *Military Small Arms of the 20th Century* (Hogg & Weeks, Arms & Armour Press, five editions 1973-1985) and the annual volumes of *Jane's Infantry Weapons* (various editors; Jane's Publishing Co, 1975 onwards) are both recommended.

Artillery development is less well-documented. *Modern Guns & Gunnery* by Bt-Col H. A. Bethell (Cattermole, London, 1904 and 1910) is perhaps the best source of information on the subject as it stood prior to the 1914-18 war. It is primarily devoted to field guns though there are useful sections on howitzers and anti-aircraft weapons in the 1910 edition. *British & American Artillery of World War 2* by I. V. Hogg (Arms & Armour Press, 1978) covers the interwar and 1939-45 wartime developments, while *Jane's Armour and Artillery* by Christopher Foss (Jane's Publishing Co), annually covers the contemporary developments.

The study of uniforms is an enormous subject and has a considerable booklist; to my untutored eye *A History of the Uniforms of the British Army* by C. C. P. Lawson (Peter Davies, Kaye & Ward, 5 vols 1940-67), appears to be perhaps the most exhaustive of the many works available. More specialised, if somewhat less detailed, are *British Infantry Uniforms Since 1660* by Michael Barthorp (New Orchard Editions, 1982) and *The Dress of the Royal Artillery* by D. Alastair Campbell (Arms & Armour Press 1971).

On the social conditions and actual employment of the Army there is an enormous choice, but *The Victorian Army at Home* by A. R. Skelley (Croom Helm, London, 1977) is a highly detailed work covering health, discipline, pay, recruiting and other aspects of military economy during the period 1859-1899. It is also valuable for the pointers it gives for further research and to sources of statistical information. *For Queen and Country* by Brian Farwell (Penguin Books, 1981) is described as a 'social history of the Victorian and Edwardian army' and gives much useful information on recruiting, social questions, education, medical and similar aspects of the army. Also by Brian Farwell, *Queen Victoria's Little Wars* (Penguin, 1973) deals primarily with the various campaigns fought between 1837 and 1900, but also includes much background information on the condition of the army during this period. It has a particularly enlightening appendix on the regimental system. *The British Infantry*

Above:
A Home Guard motorcycle Lewis gun team being inspected by Sir Archibald Sinclair, Secretary-of-State for Air, 27 August 1941. The Lewis gun is converted from an aircraft observer's gun and thus does not have the original barrel jacket.

1660-1945 by Maj F. Myatt (Blandford Press, 1983) is a valuable source of information on the organisation and employment of infantry, throughout the defined period, and it also gives some useful observations on infantry changes in the postwar world. *Gunners at War* by Shelford Bidwell (Arms & Armour, 1970) and *Fire-Power: British Army Weapons and Theories of War 1904-1945*, by Shelford Bidwell & Dominick Graham (G. Allen & Unwin, 1982) are both extremely valuable discussions of artillery employment from 1914 to the present day, and the latter book extends its brief to deal in passing with armour and infantry weapons. For a study of armour and its employment, *Tank Warfare*, by Kenneth Macksey (Hart-Davis, 1971) is a concise and accurate story of the development of tanks and their use in operations from 1916 to the present day, while *The Tank Pioneers*, also by Kenneth Macksey (Jane's, 1981) gives a first-class view of the interwar debates and theories of the tank protagonists and of how the armoured force was developed. For an insight into a rather recondite sphere of military activity, *British Military Intelligence 1870-1914* by Thomas G. Fergusson (Arms & Armour, 1984) covers the substance of its title and also gives a great deal of background information on the Army's development and reorganisation during those years. *The Education of an Army* by Jay Luvaas (Cassell, 1964) describes the principal British writers on military theory from 1815 to 1939 but provides an immense amount of background information on their contemporary army as well.

The Smoke and the Fire by John Terraine (Sidgwick & Jackson, 1980) is primarily devoted to debunking many of the myths which surround World War 1, but it has additional value in providing accurate information on such things as machine gun stocks, tanks and personnel strengths at various times, and particularly in bringing 1914-18 casualty figures into the proper perspective. *British Generalship in the 20th Century* by Maj-Gen E. K. G. Sixsmith (Arms & Armour Press, 1970) covers from the Army reorganisation after the South African War to the aftermath of World War 2 and discusses the general officers and their conduct of operations. A professional analysis, it avoids the polemics of more popular works and is the better for it.

In the matter of campaigns the choice is limitless and it would be invidious to attempt to recommend specific books about World War 1 and 2. *Britain and Her Army 1509-1970* by Corelli Barnett (Penguin 1970, 1974) is a first-class overview of the Army's progress and has succinct descriptions of major campaigns. For the Korean War, *Now Thrive the Armourers* by Robert Holles (Harrap 1952) is fiction based on fact, but is probably the best and most evocative description of the British Army of the period that can be found, while *Suez 1956: Operation Musketeer* by Robert Jackson (Ian Allan, 1980) gives a view of the Army in the mid-1950s.

1 Wellington's Legacy

The end of the Crimean War found the British Army in a peculiar position; as usual at the end of a successful war the rank and file were being hailed as heroes, but, unusually, the generals, the staff and the entire hierarchy of command almost without exception were being reviled as bunglers and worse. The root of the trouble lay in the gross mismanagement of the campaign which, though possibly not much worse that any previous campaign so far as the conditions under which the soldiers fought were concerned, was exposed in all its awfulness to the public gaze due to the attentions of the press, in particular the reports in *The Times* by William Russell. The stamp tax on newspapers had been repealed shortly before the war, and this, together with a move towards popular education, had increased the readership of newspapers with the result that Russell's reports were picked up and, perhaps with embellishments, spread throughout the country. Never before in British history had a campaign been so assiduously reported to the population at home, and certainly never before had the shortcomings of the military establishment been subjected to such criticism. From the Houses of Parliament down to the local pot-house, the cry was for reform.

Reform, however, is easy to demand, rather less easy to perform. It requires some well-defined aim and beyond the somewhat nebulous aim of 'improving things' the various voices for reform had very little useful to offer. The British Army was running on the same lines that it had been run for the previous century or more. It invariably won its wars; it had won this latest war. Yes, things might have been better organised, there were a few areas which could be improved, but wholesale reform? Towards what? By what means? To what end?

In fact the cries for reform after the Crimea began a constant movement of organisation and reorganisation which has virtually never stopped since then. One is reminded of Sir William Robertson's report of a comment made to him in the early 1900s by an elderly general:

'Never forget Robertson, that there are two armies, the Aldershot army and the field army. The former is organised, reorganised and disorganised almost daily; the latter knows nor cares nothing of all this organising; it merely picks up its rifle and falls in on parade.'

To appreciate the scale of this century of organisation, reorganisation and disorganisation, we should therefore begin by examining the army of 1855 and seeing why it required overhauling in the first place.

To lapse into modern jargon, the army of 1855 was not merely built around the 'teeth arms' — infantry, cavalry and artillery — it was virtually nothing but the teeth arms, plus a leavening of engineers. The ancillaries taken for granted today — signals, medical, dental, repair, maintenance, supply, intelligence, records — where these existed at all they were either minor services provided for themselves by individual regiments or the arms or rudimentary services provided by quasi-military organisations. Clothing, for example, was provided by the Army Clothing Depot in Pimlico against the orders of individual commanding officers, but the Army Clothing Depot was not controlled by the War Office, it was an adjunct of the Treasury. Weapons were provided by either the Royal Gun Factory at Woolwich or the Royal Small Arms

Below:
Bringing a 13in Land Service mortar into action, c1850. The squad are raising the shaft of the travelling carriage so as to slide the mortar and its 'bed' on to the ground.

Factory at Enfield or by private contractors, but all these came under the Master-General of the Ordnance whose department was under no obligation to anything the War Office might or might not suggest. So if the Commander-in-Chief decided upon an expeditionary force to some outpost of Empire, then letters had to be written to the Master-General of the Ordnance to tell him, and to request that suitable weapons and ammunition might be provided by such and such a date. Moreover, since the Royal Artillery and the Corps of Engineers were also administered and commanded by the MGO, his permission had to be obtained in order to secure elements of these regiments for the force. And if the MGO decided that one artillery brigade was sufficient, then it was no use the Commander-in-Chief arguing that two would be an improvement, one was offered and one he would get.

Supply of such things as food and clothing to such an expeditionary force would be done by the simple expedient of appointing a 'Commissary-General', a post which did not exist in peacetime but was conjured up only upon mobilisation. The unfortunate appointee (another responsibility of the Treasury) was then expected to devise a system of supply relying entirely upon hired ships and wagons and the resources of the theatre of war. The total absence of anything to be impressed or hired in the Crimea led to the formation of a 'Land Transport Corps', a military-sounding name for what was simply a collection of transport hired in Britain and shipped to the seat of war, but the lesson was so harrowing that the column was retained when the war ended and became the 'Military Train'.

Medical care, such as it was, belonged to the Medical Department which was responsible to the Secretary of State for War. The Secretary of State's office was also responsible for pay — except for the artillery and engineers, who were looked after by the MGO. The ultimate decision on how big the army was to be and how much money it was to have, though, lay not with the Commander-in-Chief, nor with the Treasury, nor yet with the Secretary of State for War but with the Secretary of State for the Colonies.

To make confusion worse, the Commander-in-Chief only had jurisdiction over the troops in Great Britain, and the British Army in India was an entirely different army, even though it was supplied with men from Britain. The Indian Army (by which was meant the combination of British and Indian troops) owed allegiance to the Queen-Empress, but did so by way of the Viceroy's office in Delhi and not the War Office in London. Indeed it has been suggested, with a good deal of justification, that the poor performance of the British Army in the Crimea was largely due to the absence of any Indian Army element which, at that time, was virtually the only British military force experienced in war. This absence was not due to any organisational reason, simply to the fact that Lord Lucan, the Commander-in-Chief in the Crimea, disliked Indian Army officers and refused to have any in his command.

(Strictly speaking the Indian Army did not exist at the time of the Crimean War, since the defence of India lay in the hands of the East India Company, but there was always a leavening of British officers and troops in the 'John Company' regiments. The Indian Army proper was formed as a result of the Indian Mutiny, when the Crown

Below:
The organisation of the British Army in the 1850s. This is a much simplified schematic to show areas of influence — in real life responsibilities were divided or overlapped.

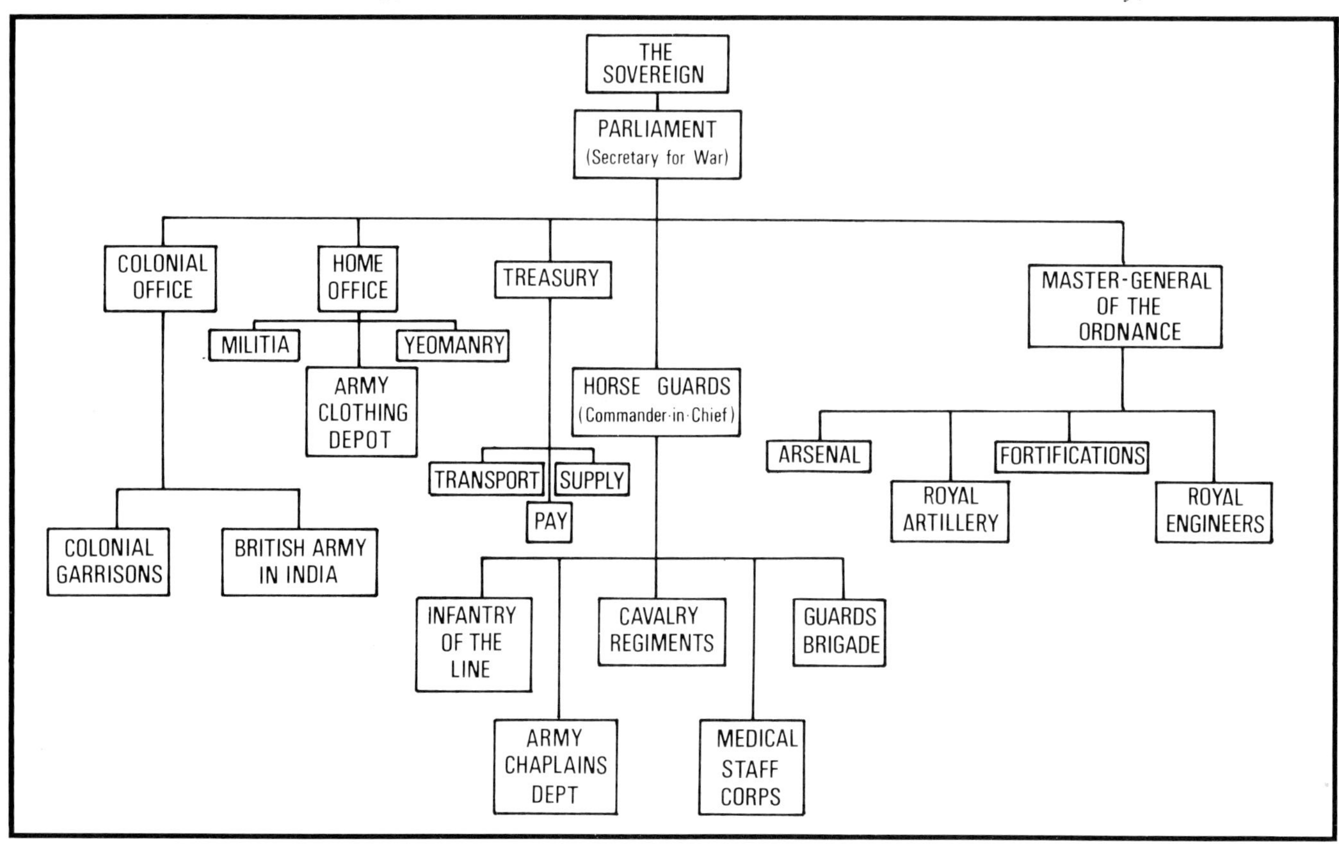

Above:
The boredom of war; a resting mortar crew outside Sebastopol, Crimea, 1854. This, and other photographs by James Robertson, were the first true pictures of war, pictures which belied the heroic flights of artistic fancy hitherto accepted as truth.

assumed the responsibilities previously borne by the Company.)

This hotch-potch of organisation was responsible for the defence of Great Britain, for the defence of much of the Empire, and for finding an expeditionary force when one was required. But the first half of the 19th century had seen a rapid increase in the number of places throughout the world in which a British garrison was necessary, or at least thought to be necessary, until by 1850 fully four-fifths of the British Army was stationed overseas. And once sent abroad a regiment could well expect to stay there for 20 years before it was posted back to England, there to stay for three or four years before being sent off to another 20-year foreign stint. When the Crimean War broke out, the only way that an expeditionary force could be sent to the Black Sea was by scouring the barracks and garrisons of Britain for every able-bodied man. Once this force had been reduced by casualties, as it soon was, there was no way of replacing it from the regular army, since there was no one left. The replacement had to be done by the desperate expedient of using the Militia, which had been reconstituted in 1852, to take over the garrisons in the Mediterranean, so releasing regular troops to feed the Crimea. At the same time the usual expedient for raising men was adopted, the payment of a bounty for enlistment. In this way about 30,000 men were raised, most of them youths, and by the time they were trained sufficiently to take their place in the line the war was all but over.

The two basic demands, then, were firstly to raise and maintain the Regular Army at its allotted strength, and seondly to build up a reserve Army which could be called upon in time of need. This had been addressed in 1847; prior to then enlistment was for life, or at least that much of a man's life that was of value to the army — as soon as he became medically unfit he was discharged. In 1847 this was changed to an initial enlistment of 10 years, after which the man could re-enlist to complete 21 years 'colour service' and thus qualify for a pension. This appeared to be a popular move, and in 1856 the question of forming a reserve was approached. At the end of the 10 years' initial service, the soldier was given the option of going to the 'Army of Reserve' or re-enlisting. This proved to be a failure, and in 1864 the idea was dropped.

What everyone knew, but what many in high office refused to admit, was simply that the soldier was poorly paid, and no man capable of finding employment in civil life was likely to enlist in the army. The basic pay for a private soldier was 1/1d (5½p) per day — £19/15/5d (£19.77p) per year. This was not exactly poverty in 1855, but concealed behind the simple 'shilling a day' slogan was the bitter truth that it was a rare soldier who ever saw 7/7d at the end of the week. There were 'stoppages'. In the first place, rations sufficient for only two meals per day were issued free; the third meal, though provided by the army, had to be paid for — by 'stoppages' from the man's pay. His initial issue of clothing was free, and subsequent replacement of major items — outer clothing and boots — was free, but underwear, handkerchiefs and so forth had to be maintained from the man's pocket — by 'stoppages'. Laundry, haircutting and damage or loss to barrack furniture, boot repairs, alterations to his uniform by the tailor, all had to be paid for, as did some medical treatment, and if the man wished to belong to a regimental library or a sports club, then he was expected to pay for the privilege.

Fortunately there was a regulation which laid down that no matter what the amount of stoppage, the soldier had to receive a minimum of one penny per day; and for some soldiers this was the saving grace which kept them alive. A survey conducted in the 1890s showed that the average private soldier was being mulcted over £7 per annum by stoppages, over one-third of his pay. In spite of complaints, in spite of reasoned argument by commanding officers, in spite of everything, the system of stoppages continued and, in a much modified and reduced degree, continues to this day.

Nevertheless, although the poor pay was obvious to all, it was an uphill struggle to make it any better. A Royal Commission was eventually invited to look into the question and in 1866 recommended an increase of 2d per day, an additional 1d per day for those who re-enlisted, and the elimination of all stoppages. A War Office Committee turned down the proposals, but eventually, in 1867, the increase in pay was granted though the system of stoppages remained. The first major step in the way of improvement came in 1870 when the basic ration became free, thus abolishing the standing 4½d per day stoppage to provide the third meal. The medical care stoppage — paid when in hospital — was reduced from 9d to 7d per day, and good conduct pay became admissible at shorter intervals. To compensate for this, the 2d per day rise granted in 1867 was cancelled.

In return for this pay, of course, the soldier was expected to work, but the work was neither mentally taxing nor particularly rewarding. It consisted simply of drills and fatigues — labouring tasks necessary for the day-to-day functioning of the barrack. This would cover the collection and delivery of coal, sweeping the area, removing rubbish, whitewashing and painting, the menial tasks in the cook-house such as preparing vegetables and washing pots, and the necessary cleaning of the man's own accommodation. The military side of his day would be taken up with foot and arms drills of the most simple kind,

Above:
Officers of the 2nd Battalion, Royal Fusiliers, pose in front of a shot pile at Gibraltar, June 1863.

repeated interminably until they became automatic. These were not just drills devised in order to make the man smart or obedient, they were, quite simply, the basic tactical manoeuvres of the battlefield. In war the troops would march toward the battle in column; on arrival at the battlefield they would require to reform into lines, to form defensive squares, to fire volleys under the command of their officers, reform into columns to move to another part of the field, reform again into line, advance, retire, charge and finally reform into column in order to advance once more. All the various ways of changing formation had been discovered over centuries of manoeuvre and had been codified into simple commands capable of simple execution. These were the subject of the daily drills, so that in one combined package the soldier was disciplined, excercised, and taught the conduct of warlike evolutions. Once a year, perhaps twice, he would be marched to an open space and allowed to discharge his firearm at a target, usually a six-foot screen placed 100 paces away. If he hit it, he qualified as a trained soldier; if not, he was allowed more ammunition until such time as he qualified. Another annual event would be the 'field day' when the regiment marched out to some convenient heath and performed its drill evolutions to simulate an actual battle, perhaps culminating in a volley of blank fire and a rousing bayonet charge. And that was the sum total of his military accomplishment; no lectures on section tactics, no lectures on weapon handling, no training films, no NBC days, no annual exercises lasting days and nights. The only excitement a post-Waterloo soldier could look forward to was the possibility of being called out to suppress a riot, and after the formation of police forces in the 1850s, even this lapsed.

If, of course, he was in the artillery or cavalry, then the training might become more involved, and the day more industrious. Both these arms were provided with horses, so that there was the interminable business of feeding and cleaning these animals, and cleaning their harness and quarters, which took up a good proportion of the day. The cavalryman's training was much like that of the infantryman, endlessly repeated drills, though performed on horseback. The artilleryman had the added interest of cleaning and maintaining his gun and its associated stores, the ammunition limbers and wagons, and the task of drilling — bringing the guns into action, aiming them, loading and firing them (though without ammunition) and taking them out of action again. As with the infantryman, once a year he would have the opportunity of taking the guns to some stretch of countryside and firing them against targets. But there was never any thought of taking elements of all three arms and exercising them together. For most soldiers the only time they ever saw a member of another arm would be either at a review or on the field of battle.

And when the day's drills and fatigues were over and the last horse had been fed and watered and bedded down, what then? The last meal of the day was provided usually at 4pm; tea, bread and the 'unexpired portion' — that part of the day's ration which had not already been eaten. The ration had been laid down in 1813 and remained unchanged for over 50 years: one pound of bread and 12 ounces of meat per man per day. Anything over and above that — potatoes, green vegetables, condiments, tea, butter, cheese — had to be purchased by the regiment and paid for by the soldier by his 4½d a day stoppage. The only addition to this would be whatever the man could afford to buy. As a result the average man's diet was a breakfast at 6.30am of tea and bread; a midday dinner of meat and vegetables, and the four o'clock supper. Cooking facilities were minimal, and the cooks were merely soldiers pressed into the job, with no training other than what they picked up as they went along. Consequently the average diet was a succession of watery stews, since boiling the tough meat was the only way to make it remotely palatable, and no facilities for more ambitious methods of cooking were provided. There was, furthermore, no dining room; an orderly from each barrack room went to the kitchen, collected the rations for the members of the room and carried the food back to the barrack, where it was distributed by the NCO in charge of the room. He then took the dishes back to the kitchen, washed them, and carted them back to the barrack room again.

So having eaten what there was of his evening meal, the soldier was free to amuse himself until 'Lights Out' at 10pm or so. For most, this meant a trip to the 'wet canteen' which sold beer, or the 'dry canteen' which sold coffee and meals, always supposing he could afford either. A man with a few coppers extra could walk out and visit a public house or music-hall, but the Victorian soldier was not held in particularly high esteem and he might well be refused admission if he set his sights on any but the worst specimens of either form of entertainment.

Should the soldier decide to marry, then he was opening the door to a fresh set of problems. In the first place, no soldier could marry without the permission of his commanding officer if he wished to have the union recognised by the army. He could, if he wished, marry without his CO's blessing, but in that case his wife was solely his responsibility; he had to find accommodation for her and support her; if he went overseas she would have to remain at home, there was no method of remitting pay to her and no allowance was made to her. Altogether an unenviable position, yet there were soldiers who risked it, usually because the wife was able to find employment.

For the man who married 'on the strength', things were better — just. He would be allowed rations for his wife and children, accommodation of a sort would be provided, and if he went overseas then, according to the luck of a draw, his family might accompany him or, if they were unlucky and had to remain at home, then allowances were made and perhaps rations provided. In return for these privileges, the woman was expected to contribute by taking in washing, nursing, or some other activity for the benefit of the regiment whereby a service was performed and in return for which she received a wage which helped support the family.

The soldier — or civilian — of today might well consider the soldier of the 1850s to have been in a miserable position; but one should consider that by the working class standards of the time he was not too badly off. He was fed, clothed and housed to a standard which, while low, was still above that of the lowest in the land. Moreover his demands were considerably less than those which became common in later years. The soldier of the 1850s was probably illiterate, probably unambitious, a man of few and simple tastes easily satisfied. True, if he was an ambitious man, then the army would assist him; he could learn to read and write and perform simple arithmetic, and as he acquired military knowledge so he could advance in the ranks, even to the rank of Regimental Sergeant-Major, Conductor or Master-Gunner, men who were respected by every level of military society as masters of their profession. But beyond that, there was an enormous gulf between the 'other ranks' and the officers, and very few men who enlisted as private soldiers ever passed it.

The officer of the 1850s was an entirely different being to the soldier, he occupied a different world, moved on a different plane. Almost exclusively from the landed gentry and upper classes, he entered the army by way of a good education followed by a recommendation from a friend of the family to a commanding officer. He then purchased his initial commission. For £450 he could become an Ensign in an infantry line regiment, though if his sights were set higher the cost would be commensurate — to be an Ensign in the Brigade of Guards cost £1,200. His advancement thereafter relied either upon good fortune — being in the right place at the right time to secure promotion in battle — or by further purchase, usually the latter, until he reached Lieutenant-Colonel (£4,500-£9,000) and the command of a regiment. Thereafter promotion was by seniority and selection.

The pay of officers in the lower grades was as niggardly as that of the soldiers, comparatively speaking. Whilst it was greater, it was nevertheless insufficient in view of the numerous expenses which an officer was expected to bear. He required a horse, even in an infantry regiment, and a servant; he had to pay his proportion of the expenses of the officers' mess as well as his own food and wine bills; he was expected to have a number of different uniforms and pay for them himself, and the expense of all these things varied with the regiment in which he served. An infantry regiment of the line from the provinces would be relatively inexpensive; £100 per year over and above his

Below:
Where the money went: the effect of 'stoppages' on the nominal 'Shilling a day'; based on annual averages, in practice 'rounded off' to the nearest halfpenny. When in hospital a flat 9d per day was stopped covering medical expenses and food. The other stoppages might well be applied in addition up to the legal minimum pay of 1d a day.

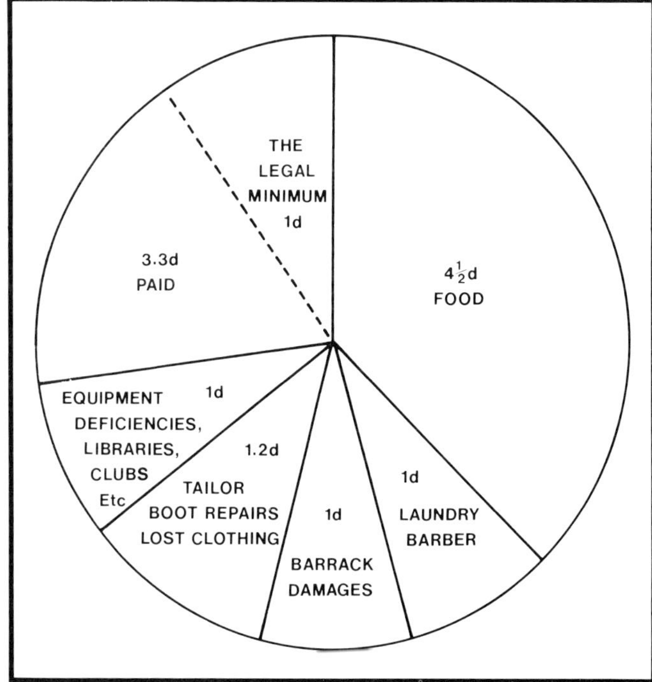

Above:
Sentries at Europa Point Battery, Gibraltar, c1866. Two more guns can be distinguished on the cliff-side above the reclining man.

pay would suffice to keep a young lieutenant comfortably. But in a Guards or cavalry regiment thrice this would be barely enough. A second lieutenant of a line infantry regiment received 5/3d (26p) per day in 1850, though an equivalent officer in the Royal Horse Artillery received 7/8d (38p).

The only officers who did not have to suffer the purchase system and whose expenses were kept to a reasonable level were those of the artillery and engineers. Controlled by the Board of Ordnance, entry to these arms was by competitive examination followed by a three or four-year course of instruction at the Military Academy at Woolwich. Thereafter promotion was by merit and seniority; and for the most part it was desperately slow, since advancement relied entirely upon the senior officers leaving the regiment and thus making space for those treading on their heels. In wartime, with a fair casualty rate, this was acceptable, but in peacetime, with no fixed retirement age — officers could serve as long as they felt inclined and were sufficiently fit — promotion became stagnant; some officers spent 20 or more years as lieutenants or captains.

One way out of the dilemma, and a way generally taken by those few who enlisted in the ranks and made the leap to a commission, was to opt for the Indian Army. The pay was somewhat better, since it was tied to the value of the Rupee, and the expenses considerably less, so that it actually was possible for a young officer to live on his pay, or at least so close to it that the gradually-amassed indebtedness could be wiped out periodically on promotion. Once the young officer had built up some seniority and perhaps a bank balance, he might be able to return to the British Army by way of a purchased commission or an exchange with someone seeking a place in India; more often he stayed where he was, accepting the Indian Army as his career. Service in the Indian Army had one considerable advantage in the 19th century, and that was simply that it was rarely without some minor campaign or fighting, and that meant opportunities to display such martial qualities as one had and reap medals, promotion and preferment. It also meant that the Indian

Army was perhaps more professional in its approach than the British Army, and certainly more skilled at fighting.

When it came to fighting, with what were these armies equipped? Broadly speaking, with the minimum of the most simple weapons. Apart from the adoption of the percussion cap in place of the flintlock in the 1830s, there was little if any equipment held by the army in 1850 which would not have been recognisable to and operable by a soldier of a hundred years earlier.

The basic infantry weapon was still the heavy-calibre smooth-bored musket scarcely changed from the 'Brown Bess' of the 18th century. Rifle regiments, however, had been issued with the Brunswick rifle in the mid-1830s, replacing the earlier Baker rifle, and it was to be expected that experience with this weapon would hasten the general adoption of rifled shoulder arms. But the Duke of Wellington was not convinced that a general issue of rifles was necessary; when he finally capitulated, in 1851, he made it clear that the weapon was still to be called a musket, 'lest the entire army clamour to be clothed in green', the colour appropriated by rifle regiments. The weapon which appeared in 1851 was the 'Enfield Rifled Musket', sometimes called the 'Minie rifle' after the supposed inventor. Still a muzzle-loader, it used an elongated bullet which was hollowed out at its rear end; thus the diameter was such that it could be rammed down the bore of the rifle, on top of the cartridge, without binding against the grooves, but once the cartridge was fired the explosion would force the rear end of the bullet to expand radially, engage with the grooves in the barrel, and so depart spinning to give better range and accuracy.

Issues of the rifle were slow, and the troops who went to the Crimea in 1854 were largely armed with the smoothbore musket, but production was stepped up until by the end of the campaign three out of four soldiers had a rifle. But it was, by any standards, a relatively poor weapon; one defect stemmed from the British Army's age-old obsession with making any one device perform the task of two, and the Minie rifle was of 0.702in calibre so that it would, in an emergency, accept the standard spherical ball of the musket. This made it a heavy and ill-balanced weapon, difficult to shoot with accuracy, but the British troops in the Crimea managed to use it effectively once they understood it.

Even before the Crimean War began a new design of rifle was being developed, and in 1852 it was formally approved as the 'Enfield Rifle Pattern of 1852', the name indicating that it had been conceived and made at the new Royal Small Arms Factory established at Enfield Lock, north of London. The Enfield rifle had a bore of 0.577in and used a 'Pritchett' bullet, very similar in concept to the Minie bullet; it was of 0.568in diameter so that it could easily be rammed, but expanded on firing to fit the three grooves of the barrel. The Pattern 1852 rifle was lighter, handier, easier to fire and accurate, and quantities appeared in the Crimea in 1855.

The cavalry, of course, was armed with either the sword or lance and with the 'pistol a tige', roughly the hand equivalent of the Minie rifle. The 'tige' was an upstanding peg in the chamber; when the powder was put in, this settled around the tige, and when the bullet was rammed it struck the tige which, due to the force of ramming, caused the hollow base of the bullet to spread into the rifling. This method of construction meant that the bullet was already expanded when the charge was fired, and that none of the energy of the charge was needed to perform the expansion. Since this expansion by gas pressure could take several inches of travel up a rifle's bore, the tige construction was adopted for pistols because of the shorter barrel. Obviously, reloading this weapon whilst in the saddle and at the charge was an impossibility, so the cavalryman tended to keep his pistol as a last-ditch resort.

The artillery was entirely equipped with smooth-bored

Below:
The 2nd (Surrey) Artillery Volunteers at practice on Plumstead Marshes (near Woolwich Arsenal) in 1865. The guns are probably 18pdrs and are in a siege battery, with a protecting rampart and ground platforms.

Table 1: Standard Weapons at the Close of the Muzzle-Loading Era

Rifles	Title	Calibre	Length (in)	Weight lb/oz	Magazine Capacity	Bullet Weight (gr)	Muzzle Velocity (ft/sec)	Muzzle Energy (ft/lb)	Effective Range (yd)	Remarks
1852	Enfield Musket P'52	.577	55	8/14	—	530	1,200	1,690	200	
1867	Snider-Enfield	.577	55	8/14	—	480	1,240	1,645	300	First breech loader

Title Artillery	Class	Calibre (in)	Barrel Length (calibres)	Shell Weight (lb)	Charge Weight (lb)	Muzzle Velocity (ft/sec)	Mounting	Weight in Action (tons)	Maximum Range (yd)	Remarks
68pr of 95cwt	Coast	8	15	68	22 P	1,579	Garrison	6.2	3,170	
10in Shell Gun	Siege	10	11.2	93	12 P	1,257	2-wheel	5.5	1,700	
8in Shell Gun	Siege	8	13.5	46	9.5 P	1,488	2-wheel	4.2	2,000	
32pr of 58cwt	Siege	6.17	19.45	32	10.6 P	1,690	2-wheel	3.75	2,900	
24pr of 52cwt	Siege	5.6	21.4	24	8 P	1,720	2-wheel	3.75	2,400	
18pr of 42cwt	Field	5.09	22.4	18	8 P	1,690	2-wheel	2.8	2,300	
12pr New Medium	Field	4.52	17.25	12	4 P	1,770	2-wheel	1.75	1,400	
6pr Medium	Horse	3.57	23.5	6	1.5 P	1,485	2-wheel	1.15	1,400	
24pr Howitzer	Siege	5.6	10	17.5	2.5 P	1,223	2-wheel	1.25	1,025	

Note that the maximum ranges quoted for artillery might more properly be called 'maximum *effective* ranges' since the guns could doubtless fire further but were constrained firstly by maximum elevation possible on their simple carriages and secondly by the limitations of current fire control techniques. It was pointless to fire a projectile to a distance at which impact could not be observed or corrected. Moreover the tactics of the period did not call for long range fire.

muzzle loading cannon whose essentials had scarcely altered in the previous three centuries. The standard armament of Horse Artillery was a mixture of 6pdr guns and 12pdr howitzers, while the Field Artillery had a mix of 9pdr guns and 24pdr howitzers. One battery would have four or five guns and one or two howitzers, so that any field unit could provide a mixture of projectiles at demand. Beyond this support element came the Siege Train, whose principal task was the reduction of fortresses. For this they were equipped with the heaviest artillery which could be brought into the field by a manageable team of horses, the 18pdr, 24pdr and 32pdr guns and the 8in and 10in 'shell guns' or howitzers. In addition there was a collection of mortars, short-barrelled weapons ranging from the 4⅔in Coehorn to the enormous 13in Land Service Mortar. All these weapons were heavy — the lightest of them, the 18pdr, weighed 65½cwt (3.25 tons) behind the team — and taking them into action was a slow and deliberate business.

The projectiles fired by these weapons ranged from solid shot to exotic forms of incendiary bomb. The solid shot was simply a sphere of cast iron, and it remained in use from the first to the last days of muzzle-loading guns. There is a record of an instance during the Battle of the Alma in the Crimea of a group of 15 men all killed by a single solid shot whilst standing aligned with the line of fire. Far more lethal was the Shrapnel Shell or 'Spherical Case Shot' which had first been used in the Peninsular War. This was a hollow projectile containing a small charge of gunpowder, several musket balls, and a rudimentary time fuze. When fired, the flash ignited the fuze, and at the end of its burning the gunpowder charge exploded, splitting open the shell and so allowing the musket balls to fly free along the shell's trajectory; the effect was that of musket fire at long range, and the cone of balls ensured a devastating effect against close-packed troops.

For close-quarter work, to repel a charge, case shot or grape shot were used. Case was a canister of tinplate containing musket balls and no explosive; on firing it ruptured in the gun barrel and spewed from the muzzle a mixture of tin fragments and lead balls like a charge from a sawn-off shotgun. Grape shot were larger balls and less of them, wrapped in canvas and rope to resemble a bunch of grapes; their effect was similar to case, but since the balls were larger they had a greater carrying power and could be used at longer range.

Common shell was the term used for a hollow 'cannonball' containing gunpowder and fitted with a fuze. These were mainly used by the larger howitzers and produced a formidable explosion at the target, provided the gunner managed to get the fuze timing correct. More effective was the 'carcass', a hollow iron sphere filled with a mixture of saltpetre, sulphur, resin, Russian tallow, antimony sulphide and Venice turpentine. This was ignited by the explosion which shot it from the gun, sailed smoking through the air, and then landed to burst by the force of impact and splash the viscous burning mixture in all directions. As a method of burning out defended towns it was without equal. And finally, a surprisingly modern idea to find in the 1850s, came the 'Boxer Parachute Light Ball', developed by Colonel Boxer the Superintendent of the Royal Laboratory at Woolwich. This consisted of two thin hemispheres of metal containing a parachute and a suspended canister which contained an illuminating flare. Fired into the air it would burst, allowing the parachute to open and lower the burning flare to the ground, lighting up the area beneath as it did so.

It was with this combination of simple and robust weapons, simple tactics and hardy soldiers that the British Army had gone to war in the Crimea, relying upon using them in the same way that they had been used in the Peninsula and for years before that, and with the same good effect. Insofar as the tactics and weapons and men were concerned, the war went more or less as expected, but the appalling waste, the death-toll due to disease and exposure as well as wounds, the total collapse of the supply system and the obvious incompetence of most of the military staff left a sour taste in the mouths of most onlookers. Here we were half-way through the 19th century, with the benefits of science and industry all around us, steam engines, the electric telegraph, all manner of new inventions, and yet the army seemed to be stuck in the dark ages. It was indeed time for a change.

Dress

The study of dress in the British Army is one which could fill a number of volumes — and has done. Basically the problem has always been to produce a style of dress which is on the one hand smart and orderly, and on the other hand suited to the strenuous activities of the soldier. The compromise has usually been conditioned by the type of activity the soldier has been called upon to perform. In the early 19th century soldiering, though arduous, was not as strenuous as it is today, and the dress which looked good on Horse Guards Parade was not ill-suited to wear during the formal evolutions which passed, at that time, for combat manoeuvre. As warfare became less formalised, however, the dress had to adapt accordingly; the repeating rifle brought a demand for more ammunition stowage, long range rifle fire a demand for less obvious styles of dress, and warfare which took no notice of the 'campaign season' demanded better protection from the elements.

The development of uniform might be said to have been evolutionary until 1938, when the revolutionary 'battle-dress' was introduced. Learned commentators have decried it on various aesthetic and technical grounds, but to those of us who wore it, battledress was comfortable and practical, and capable of being pressed and tailored into a reasonably smart parade dress. Nevertheless, the introduction of 'Number Two Dress' in 1960 made the wearer feel more like a soldier, and the combat clothing, first introduced during the Korean War, was the most practical battle clothing ever developed and was, indeed, the envy of other armies at the time. As is common, though, economy ruled the day, and the original high quality combat dress and 'Boots, Cold Wet Weather' of Korea soon slipped into a lower quality, thinner form of suiting and 'Boots Directly Moulded Sole' which proved worse than useless when put to the test in the Falklands in 1982. That campaign acted very much like the Crimea in exposing sundry minor shortcomings to the public eye, and as a result the army's combat dress has again been overhauled, and new equipment of better quality is expected to reach service in the late 1980s.

Far left:
A private of the 74th Regiment, 1864. He wears Crimean medals and is armed with the percussion Enfield Rifle Musket. The 74th became the Highland Regiment and, after 1881, the Highland Light Infantry.

Below centre:
An officer of the 3rd Battalion, Grenadier Guards, about to embark for Egypt in 1882.

Below:
A typical mounted infantryman, Sergeant Seymour of the 2nd Battalion, Gordon Highlanders, attached to the Highland Mounted Infantry Company, 1896.

Above:
A sentry of the Royal Scots Fusiliers at the Tower of London, 1896.

Above centre:
A corporal and private soldier of the Lincolnshire Regiment, 1895.

Above right:
The Brigade of Guards, 1897; left, Grenadier; centre, Coldstream; right, Scots Guardsman. Note the arrangement of buttons on jacket and cuffs, distinguishing the various regiments. Note, too, that the Scots Guardsman is cleanshaven, which appears to conflict with Queen's Regulations in force at that time: 'The chin and underlip will be kept shaved but not the upper lip'.

Right:
A Lancer of the 16th Queen's Lancers, 1897. The 16th was the only Lancer regiment to wear a scarlet uniform, and their helmet was derived from the Polish 'czapka'.

Below right:
Sgt A. C. Russell, 1st Battalion Scots Guards, in South African dress, 1899.

Below:
Members of a Royal Garrison Artillery siege battery prior to embarking at Southampton for South Africa in 1900.

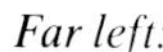

Far left:
A senior NCO of the King's Dragoon Guards, Umballa, India, 1913.

Left:
A soldier of the 4th Hussars, c1915.

Below left:
A private of the Seaforth Highlanders in his best 'walking-out dress', 1914.

Below:
An officer in the Royal Engineers Signal Service, c1916; he appears to have acquired a corporal's greatcoat for additional warmth in the trenches.

Bottom:
The 2nd Battalion, Highland Light Infantry, indulging in some ceremonial during the 1928 summer manoeuvres.

Above:
A patrol from the Medical Section of the Logistic Support Battalion during Exercise 'Hardfall 82' in Norway. Wearing snow shoes for uphill work and carrying their equipment and skis they also pull a sledge carrying their tent, food and equipment.
Crown Copyright

Left:
Mounting guard, 1948; the Royal Welsh Fusiliers in Germany. Note the characteristic black flash of the RWF at the collar, carefully worn outside his leather jerkin by the Regimental Sergeant-Major, and the 'Caps, General Service', probably the ugliest and most uninspired headgear ever inflicted on the Army.

Below left:
The DPM (Disruptive Pattern Material) combat suit, with Pattern 1958 web equipment, worn by a member of 1st Battalion, the Green Howards, 1978.

Above right:
British troops in Northern Ireland, 1977, wearing fragmentation jackets (commonly called 'flak jackets' after the original soft body armour worn by US aviators during World War 2) to protect them from the effects of mines and grenade splinters and, to a lesser extent, sniper fire.

Right:
An officer of the Irish Guards, 1984, demonstrating the new designs of helmet, respirator, NBC suit and web equipment scheduled for adoption in 1985. The rifle is an American M16, being used here to represent the British Enfield L85 which had not then entered service.

Far right:
NBC protective suits, 1978. These suits were of impervious material and after being worn for any length of time tended to make the wearer perspire freely.

2 Armstrong's Benefice

The Battle of Inkerman has come down to us as the 'Soldiers Battle', since it was fought in a miasma of fog and powder smoke so thick that the officers could not see their men and the soldiers and NCOs fought the battle as they saw fit. But Inkerman revolved around relative artillery strengths as well, and the British were at a disadvantage in having to bring up guns to deal with the Russian batteries. Manhandling an 18pdr through the mud and filth of the Inkerman Ridge on a foggy November day was a dismal task, performed against time and in the face of enormous difficulties, and Russell's report of this in *The Times* had an effect far beyond anything Russell could have dreamed. The report was read by William Armstrong, a solicitor by profession but with an interest in an engineering works, and a man given to looking forward and to discovering the most modern and effective way to harness engineering skill to the problems of the day. In his view a cannon which threw a mere 18lb ball and yet weighed some 3¼ tons was an anachronism and a gross waste of effort. According to legend he immediately sat down and sketched out a totally new design of gun on the spot; indeed, the story goes that he sketched it on a piece of blotting paper, a detail which always appears to be gilding the lily, given the properties of blotting paper for retaining fine detail. But however he sketched it, he laid down some basic principles which governed gun manufacture for many years afterwards.

To understand what Armstrong's proposals meant, it is first necessary to consider the artillery gun as it stood in 1850. It was of cast iron or bronze, cast in one piece and then smoothbored from the muzzle, the boring stopping before it reached to the end of the casting so as to leave a solid breech end. Into this 'bore' a vent was drilled, down from the top surface of the cannon. The casting had been made with two short arms at roughly the point of balance — the 'trunnions' — which were turned smooth and then fitted into semi-circular receptacles on the gun carriage and secured there by flaps of cast iron — 'capsquares'. The trunnions permitted the gun to be elevated and depressed. To direct the gun in azimuth — to point it to a

Below:
Inkerman; a plate from the *Illustrated Naval & Military Magazine*, 1886.

Above:
The actual .42in calibre Gatling machine gun demonstrated at Woolwich Arsenal on 11 August 1870 by Dr Richard J. Gatling himself.

Below:
Volunteer artillery firing a 10in rifled muzzle-loading coast defence gun at the Shoeburyness School of Gunnery about 1880. The emplacement is representative of a fortress gun emplacement, a shield of wrought iron plates between two wings of granite.

target to the left or right — it was necessary to heave the entire carriage round bodily.

Because the recoil of the gun bore directly on to the carriage, through the trunnions, the carriage itself had to be massive, and because it was a relatively simple affair, and because it had to be capable of ready repair in the field, miles from any sort of workshop, it was of wood. Wood was always available and carpenters could always be found. Because the explosion of the gunpowder propelling charge was quick and violent, the cast iron was made of ample thickness to withstand the internal pressure, and so what with the thick and massive cast iron gun and the thick and massive oak carriage, the end result was a ponderous piece of equipment.

Armstrong changed the gun; he could do little about the carriage for the moment, but he could certainly see a way of improving the gun. In the first place cast iron was out of date; wrought iron was the material of the age and it had certain advantages in that its strength could be more precisely calculated and guaranteed, and it had the happy property of yielding gradually when it began to fail. Thus a wrought iron gun developing a fault would tend to split gradually rather than burst violently asunder as did a cast iron gun. Armstrong therefore built the barrel of his gun from a tube of wrought iron, and to provide the necessary strength to resist the internal pressure he made additional tubes — or 'hoops' as he called them — and, after heating them so as to expand, slid them over the wrought iron barrel and allowed them to cool and contract. This built up the thickness of metal in the right places — over the chamber — and also, by careful dimensioning, he ensured that the contracting hoop placed the barrel under pressure, so that it added to the resistance to internal explosion. By building up a barrel and a succession of hoops, he could develop a gun to withstand any given degree of pressure without wasting material in over-insuring.

For the next refinement, Armstrong rifled the interior of the barrel, cutting a number of helical grooves into the metal. The projectile to be fired from this rifled gun was not the well-understood spherical ball but an elongated shell, with rounded nose, coated with a layer of lead.

Finally, the gun was arranged to be loaded from the rear, not from the muzzle. The hoops surrounding the barrel were formed into a 'breech ring' at the rear of the barrel into which a 'vent piece' or breech block could be dropped vertically; it was then secured by turning a large screw in the breech ring, lying in an extension of the barrel axis, so that it clamped the vent piece securely against the back of the barrel. The meeting faces were fitted with copper rings so that there was a gas tight joint.

To load, the screw was slackened and the vent piece lifted out; the lead coated shell was then inserted into the breech of the gun (through the screw, which was hollow) and rammed until the lead coat bit into the rifling grooves. A powder charge was placed in the chamber behind the shell, the vent piece dropped into position and the screw tightened against it. A 'friction igniter', based on the same principles as a common match, was inserted into a vent in the vent piece and was ignited; the flame went down the vent, igniting the powder charge which exploded, and the shell was driven up the barrel, the rifling grooves and the lead coat causing it to rotate and take up spin.

Armstrong delivered the first of his new models, a 3pdr

in July 1856, and for the next two years an extensive series of trials was carried out not only on Armstrong's gun but also to discover if there was a cheaper and simpler way of arriving at the same result. After the trials were completed, in August 1858, the Secretary of State for War appointed a Special Committee 'to ascertain the best form of rifled guns for garrison and field service then known to the War Department'. Seven different designs were considered, and in November the Committee reported that they 'have now the honour to recommend the immediate introduction of guns rifled on Mr Armstrong's principle for special service in the field'.

Armstrong, once informed that the Committee's recommendation had been approved, assigned all his gun patents to the Secretary of State for War by deed of gift, a gesture which was duly rewarded in February 1859 by his being appointed 'Engineer of the War Department' and later, in November of the same year, Superintendent of the Royal Gun Factory at Woolwich Arsenal. Production began almost immediately, and by the end of March 1860 162 12pdr field guns had been issued; 12 of these were lighter models which were issued for the 'special service' referred to in the Committee's report, which was in fact service in China during the Third China War (the 'Arrow' war). In 1861 more were tested in the field during the Maori Wars in New Zealand, and in both cases the reports were generally enthusiastic but referred to problems with the sealing of the breech and with the fuzes fitted to the shells.

The Royal Navy had also adopted the Armstrong gun in various calibres, so that eventually, when manufacture of Armstrong's 'Rifled Breech Loader' (RBL) ceased in 1864, a total of 4,540 guns in six calibres and 10 different models had been made, either in the Royal Gun Factory or in Armstrong's own factory, the Elswick Ordnance Company. As might be imagined this monopoly position

Above:
A Royal Artillery Gatling gun section in Zululand, 1879. It can be seen that these guns have a more practical carriage — wider and thus more stable — that Gatling's demonstration model.

Above right:
The town of Gibraltar lying under the old Moorish castle, and with one of the many harbour defence batteries in the foreground, c1880.

Right:
'Touting for recruits at George Street, Westminster', a drawing from the *Illustrated Naval and Military Magazine*, 1885 which gives a fairly accurate representation of the recruiting practice of the period.

caused some comment by other ironmasters and inventors, but even when other designs were put forward, the Armstrong invariably proved better on trial. Some £35,000 was expended on a trial between designs by Joseph Whitworth and Armstrong, and to Whitworth's eternal chagrin, the Ordnance Select Committee found in Armstrong's favour yet again.

But the Armstrong certainly had its defects, the principal one of which was that unless the gunners were careful in locking the vent piece into the breech, it was liable to be blown out when the gun was fired. Moreover the sealing faces of copper were soon eroded and required frequent refacing. The greatest defect, though, was simply that the breech system was insufficiently strong to stand the firing of heavy charges in large-calibre guns; the largest Armstrong gun ever issued was of 7in calibre, and it had the relatively low muzzle velocity of about 1,200ft/sec. This was no particular drawback in field artillery use, since it was sufficient to send a shell to the

fighting ranges desired in those days, but for naval and coast defence use it was quite unsatisfactory.

In 1858, just as the manufacture of Armstrong guns was getting well under way, the French launched *La Gloire*, the first ironclad warship. In answer the Royal Navy laid down *Warrior*, *Black Prince*, *Defence* and *Resistance*, also ironclads, and the race for naval parity had begun. The French were arming their ships with 'shell guns' which could stand away and wreak havoc on unprotected wooden ships, while the obsolete muzzle-loaders of the Royal Navy were outranged and, moreover, could scarcely make an impression on the iron armour. What the Royal Navy needed were powerful guns capable of firing a heavy shot which would pierce iron armour; and since there was the constant fear that Napoleon III would send this ironclad fleet acros the Channel, then the defences of the British coast also needed similar guns. And the Armstrong gun was simply incapable of producing the required force.

During the expensive trial against the Whitworth gun, Armstrong had produced a rifled muzzle loading (RML) design; this was built up in the same way as the breech loader but had only three rifling grooves. The shell was fitted with two rows of three soft metal studs, and when the shell was loaded into the muzzle these studs were carefully engaged in the rifling grooves. When the gun fired, the action of the studs riding in the grooves gave the shell the desired spin. The advantage was that the gun, without any breech fittings, could stand the heaviest charges and the highest velocities, and was the obvious solution to the armour-defeating problem. The RML was adopted first as a heavy gun for naval use and for coast defence, and then universally, replacing the RBL pattern throughout the army and navy. While the advantages of the RML were not so pronounced in the small calibres, it made sense to arm with a single type of weapon until the breech-loading principle could be improved. For there was no doubt in the minds of the British Army or Royal Navy that breech-loading rifled guns were the ideal; their only reservation was that at the current level of technology they could not be made to perform all the tasks required of a gun.

At the same time as the gun question was being addressed, the possibility of Napoleon sending his ironclad fleet across the Channel to raid harbours and naval bases or even land a military force on the coast set Britain in an uproar, and in 1859 Lord Palmerston set up a Royal Commission to enquire 'into the state, sufficiency and condition of the Fortifications existing for the Defence of Our United Kingdom and an examination had into all works at present in progress for the improvement thereof, and consideration given to the most efficient means of rendering the same complete, especially all such

Works of Defence as are provided for the protection of Our Royal Arsenals and Dockyards' and to offer 'such suggestions as may seem to you meet as, regard being had to the works completed and in progress, and to the ordinary number of Our Royal Artillery voted by Parliament, will render Our United Kingdom in a complete state of defence'.

The Commission reported in February 1860 and recommended fortifications to the value of £11,850,000 be erected to protect Plymouth, Portsmouth, Pembroke, Portland, the Thames, the Medway, Chatham Dockyard, Woolwich Arsenal, Dover and Cork. But it can be seen from the Commission's charge, quoted above, that the whole defensive scheme was to be carried out having regard 'to the ordinary number of Our Royal Artillery voted by Parliament'; in other words there was no question of increasing the regular strength of the Royal Artillery to man these extensive works. The manpower was to come, according to the Commission, from elsewhere. 'Your Commissioners . . . are of the opinion that the description of duty and amount of training required for the service of Garrison Guns are comparatively of so simple a nature, that to employ solely for that purpose a highly trained and specially educated body of men such as now compose the Royal Artillery is not absolutely necessary . . . We feel justified, therefore, in expressing a belief . . . that previously untrained men of average capacity can be taught the ordinary duties required for such service in about a month . . . when supported by a due admixture of full trained men and commanded by properly qualified officers.'

Numerous people are of the opinion, even today, that in time of war it is possible to produce a fighting force by simply rounding up anyone standing on street corners, furnishing them with weapons, and sending them off in the direction of the nearest battle. It is surprising that the Royal Commissioners, consisting as they did of three major-generals, a colonel, a rear-admiral and a captain RN, made this same elementary mistake of thinking that by impressing the local ploughboys and giving them a month's basic training they would provide garrisons for major fortifications. History shows that probably the most important element of a fortified defence is the morale of the garrison inside it, and a half-trained force of this nature would be lost before it started. It is worth noting, in this context, an American report of the 1880s which recommended the provision of some 3,000 guns to defend 27 ports in the USA and proposed to man them in much the same way; the United States Artillery soon pointed out the defect:

'. . . these guns, numerous as they are and formidable as they ought to be, are only buried capital unless they be properly manned — not merely manned but *properly* manned. To take a man from the plow and set him to run a locomotive would be deemed criminal by an intelligent man, but the criminality is trivial compared to setting him to operate any of the great engines of war now included in the term cannon.'

As the Commissioners were preparing their report, however, the 'French Invasion' scare of 1859 led to the revival of the 'Volunteers'. This force had originally been raised during the Napoleonic Wars, when some 400,000 men joined locally-raised units to defend their local area. The idea did not go down well with the regular Army, since it found difficulties in reconciling the military need for discipline with the essentially independent spirit of the Volunteers, and it considered the force to be depriving the regular army of valuable recruits. The force was disbanded after Waterloo, but in 1859 it was revived, and whilst most Volunteer units were rifle corps, several formed Volunteer Artillery Batteries based on the forts in their locality, from Sussex to the Orkney Islands. Their organisation and duties were never properly defined; some were 'position artillery', with obsolete armament firmly anchored in the ground, while others were loosely allied to coast defences, but it seems probable that had an invasion materialised, some of these Volunteer forces would have been among the defending garrisons in the fortifications.

The formation of the Volunteer Rifle Corps led to a demand for rifle ranges, which were built all over the country, and to the formation of the National Rifle Association to encourage competition and the improvement of rifle-shooting as a sporting skill. The Enfield rifle

Top:
A mobile field bakery, from the *Illustrated Naval and Military Magazine*, 1885. One wonders how long it had to cool down after use before the driver could take his seat.

Above:
A typical siege gun in its field emplacement, built up from sandbags and wickerwork, barrels and timber.

Above:
Drill on a 12.5in rifled muzzle-loading gun at Southsea Castle, c1885. The gun captain, on the rear platform, looks across the sights while two men alongside the gun turn elevating handles and two beneath the platform crank the traversing handle. The ammunition supply men (shell on the left, powder on the right) stand rigidly to attention, and the instructor takes assiduous notes.

was the standard weapon, but in 1864 the success of the Prussian Army, armed with the breech-loading Dreyse Needle-Gun, over the Danes had shown the superiority of this type of weapon, and the British Army set about discovering a suitable breech-loader. As usual, finance carried a good deal of weight in the deliberations, and the search was more for a practical method of adapting the existing muzzle-loaders to breech loading than for an entirely new rifle. The result was the Snider conversion, in which the Enfield rifle was converted by fitting a hinged breech block which allowed a primitive metallic cartridge to be loaded from the rear. It was realised that such a conversion could only be a temporary measure, and in 1881 came the Martini-Henry rifle, a properly designed breech loader which used a lever below the butt to open a vertically-moving breech block. The calibre was 0.45in, and it used a cartridge constructed from wrapped brass sheet which was formed into a 'bottle-neck' so as to contain the large powder charge in a convenient length. Since most of the British Army's fighting of that period was in dusty tropical climates, this cartridge was to give a good deal of trouble before it was finally perfected; the piecemeal construction was liable to tear apart when the the empty case was being extracted, due to dust anchoring it too firmly in the chamber.

In December 1868 Edward Cardwell was appointed

Table 2: 1870 The Armstrong Rifled Breech-Loading Guns

Title	*Class*	*Calibre* (in)	*Barrel Length* (calibres)	*Shell Weight* (lb)	*Charge Weight* (lb)	*Muzzle Velocity* (ft/sec)	*Mounting*	*Weight in Action* (tons)	*Maximum Range* (yd)
6pr of 3cwt	Field	2.5	21.2	5.75	12oz P	1,046	2-wheel	0.75	2,235@11°
9pr of 6cwt	Horse	3.0	17.6	8.5	1.2 P	1,055	2-wheel	1.3	2,675@9°
12pr of 8cwt	Field	3.0	20.4	11.25	1.5 P	1,172	2-wheel	1.6	3,100@9°
40pr of 35cwt	Coast	4.75	22.4	41	5 P	1,180	Sliding	3.9	4,300@13°
110pr of 81cwt	Coast	7.0	14.2	90	11 P	1,165	Sliding	7.45	3,250@10°

Absolute maximum range was still not a criterion; the important ballistic parameter was the maximum range at which shrapnel shells were lethal. The ranges quoted here are taken from various trial reports of the period and indicate the elevation at which the range was attained. In some cases this was not capable of being achieved on the service mounting

Top:
A Royal Artillery mountain battery, c1890, on the Northwest Frontier of India. They are armed with the 10pdr 'screw-gun' of which Kipling wrote, dismantled and carried piecemeal on mule-back.

Above:
The Moncrieff disappearing mounting, carrying a 7in rifled muzzle-loading gun. The gun is in the 'down' position, for loading; when released, the counterweight would lift the gun to the firing position, clear of the mounting and any parapet, and when fired the recoil would bring it down again.

Secretary of State for War, and he immediately set about a vigorous reform of the army's organisation. Events in Europe, notably the activity of the Prussian Army in defeating Denmark and Austria in quick succession, pointed to a need to have adequate forces in the United Kingdom rather than scattered throughout the Empire, and Cardwell's first move was to reduce the overseas demands for manpower. The 'white colonies' — Canada, Australia, New Zealand — were made responsible for their own defence, while the 'native colonies' were garrisoned by locally-raised troops under command of British officers. By 1870 the number of infantry battalions in Britain had been raised from 48 to 68. This was followed by a change in the terms of enlistment so that soldiers joined for 12 years 'with the colours' followed by a varying period on the Reserve, a step calculated to build up a useful reserve force which could be called upon in time of war.

Cardwell's next suggestion was that all infantry, whether regular, volunteer or militia, should be brought into a unified structure by means of a system whereby the existing numbered regiments would be linked in pairs, becoming two battalions of a single regiment. One battalion would be serving abroad, one would be serving in Britain, and one company from each battalion would form the 'home depot' where records would be kept, recruit training performed, and the volunteer and militia elements commanded and trained. This meant the formation of some 70 new 'sub-districts' in Britain in which the depots were to be established, and this, in turn led to a vast barrack-building programme. Most of the barracks remaining in county towns of Britain date from this period, severe but elegant Victorian piles, often brick-built but occasionally of local stone, usually with a rectangular 'keep' as a gesture toward fortificational theory. Some appear to have had notions of defensive capability, their keeps being provided with steel-shuttered windows and rifle slits in the exterior walls. Although there was a certain amount of friction between the various battalions forced into these new alliances, the system certainly worked and it had the advantages of giving the units a permanent base and a steady supply of recruits.

Cardwell's other great change of 1871 was the abolition of the purchase of commissions. As might be imagined this ran into a vast amount of opposition from those who considered it the natural method of advancement, from those officers who, having invested large sums of money felt that their investment was about to vanish, those who feared that the abolition would open the doors to officers who were not of the quality or breeding thought desirable . . . there were hundreds of arguments put forward. But Cardwell succeeded, even though his hardest task was to persuade the Government to recompense officers for their investment at the market rate then current, rather than at some arbitrary (and grossly undervalued) rate calculated by the Treasury. It cost the government £6,150,000 to recompense the officers and 'buy back the army'.

The final great change came in 1881 with the conversion of the linked battalions into two-battalion regiments of the line, abandoning their numerical identification and giving the new regiments titles, mostly based on the location of their depot. This new designation was usually based on the senior of the two battalions, so that, for example, the 39th (Dorsetshire) Battalion and its link, the 54th (West Norfolk), became the Dorset Regiment with its depot at Shaftesbury. Some amalgamations were fairly logical, such as that of the 44th (East Essex) and the 56th (West Essex) into the Essex Regiment; but what can one make of allying the 100th (Royal Canadians) and 109th (Bombay Infantry) and calling the result the Leinster Regiment?

While the infantry concerned themselves with reorganisation, the artillery and engineers, as befitted the 'most scientific corps', were making themselves responsible for the advance of technology within the army, albeit inadvertently. Armstrong's muzzle loading guns had increased in size and power (and cost) by leaps and bounds, until the standard coast defence heavy gun was a 12.5in weapon firing an 800lb projectile capable of piercing 18in of iron armour at 1,000yd range. Guns of this and other calibres were installed by the score in forts throughout the Empire and they brought in their train problems of fire control, range-finding and communication. The programme of fortification which began in the

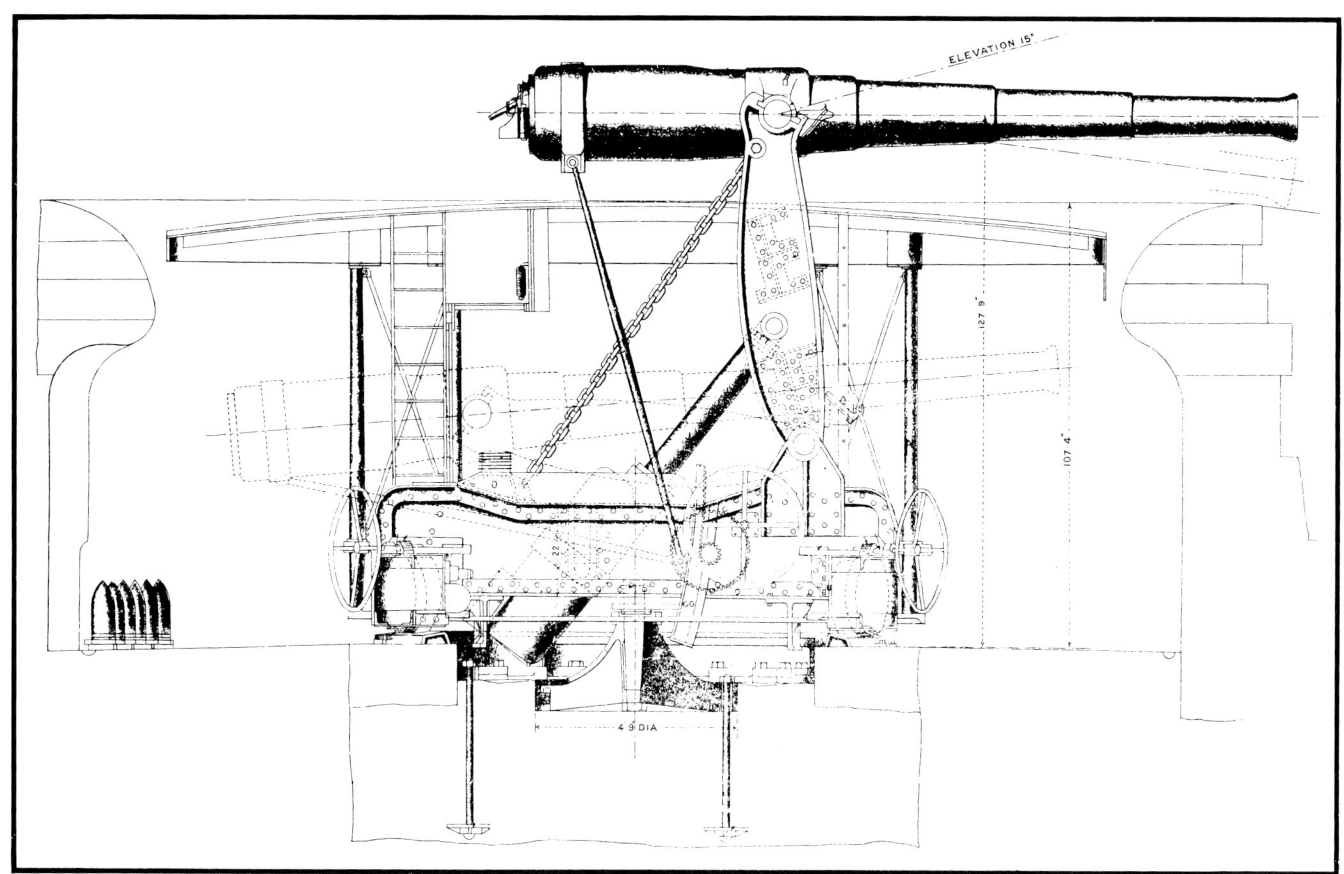

Above:
Drawing, from the gun handbook, of the 6in disappearing coast gun, which was mounted in forts throughout the Empire in the 1880-1900 period. The mounting carries an overhead shield with a slot through which the gun rose and fell, and the gun's movement was controlled by an hydraulic ram.

Left:
Plymouth Breakwater Fort. The lower level is of granite, the upper, carrying the small gun ports, of wrought-iron armour. The buildings on the roof are Naval and Coastguard signal stations, added after the fort was abandoned as a defensive work.

middle 1860s and continued almost until the outbreak of war in 1914 was the largest, most expensive and most technical effort the armed services had ever attempted and its repercussions were felt throughout the army.

The forts themselves went through a series of changes. The science of fortification had been taught in military schools and self-taught by reading innumerable continental tomes on the subject, but in truth it was a science which had been very little practised in the British Army. Continental countries with land borders had built and rebuilt forts for centuries, which was why all the 'systems' of fortification were of continental origin, but the number of works capable of being called forts in the United Kingdom could be counted on the fingers, and those had been largely modelled on continental ideas. With the fortification programme ordered by the Royal Commission of 1859, something rather more modern and certainly quicker and cheaper than the classical bastioned trace was wanted. Fortunately, as is frequently the case, the hour produced the man; Colonel (later Lieutenant-General Sir) W. F. Drummond Jervois.

Jervois was the Deputy Director of Fortifications and Works under the Inspector-General of Fortifications, General Sir John Fox Burgoyne. Burgoyne was approaching the end of a long and distinguished career (he was to retire in 1868 at the ripe old age of 86) and was content to hand over to Jervois the responsibility for implementing the ideas of the Royal Commission. Jervois had made fortification his life's study, and he threw himself into the task with a formidable dedication. No Committee was too small for him to appear before it or become a member if it had the remotest connection with imperial defence or fortification; no journey was too difficult, no distance too far, if there was the prospect of designing and building a fort or a battery at the end of it. Not only was he occupied, in the 1860s, with the defensive plan for Britain, but he was very nearly commuting back and forth across the Atlantic to superintend the construction of the defences of Bermuda, Jamaica, Halifax, Quebec, Esquimault and the Windward Islands. With those areas secured he then

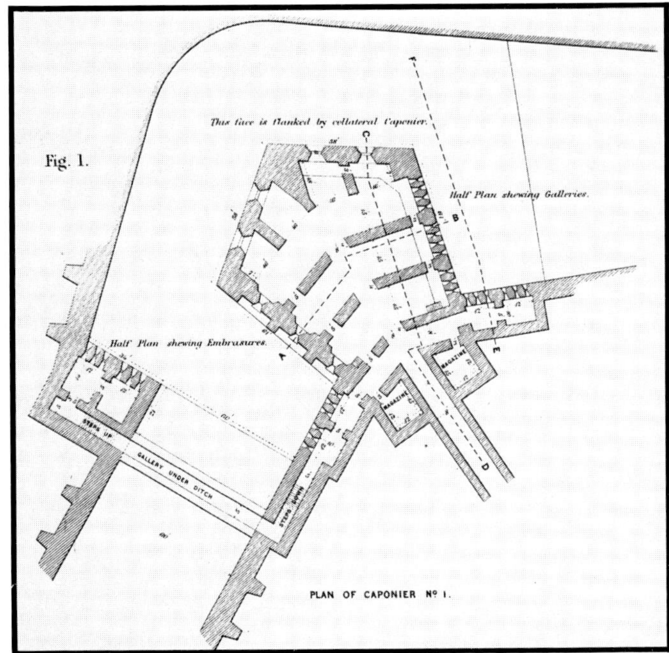

Right:
Plan of a caponier designed by Jervois, Inspector-General of Fortifications, for Fort Brockhurst, Portsmouth in 1864. The caponier protrudes into the ditch around the fort so that fire from its embrasures will sweep the ditch and prevent an attacker reaching the fort's rampart. Note the intricate arrangements for cross-fire to cover every face of the various works.

Below right:
The sea face of Bovisand Fort, Plymouth Sound, showing the individual casemates with their armoured shields between granite piers, each shield pierced by a gun port. These casemates contained nine 9in and 14 10in RML guns in the 1880s.

moved eastward, and the defences of such places as Gibraltar, Aden, Bombay, Singapore, Hong Kong and the Australian ports all bear the stamp of his genius. For if genius is the capacity for taking infinite pains, Jervois was certainly a genius. His method was remarkable in its simplicity; he developed a handful of what might be called 'master plans' of forts and gun batteries to suit particular circumstances — sea-level batteries, cliff-top batteries, batteries open to bombardment at close range and so on — and instructed a small coterie of engineer officers in their application and, more important, in how they could be adapted to suit different terrain or circumstances. Having thus indoctrinated his squad, he sent them forth like disciples to do the actual design and construction work. Thus Capt Crossman (later Sir William Crossman MP) built most of the Portsmouth defences, two forts near Plymouth, and the Verne Citadel at Portland (now a prison), while Capt Du Cane (later Sir Edmund du Cane of the Home Office) built most of the Dover and Plymouth works; Capt Siborne was responsible for the whole of the Thames Defences, and Maj Porter built at Milford Haven and Plymouth Sound; Capt Edwards made the Isle of Wight secure, while Lt-Col Fisher fortified Cork harbour.

The forts were massive structures which, due to the frequent improvement of the guns to be mounted, demanded frequent rebuilding and remodelling, and the technical problems involving earthshifting, masonry and mechanical engineering all demanded new solutions. When plans were first drawn up, in 1860, gunnery was still a fairly primitive art; muzzle-loaders at short range were the norm, and the design of the forts reflected this. The preferred form was a 'modern pentagon', five straight faces with 'caponiers' — galleries loopholed for musketry and short range cannon fire — sticking out at the angles so that they could sweep the faces of the forts with fire and thus discourage attackers. The seaward-facing portion, which was, of course, the prime reason for the forts in most cases, was provided with casemates — vaulted chambers for guns — faced with immense thicknesses of wrought iron 'armour' with a loophole through which the muzzle of the gun poked for firing. Once fired the gun was run back into the casemate, loaded and run out again to fire, a process taking two or three minutes; this meant that a moving target on the water could move some fair distance while the gun was loading, and thus the only way to ensure that a naval attack was repelled was to provide a sufficiency of guns, so that there was ample firepower even though half of them might be reloading at any one time. Hurst Castle, at the entrance to the Solent, was given 61 casemates for 7in muzzle-loaders, while Picklecombe Fort, guarding Plymouth Sound, has 42 9in and 10in guns in two tiers of casemates.

History can show innumerable examples of coastal forts overwhelmed by attacks from the land (Singapore being only the most recent) and the designers of 1860 were alive to this possibility. The great naval ports of Plymouth, Portsmouth and Chatham had rings of land forts built so that an enemy landing somewhere else on the coast and advancing on the rear naval bases would be kept out of gunshot range. But as the construction of the forts went forward, so did improvement in artillery; the planned ring of forts around Plymouth had to be moved further out and the number of forts increased before work began, simply because the range of artillery had suddenly become greater than the distance of the ring from the dockyard. Similarly, the defences had to be given even heavier guns to meet the potential threat; Hurst Castle had been planned for 7in RML guns but before the casemates were completed the plans were changed to 9in guns; two were installed for test, but before the remainder could be moved in the fort was handed back to the Royal Engineers to have armour plate fitted in the casemates. The 9in guns eventually moved in in 1873, but within two years the casemates were cleared and remodelling began so that 12.5in guns could be installed. Eventually, some time in the 1880s, Hurst Castle received its final armament, a collection of five 9in, two 64pdr smoothbore, 23 10in and 10 12.5in, an arrangement which still left 21 casemates empty.

But it gradually became apparent that as the power of guns increased, so did the possibility of warships standing well off shore and pounding the coastal forts into silence; though in fact there was little chance of that since naval gunnery was by no means advanced. Nevertheless, the point was raised that making forts of granite, with prominent casemates, and siting them at the water's edge merely provided the enemy with a well-defined target, and even if he could not demolish them with a single shot, he could certainly make life intolerable for the gunners. This dilemma was resolved by the invention of the 'disappearing gun' by Capt Moncrieff of the Edinburgh Militia Artillery in the late 1860s. Moncrieff's carriage supported the gun at the top of two wrought iron curved arms which had at their lower end a large iron box of ballast. The carriage was emplaced in a pit some 11ft deep, so that the muzzle just cleared the edge and was virtually invisible to an observer at sea. On firing, the recoil drove the gun backwards, and the action of the curved arms and the counterweight caused it to descend into the pit, where it was then held by a ratchet device. The gunners could load in safety and then release the ratchet so that the counterweight swung down and the gun went up again. Then by means of a mirror sight it could be aimed from in the pit and fired once more.

This invention took some time to perfect, but it was taken to with considerable keenness, one reason being that providing a pit and a Moncrieff carriage for a 7in RML gun was a great deal cheaper than making a granite casemate and an armoured shield. But the design was incapable of operating with anything greater than a 9in gun and since the calibres soon surpassed that figure, the Moncrieff carriage found but limited application. Nothing daunted, Moncrieff went to Sir William Armstrong with his ideas and they began to develop a design capable of supporting heavier weapons.

The Royal Carriage Department in Woolwich Arsenal had been examining the problem of taming the recoil of massive guns, and called on Sir William Siemens, inventor of the regenerative steel furnace and later President of the British Association. He suggested an hydraulic brake which eventually became the accepted method of recoil control, still in use today. Armstrong and Moncrieff now adapted this hydraulic system (and bear in mind that Armstrong had made his engineering name by the application of hydraulic devices) to the disappearing carriage, but it was to be some time before the idea bore fruit in a practical manner.

In 1881 the Royal Navy suffered an unfortunate disaster when a muzzle-loading 12.5in gun was inadvertently double-loaded and burst upon firing, killing several men. Even before this time Armstrong had appeared at the War Office with designs for a new type of breech-loader, and the burst naval gun was probably the clinching factor. Guns had been getting longer and longer and more inconvenient to load from the muzzle, and Armstrong's breech-loader design was adopted. This used the same built-up construction as before, but in steel, and used a breechblock which was a cylindrical plug with screw-threads on the external surface. One-third of these threads were cut away, as were the corresponding threads in the gun breech, so that the plug could be pushed in, its protruding threads passing into the spaces cut out in the gun, and then given a one-third turn which brought the two sets of threads into engagement. Sealing was done by a soft metal cup on the face of the block which entered tightly into the chamber and was expanded against the sides by the explosion of the cartridge. This sealing system was later abandoned for the 'De Bange' system, invented in France, in which a resilient pad in the face of the breechblock expanded radially under pressure and formed the seal.

The final improvement in artillery was the arrival, also in the early 1880s, of the 'Quick-Firing' gun. Quick firing in this case really meant rapidity of loading, since the breech was sealed by a simple slab of steel which slid sideways away from the chamber; the cartridge was of brass, carrying the charge inside it and having the shell gripped in its mouth so that the entire round of ammunition could be loaded in one movement. The breech was then slid closed, and a simple hammer mechanism drove a firing pin into a cap in the base of the cartridge; the whole thing, in fact, was simply an enlarged rifle. This type of gun, introduced as the Hotchkiss 6pdr for Naval service, was employed for anti-torpedo-boat firing, and completed the re-equipping of artillery with modern systems to replace the rifled muzzle loaders. With minor improvements, both the breech-loading (BL) and quick-firing (QF) guns have remained the standard patterns ever since.

While the artillery had thus been brought up to an efficient standard of equipment, the infantry had not been neglected. The Martini-Henry had been improved by the adoption of a solid-drawn brass cartridge which reduced the possibility of breaking during extraction, but the late 1870s and 1880s were thick with proposals for 'magazine rifles', weapons which would carry a supply of ammunition within themselves so that they could be quickly reloaded. Several nations took the cheap way out and retained their single-shot rifles, adopting 'quick-loaders' which were no more than clips which held a number of cartridges on the outside of the rifle so that they could be quickly grasped and loaded into the breech. But in 1873 the American Winchester carbine had appeared, using a tubular magazine under the barrel, and it had been used with considerable effect by the Turks against the Russians at Plevna. In 1884 the Germany Army adopted a Mauser rifle with tubular magazine, and in 1886 the French Lebel rifle was introduced, another tubular magazine design. In 1883 the Small Arms Committee was formed, to report 'on the desirability or otherwise of introducing a magazine rifle and as to the best pattern of such arm should the Committee decide to recommend one for adoption'. A large number of designs were examined, most were rapidly eliminated, and three appeared to show promise; the Lee Magazine rifle; the Improved Lee Rifle with Bethel-Burton magazine; and the Owen-Jones rifle. Eventually the Owen-Jones was discarded and the Lee design, using a Martini-Henry barrel of 0.45in calibre, was further tested.

James Paris Lee was a Scotsman who had emigrated to Canada and then moved to the USA. He set up the Lee Firearms Co in 1860 and in 1879 had patented a bolt-action rifle with a removable box magazine underneath the bolt, the first of its kind. This was the design, which was now adopted by the Royal Small Arms Factory at Enfield, but before it could go much further the French introduced the Lebel rifle in 1886. This was a notable weapon because it was the first small-calibre rifle firing a bullet of more or less modern type. The calibre was 8mm (0.318in), far smaller than any military rifle had been in the past, and the propellant was smokeless powder, which promised to conceal the position of the firer. Before this surprise had time to register, came the news that the Germans would adopt the magazine Mauser in 7.92mm calibre. Britain, holding to the 0.45in calibre, looked like being left behind in the ballistic race. Aided by Major Rubin of the Swiss Army, the pioneer of small-calibre cartridges, a new cartridge in 0.303in calibre was developed, but since the Royal laboratory was somewhat suspicious of the new smokeless powders, a charge of compressed gunpowder was adopted. Special rifling, devised by William Metford to counter powder fouling, was adopted, and in 1888 the Lee-Metford rifle was introduced into British service, a 0.303in calibre rifle using bolt action, the Lee magazine holding eight cartridges. In deference to those who averred that, given a magazine rifle, the soldier would blaze all his ammunition off at the first thing he saw, the rifles had a 'cut-off' which prevented cartridges leaving the magazine. With the cut-off pressed in, the soldier used the rifle as a single-shot weapon, loading each round separately as he fired. When the enemy formed up for the final assault, however, then the cut-off was pulled out of engagement and the soldier had the eight rounds in his magazine to deal with the rush.

The last weapon to be brought into service in this period was the machine gun. The American Gatling Gun had been adopted by the British Army in 1870 after exhaustive tests, and it was followed in due course by the two-barrelled Gardner and four-barrelled Nordenfeldt guns in 1880. These were all mechanical guns, worked by the gunner turning a handle or, in the case of the Nordenfeldt, pushing a lever back and forth, and they were all more or less prone to jams and mechanical problems. Nevertheless they were used in action on numerous occasions, particularly in some of the smaller engagements in Africa.

In 1884, however, Hiram Maxim demonstrated his first 'automatic machine gun' to the Duke of Cambridge and several other high-ranking military men. Maxim's gun achieved its automatic action from the recoil of the cartridge, so that there was no handle to turn, and the gun could be aimed quite steadily, as opposed to the upsets caused by the movement of the handle. It could fire 0.45in cartridges at any rate from one to 600 rounds/min. The Duke and his entourage were impressed, but non-committal; one can imagine Mr Maxim being given the 1884 equivalent of 'Don't call us, we'll call you'. But some of the officers present were sufficiently interested to approach Maxim and discuss various improvements which might be made in the general design — for the original Maxim gun was a cumbersome device — and Maxim duly went away and in 1885 represented himself with his improved model. This was a considerable improvement, and while the army considered the matter Maxim formed a company and began selling the gun around the world. By 1890 it was in use in Russia, Britain, Austria, Switzerland, Italy and Germany.

The first use of the Maxim was in the newly-formed colony of the Gambia, on 21 November 1888. A small punitive expedition under General Sir Francis de Winton had been sent out to deal with a tribe who had been raiding various settlements, and among the armament was a 0.45in Maxim gun. On arriving at the defended village of Rohari, the General himself set up the gun and opened fire. 'The bullets rained in through the portholes and between the planks, killing numbers of the enemy. The breastwork and other towers were treated in the same manner, and in a few minutes . . . the garrison were fleeing for their lives.'

The weapons were provided; all that was now needed was a tactical framework in which to employ them.

Table 3: The Late Victorian Years of Technical Development

Small Arms	*Title*	*Calibre*	*Length* (in)	*Weight* (lb/oz)	*Magazine Cap*	*Bullet Weight* (gr)	*Muzzle Velocity* (ft/sec)	*Effective Energy* (ft/lb)	*Range* (yd)	*Remarks*
1871	Martini-Henry rifle	.45	49.5	8/10	—	480	1,350	1,948	400	
1871	Gatling 10-barrel MG	.45	59.4	360	240 drum	480	1,350	1,954	1,000	800rd/min Wheeled mounting
1884	Gardner 2-barrel MG	.45	53.5	290	100	480	1,350	1,954	1,000	650rd/min First 'Machine Gun'
1884	Nordenfeldt 5-barrel MG	.45	46.0	154	Hopper	480	1,350	1,954	1,000	400rd/min
1889	Maxim Automatic MG	.45	43.5	60	250 belt	480	1,350	1,954	1,000	600rd/min First automatic gun
1881	Pistol, Enfield Mk 1	.476	11.5	2.5	6-cyl	272	670	272	15	First cartridge revolver
1887	Pistol, Webley Mk 1	.442	10.2	2.1	6-cyl	265	600	212	15	

Title **Rifled Muzzle-Loading Artillery**	*Class*	*Calibre* (in)	*Barrel Length* (calibres)	*Shell Weight* (lb)	*Charge Weight* (lb)	*Muzzle Velocity* (ft/sec)	*Mounting*	*Weight in Action* (tons)	*Maximum Range* (yd)	*Remarks*
9pr of 8cwt	Field	3.0	21	9	1.75 P	1,330	2-wheel	1.05	3,000@9°	
16pr of 12cwt	Field	3.6	19	16	3.25 P	1,355	2-wheel	1.50	3,000@8°	
40pr of 34cwt	Siege	4.75	22	38	7 P	1,380	2-wheel		3,655@9°	
7in of 7 tons	Coast	7.0	18	114	30 P	1,525	Casemate	12.4	4,600@10°	
9in of 12 tons	Coast	9.0	13.8	249	43 P	1,445	Casemate	27.3	4,500@10°	
12.5in of 38 tons	Coast	12.5	15.8	802	160 P	1,463	Casemate	52.35	3,850@7°	
16in of 80 tons	Coast	16.0	18	1,700	450 P	1,540	Turret	895	5,500@8°	Special to Dover
17.72in of 100 tons	Coast	17.72	20.5	2,000	450 P	1,548	Barbette		6,800@12°	Special to Gibraltar and Malta

Communications

The Crimean War saw the arrival of the electric telegraph on the military scene, firstly as a means of permitting the War Department to give instructions to the field army, but then, at a lower level, to permit communication between elements of the army itself. With the universal adoption of the Morse Code in the 1850s, flag signalling appeared for short distance communication, followed in 1882 by the adoption of the heliograph, which used reflected sunlight to send messages over quite long distances — in India distances of up to 70 miles were recorded. It had the advantage of being impossible to jam (although that aspect was little thought of in those days) and was reasonably discrete, since only those on the sight line could see the flashes distinctly.

World War 1 saw the adoption of wireless telegraphy, which brought in its train the problem of security, since a wireless signal could be heard by anyone with the necessary receiver, leading to the adoption of codes and ciphers for field use. Field telephones were considered more secure, for short-range communication, but these could be tapped by means of induction coils, and devices such as the 'Fullerphone', which used buzzer signals, were adopted in the search of security. Wireless telephony — the use of speech in radio communications — came with the invention of the thermionic valve, but the lack of robustness of early radio equipment kept it as a rear-area system for many years.

In the early 1930s improvements in technology allowed radio to be fitted inside tanks to permit the control of field operations, and from then on the use of radio began to spread throughout the rest of the army. World War 2 produced smaller radio sets, allowing infantry platoons and sections to enjoy speech communication, while the adoption of crystal-controlled frequencies made operation much simpler and more reliable.

The electronic revolution of the 1960s, begun by the transistor and continued by the micro-chip circuit, has allowed radios to be reduced in size whilst being increased in ability; today military radios use highly advanced technology to permit memory-held frequencies, frequency-hopping to prevent jamming or interception, automatic coding and speech 'scrambling' and many other facilities. The coming step is the adoption of digital message entry systems which will permit observers or field units to transmit messages directly into data processing systems where the information is automatically collated and re-distributed to interested parties with the minimum delay.

Below:
A field army satellite station, capable of sending and receiving signals from a military satellite to give instant communication between any parts of the world.
Royal Signal and Radar Establishment

Above:
A heliograph relay station on the Northwest Frontier of India in the 1890s. The party at the rear is receiving a message and dictating it to the NCO in the centre, after which it is retransmitted down the next leg of the system by the men on the right.

Left:
A portable tactical radio set with digital input. *MEL Ltd*

Below:
A modern manpack radio capable of operating on any of 2,320 channels with an output power of 20W. *The Plessey Co*

3 The South African Effect

It is tempting to contemplate what the result on British armament might have been had the South African War been fought somewhere else against a different enemy. The peculiar conditions of the terrain and the enemy combined to give emphasis on long-range rifle fire which was to provide the infantryman with an unnecessary burden for the next half-century or more.

The British Army in the 1890s was primarily equipped and organised for Imperial policing — keeping the Empire quiet and free from invaders. Secondly it was intended for a war on the Continent of Europe, though this was generally discounted as an unlikely prospect. But neither of these aims was ever given official recognition in so many words; indeed, as late as the 1930s the Chief of the Imperial General Staff found himself in hot water when he attempted to get the politicians to define precisely what was the purpose of the British Army's existence. Of course, without an officially declared aim, it was difficult to formulate a tactical or even a strategic policy to which the army could be effectively trained. So, in effect, the army continued to be trained in the manoeuvres which had proved successful at Salamanca and Waterloo, slightly conditioned by reports from the Franco-Prussian War.

The condition of the soldier had improved slightly during the last half of the century. Although there had been no significant increase in pay, various small measures — the abolition of the ration stoppage, provision of more clothing as free issue, additional pay for long service and for passing simple tests in proficiency — had improved matters to the point where the average infantry private might be in receipt of as much as 15/- (75p) a week. At the same time, though, the average civilian wage for a semi-skilled labourer (the official equivalent of a soldier's wage) had increased in line with the generally-increasing prosperity, while the cost of civilian living had dropped, so that by the 1890s there was still a considerable differential between the soldier and his civil equal. In 1899 the

Right:
The never-ending task; 3rd Hussars cleaning stables at Aldershot in 1895.

Below:
Musketry drill, seen here being performed by Coldstream Guardsmen in barracks in 1896, had scarcely changed since Waterloo except that the Lee-Enfield rifle had replaced Brown Bess.

average labourer's wage was 30/- and the semi-skilled artisan could expect about 42/-. The army and the Treasury argued that there were such invisible benefits as accommodation, clothing, food and so forth which made up the difference, but few soldiers were convinced.

The accommodation was largely in the barracks which had been built as a result of Cardwell's regimental reforms. They may have been thought adequate, even luxurious, at the time they were built, but men's aspirations and civil accommodation change — certainly those of us who were quartered in some of these same barracks during World War 2 felt that they were but one step removed from a penal institution. The general design was of two two- or three-storey blocks, each floor forming a barrack room for 30 to 50 soldiers, the two buildings being linked by an arrangement of open stairways with 'ablution blocks' — cold-water washrooms and lavatories — on each landing. The rooms had a fireplace at the end, were lined with beds around the sides, and each man had a steel wall-locker for his belongings and a rack for his rifle. The bed was of iron, with a wooden board foundation for a mattress stuffed with straw, or, towards the turn of the century, a telescoping iron frame with spring foundation upon which a three-piece mattress stuffed with coir — known universally as 'biscuits' from their square shape — was laid. On top of this went four blankets in winter, three in summer. Some regiments might provide sheets and pillows, most did not.

The advantage of the folding bed and biscuit arrangement was that it could be made into a species of chair, by piling two biscuits as a seat and the other as a back-rest, during the day (since it was forbidden to 'make down' a bed until 6pm). But for the first part of the day, until noon, the biscuits were neatly piled, surmounted by carefully-folded blankets and a selection of equipment, for inspection. The man's locker would also be open to show his spare clothing carefully folded and arranged in accordance with the regimental 'kit plate', a formal layout which allowed an inspecting officer or NCO to make a rapid check to see that the man had everything which had been issued to him. There was no place for personal belongings in this; such personal things as the man had were stuffed into his kitbag and hidden away.

The introduction of short service terms of enlistment in 1870 had made one significant difference to the soldier, and that was in his prospects of promotion. When soldiers had enlisted for 21 years, promotion became slow and was often (in the expressive soldier's phrase) a case of 'dead men's shoes', waiting for the man above to die or retire. But rapid turnover of men and NCOs meant that by the 1890s a smart soldier could expect to begin his rise up the promotion ladder after no more than two or three years of service and, if he re-enlisted at the end of his five or seven years, could anticipate being a sergeant after eight to 10 years. This brought extra responsibility, so not every man who was eligible was willing to accept promotion, but it also brought some tangible rewards. Since the army was aware that the NCOs were the cement which held the whole facade together, there was less resistance to finding additional pay for them as there was to increasing pay across the board, and by 1890 a corporal was in receipt of about 3/- and a sergeant 5/- per day. On the other hand any good conduct pay which had accrued during the man's service as a private was lost on promotion; NCOs were

expected to conduct themselves well without further incentive.

NCOs were more liberally treated in the matter of marriage; all warrant officers and staff-sergeants, and 50% of the unit strength of sergeants, were automatically permitted to marry and receive quarters, rations and allowances. A final source of additional income was the astonishing number of sergeants and warrant officers seconded to employment with the War Office and given additional pay. Over 1,000 were so employed, in posts where today a captain would be considered barely sufficient. It is a measure, one supposes, of firstly the lesser technical requirements of the 1890s and also of the Victorian tendency to place considerable responsibility upon comparatively junior ranks. For example, the Topographical and Survey Department of the War Office (which was the original military intelligence organisation) consisted of a captain, a subaltern and a sergeant-clerk in 1870; the Superintendent of Research at Woolwich Arsenal in the 1860s was a captain; and as we have already noted much of the construction of fortification was in the hands of captains.

Such responsible posts for NCOs were probably due to the improvement in education which had spread throughout the army between 1865 and 1895. In 1864 13.2% of the army was totally illiterate, 19.7% could only read and but 7.4% was graded as having 'superior

Above left:
The interior of a barrack room, 1896. Note how the beds have been telescoped and the mattresses folded and strapped to form rudimentary easy chairs. Except for the dress and the addition of electric light, this scene saw little change until the 1950s.

Left:
Major-General H. M. Bengough CB, Commanding 1st Brigade Aldershot, with his aide-de-camp and Brigade Major in 1896.

Above:
Drawing rations, 1896. This appears to be outside the regimental butcher's shop and under the supervision of the Quartermaster. The regiment is unknown but the locale is possibly Fermoy, in County Cork, Ireland.

Below:
2nd Battalion the Dorset Regiment (54th Regiment) on parade, presumably at the regimental depot Dorchester, c1896.

education', though this latter term really implied nothing more than a basic competence in reading, writing and simple arithmetic such as might be expected from a 10-year old child in an elementary school. In the 1860s Army Educational Certificates were introduced and became a necessary step in obtaining promotion, and army schools and schoolmasters (who were civilians but given authority and privilege in accordance with a graded system of military rank) became features of every barrack. By 1889 the percentage of illiterates had dropped to 1.9 and those possessing the 'superior education' (now defined as the Army Third Class Certificate of Education) was 85.4%. Indeed, by 1893 the Director-General of Military Education was complaining the civilian education was so poor he was having to give basic literacy instruction to much of the intake of recruits.

Following on the improvement in literacy came improvements in welfare facilities. As early as 1840 the establishment of a soldiers' library in major military establishments had been authorised, and by the 1860s every barracks was expected to provide a library which would be stocked from a central depot with a standard selection of books; these could then be augmented by the regiment if it so desired. By 1871 the library service had 210,000 books and there were over 130 unit libraries throughout the Empire. Bearing in mind that regulations decreed that the purpose of the library was 'to encourage the soldiery to employ their leisure hours in a manner that shall combine amusement with the attainment of useful knowledge and teach them the value of sober, regular and moral habits' they were unlikely to find 'Ally Sloper's Half-Hour' on the tables or anything remotely racy on the shelves; Dickens was probably the lightest fare they were allowed.

The soldier also benefited from the growing Victorian concern with moral welfare. The neighbourhood of most

barracks had accumulated a rundown collection of sordid public houses, brothels masquerading as dance halls, 'houses of ill-repute' and gin-palaces solely aimed at separating the soldier from his money as rapidly as possible, and the bigger the barrack, the bigger the stews. Garrison towns such as Aldershot, Colchester and Portsmouth were notorious. In 1863 the Earl of Shaftesbury laid the foundation stone for a 'Soldier's Institute' in Aldershot, the result of the efforts of a Mrs Daniell, widow of an Army officer. This was followed in 1874 by a Soldier's Institute at Portsmouth, the work of a Miss Robinson who had studied under Mrs Daniell. Miss Robinson, after a difficult starting period during which she was heartily reviled by all those with a financial interest in the existing system, was to open a series of similar institutes and missions in Britain and overseas, and she was followed by others. None appear to have attained such lasting fame as Agnes Weston, founder of numerous Sailors' Homes and a byword throughout the Fleet, but nonetheless their efforts were deeply appreciated by the rank and file. For, contrary to received opinion, there were plenty of soldiers who preferred tea, biscuits and chess to beer, cheese and doxies. In return for, perhaps, singing a hymn or paying attention to a short Bible lesson, the soldier had something approximating to the comforts of home at his disposal for the first time.

When the South African war began, therefore, the troops might be said to have been in good heart, and they were certainly confident that they could teach a bunch of unruly farmers a short sharp lesson. But unfortunately their training did not fit them for this particular war in any respect. The theoretical level of training was based on Continental experience, as evinced by the Franco-Prussian war — skirmishing lines of infantry, batteries of artillery coming into action on forward slopes where they could see the enemy, enveloping movements round unprotected flanks and finally the assault, with bayonets, against the enemy. But the principal warlike activities of the British soldier over the previous 40 years had been in small wars against untrained natives, where the tactics of the Napoleonic Wars, close columns, squares, volley firing and massed advances were entirely sufficient. The only place which saw any variation was India, where the actions on the North-West Frontier against a dispersed enemy tended to teach more practical forms of tactics, but these were considered peculiar to India, and the disregard in which the Indian Army was held in London ensured that very little of its experience was allowed to filter

Top:
One of the many 'cyclist' regiments of the period, the 20th Middlesex Volunteers (the 'Artists') was raised in 1860; in 1897, when this photograph was taken, it mustered 828 of all ranks.

Above:
The regimental cookhouse of the 3rd Dragoon Guards, about 1895. The men at the right appear to be cutting up meat, while at the left rear cloth-wrapped puddings are being prepared. In the foreground the cook is adding sugar to several buckets of tea.

Below:
The Maxim gun section of 2nd Battalion, the Worcestershire Regiment, at practice in Malta, 1897. At this time the Maxim was still operated from its wheeled carriage and was still something of a tactical orphan.

through into the tactical instruction of troops at home.

The enemy confronting the British in South Africa was something entirely outside their experience. The Boers were not a regularly formed army, more a militia, provided with excellent modern magazine rifles firing smokeless ammunition, mounted on tough and fast horses, familiar with the country over which they fought and unfettered by any preconceived notions of tactics. Their operations were largely mobile, though they could put up a dogged defence when called upon; but more often they would occupy a piece of high ground and have to be dislodged by artillery and infantry fire. This initial tactic proved fairly easy for the British to deal with, since the hill-tops made excellent targets, and it was not long before the Boers learned to locate themselves at the foot of the hill, allow the artillery to blast the top and then shoot down the infantry as they advanced for what they thought would be the final assault.

The British tactic against this was simply to sweep forward across the veldt in a strung-out line, which, in the face of excellent shots, well concealed, was suicidal. Once the initial shooting had become serious, usually at about 500yd from the Boer position, the infantry would go to ground and begin advancing in short rushes, 30 to 50yd at a time, one section advancing while others fired in order to keep the Boer's heads down. Eventually, when all the advancing sections had arrived to within some 150-200yd, the assault would take place.

Ever since firearms appeared in the hands of infantry, the ultimate problem has been to get the assault over those last few yards in the face of the enemy's fire. When muzzle-loading muskets were the order of the day, provided one survived the one or two volleys possible in the time, then there was every likelihood of reaching the enemy and coming to grips with the bayonet. But the magazine rifle changed all that; in the time taken by a fully-laden infantryman, already tired from the advance, to run across those last 200 or so yards, the magazine rifle could pour in 30 or 40 shots, and the odds against reaching the enemy position lengthened enormously.

The solution finally arrived at was to ignore the frontal attack and go for the enemy's flanks, since the Boer was always apprehensive about being surrounded and cut off — as, indeed, any sensible enemy is. But this demanded a higher mobility than the marching British troops possessed, and eventually 'mounted infantry' formed a high proportion of the British force. Mounted infantry companies had been adopted some years before in theory; numbers of men were detailed off, sent away to learn to ride, taught some rudimentary tactics, and then returned to take up their place as foot troops once again, so that the theory of mounted infantry was not strange. But there is more to being a mounted infantryman than knowing how to stay on a horse, and it took time for these forces to become effective.

Top:
The Victorian barracks built as a result of Cardwell's reforms lasted a long time: a misty November morning at Woolwich in 1952, showing the typical 'verandah' form of construction, with store-room and offices at ground level and barrack rooms above, all surrounding the parade square.

Above:
The Jubilee Shot. In 1887, the year of the Golden Jubilee, this 9.2in gun was wedged up to 45° elevation and fired in order to discover if the range achieved matched the ballistic theories of the day. The shot landed 21,203 yards away, proving several theories wrong and set ballisticians arguing for years.

But the feature which stuck in the minds of most people concerned with South Africa was the effect of Boer rifle fire at ranges hitherto undreamed of. Musketry in Europe had been largely practised at ranges of 200-300yd; the small-calibre magazine rifle now permitted accurate fire to much greater ranges, and some sharp-eyed Boers were capable of making life extremely hazardous at ranges as great as 1,000yd and even more. As a result, there grew up a firm belief that long-range rifle shooting was the ultimate soldierly requirement, and it was henceforth built in to any specification for an infantry rifle. This meant a heavy rifle with a long barrel, firing a heavy bullet of

Above:
The interior of Hanley Grove Redoubt, one of a chain of infantry strong-points built along the south Downs in the late 1890s to act as a defensive line between London and the south coast. Photograph taken in the 1970s, long after the redoubt had passed out of military use.

Right:
A Seaforth Highlander displays his kit and equipment for inspection. He wears two good conduct badges, denoting 'six years of undetected crime' as the soldiers had it. The photograph appears to have been specially set up outdoors and was probably for a 'Kit Plate' to be displayed in every barrack room as a guide.

Below:
'Bobs Bahadur' — Field-Marshal Lord Roberts VC, GCB, one of the few soldiers ever to best the Afghans, the general who won the South African War, and one of the rare generals to be genuinely loved by his soldiers.

Below right:
Men of the Cape Garrison Artillery using 15pdr BL guns at the Battle of the Modder River, South Africa, 1890. Notice that the observer is among the guns and directing the fire; the use of forward observers was to come out of the South African experience.

7-8mm calibre, with a powerful charge of propellant. The Lee-Enfield in 0.303in, the Mauser in 7.92mm, the American Springfield in 0.30in, the French Lebel in 8mm, the Russian Mosin-Nagant in 7.62mm, all these service rifles followed this line of reasoning. And the soldier was burdened with 10lb of rifle, a bayonet of 15-18in length (for the bayonet was still considered to be the ultimate infantry weapon) and a bandolier of 200 cartridges weighing another 18lb.

The Boer rifle fire made life difficult for the artillerymen. They were accustomed to taking up a position in the open, wheel to wheel, where they could both see the enemy and be seen by their own infantry; it was an article of faith that the artillery's presence was a morale booster for the foot soldiers and that the gunners had to be seen to be taking the same risks as the men they supported. But with Mauser bullets flying about the gunners began to suffer; it was the same problem which had brought about rifled artillery, that of being outranged by enemy musketry, and the solution was to give up the noble concept of being seen and hide the guns somewhere where the enemy could no longer see them. This brought some serious technical problems in its train.

The basic problem which would occur to any layman was that if the guns were hidden so that the enemy could not see them, they, in turn, could no longer see the enemy, and their traditional method of shooting 'over open sights', was no longer possible. In fact the gunners were no strangers to this; the only difficulty was that the guns sent to South Africa did not have sights which would permit 'indirect fire'. The solution to indirect shooting is simply to determine the direction in which to shoot and then, by simple methods of angular measurement from a visible point of known azimuth, set off on a special 'goniometric' sight the displacement angle which will result in the barrel pointing towards the target. The range to be reached corresponded to a specific angle of elevation of the gun barrel, and this could be set by scale or by a form of adjustable spirit level called a 'clinometer'. So the necessary instruments had to be acquired and sent out.

The more serious problem was to discover by how much the shots were missing the target and then to correct them until they hit. This demanded an observation and communication system; previously the battery commander, at the gun position, had performed his own observation and correction and merely shouted his corrections to the guns. Now it became necessary to deploy observers and develop signalling sections, with flags and heliographs, so that the information could be passed back to the guns and the proper corrections made.

The Boers also had artillery, most of it manned by European mercenaries, and most of it superior to the equipment fielded by the British. One particularly nasty surprise was the Maxim 'Pom-Pom' gun. This was a 37mm calibre Maxim machine gun which fired small explosive shells to a range of 4,500yd at about 200 rounds/min. This resulted in the shells detonating with regular 'pom-pom-pom' which gave the gun its euphonious name; more officially it was the 'Maxim One-pounder' which had been offered to the Army in the middle 1890s and turned down since it appeared to have no particular tactical purpose. The Boers, being less doctrinaire, found it an excellent weapon for bombarding troops in the open at ranges well out of reach from rifle fire, and in sheer self-defence the British were forced to purchase a number of Pom-Pom guns for their own use.

The larger Boer artillery was of Krupp manufacture, 75mm field guns of a design more modern than the guns in British service. The Krupp weapons had sliding block breeches, used brass-cased fixed rounds of ammunition, and were provided with on-carriage recoil systems which, whilst perhaps somewhat primitive in execution, were sufficiently practical to allow the Boer gunners to remain clustered close to the gun, under the protection of its bullet-proof shield, when it fired. In opposition the British horse and field artillery were provided with breech-loading 12pdr and 15pdr guns, using screw breeches, separate-loading bag charges, and with one of the most ridiculous recoil-checking mechanisms ever devised, the 'spring spade'. This was an arm hinged to the gun carriage and carrying a sharp spade on its free end. It was lowered to the ground beneath the trail in such a way that as the gun and carriage recoiled, so the spade dug into the ground, and as the carriage moved back so a powerful spring attached to the spade extended. Eventually the force of the spring overcame the force of recoil, the movement of the carriage stopped, and as the spring asserted itself so the carriage was moved forward and into its former firing position. That, at least, was the theory; the practice sometimes failed to achieve this level of efficiency and the gun had to be heaved back into position by the gunners adding power to the spring.

At the outbreak of the South African war the Royal Artillery had 21 horse and 80 field batteries; the difference between these lay in their employment (horse with cavalry, field with infantry) since all were horse-drawn, and in their equipment — 12pdr to the horse, 15pdr to the field. But by the end of 1899 South Africa had swallowed up seven horse and 30 field batteries for supporting the three cavalry brigades and two army corps in the field. In addition, though, there were 18 battalions of infantry and some 42,000 Militia, Yeomanry, Volunteers and Colonial forces with only about 30 guns between them, and to provide this force with the correct proportion of artillery (then set at 4.25 guns per thousand infantry) demanded a further 37 batteries. On top of that another division was earmarked for South Africa, bringing the requirement up to 43 batteries. The final factor in this difficult equation was the home army (one army corps and one cavalry brigade) which required three horse and 18 field batteries for the defence of the United Kingdom.

Simple arithmetic shows that there was a serious deficit in artillery, and in February 1900 Parliamentary approval was obtained for an increase of seven horse and 56 field batteries. The provision of these batteries required two things — men and guns; finding the men, and the officers to command them, was difficult enough, but providing the guns was almost impossible. There were insufficient guns in the reserve and manufacturing more would take years. Moreover the 12pdr and 15pdr guns were technically obsolete in comparison with the Krupp guns which the Boers were using.

Fortunately once again the time produced the man: General Sir Henry Brackenbury, who had been appointed Director-General of Ordnance in October 1899. Sir Henry had served with artillery in the Indian Mutiny, had been Wolseley's Military Secretary in Ashanti in 1873, private secretary to the Viceroy of India, Military Attache in

Paris, Chief of Staff in the Sudan. He was a brilliant officer and not one to suffer fools gladly, and he made it a condition of accepting the appointment that manufacturing facilities should come under his charge and that certain conditions should be met. He demanded that the reserves of guns for coast defences should be maintained at 10%, for field artillery at 25%, that whenever reserve artillery was issued it must be replaced by fresh manufacture, and that each year the Army Council must certify that this reserve was intact. His conditions accepted, Sir Henry then set about arming the new batteries.

Since the British facilities could not produce weapons of the required modernity or in the required time, he took the unprecedented step of going abroad to purchase weapons. His staff discovered that the 'Rheinische Metallwaren und Maschinenfabrik' of Dusseldorf had developed a field gun to the designs of Herr Erhardt, a 15pdr (3in calibre) gun with on-carriage recoil system, fast-acting screw breech, and separate-loading brass-cased ammunition. Demonstration of the gun showed that it was possible to balance a penny on the wheel and fire the gun without the coin being jarred off, so efficient was the recoil system. 108 guns, complete with ammunition wagons, ammunition, sights, spare parts and accessories were ordered forthwith, the entire transaction being carried out in complete secrecy for not only would the purchase of German guns have caused an uproar in Britain, it would not have been very well received in Germany, due to the considerable pro-Boer feeling of the populace.

The equipment was delivered in the autumn of 1900 and duly despatched to South Africa. At the same time heavier weapons, 6in and 9.45in howitzers (the latter bought from Austria by Brackenbury) were sent out to deal with fortified positions. These posed a new problem, since the 6in howitzer, on its field carriage, weighed

Below:
A Nordenfelt three-barrelled .45in machine gun on field mounting. The cartridges were fed into the breeches through the vertical hopper.

Below right:
'Dignity' (a 16.25in gun on a proof mounting) and 'Impudence' (a 7pdr rifled muzzle loader on a field mounting) at the Woolwich Arsenal Proof Butts c1900. The 16.25in was a naval gun; note how the enormous breech block was completely removed on to a trolley for loading.

Bottom:
10th Mountain Battery — Major H. Montgomery-Campbell commanding — at drill near Pietermaritzburg, Natal, 1896. The battery was armed with six 2.5in jointed RML guns; five mules carried each gun in pieces and a sixth carried the ammunition.

12 tons, more than twice the limit for animal draught. It was just possible to move them by using large teams of oxen, but these were slow, and for moving long distances the steam traction engine was introduced, the first move towards mechanisation. Traction engines were being used to tow stores about the country, and their application to artillery towing was a logical step. Only once was a steam engine tried as a means of actually taking the gun into its firing position, and the cloud of steam and smoke rapidly drew such intense counter-fire from the Boers that the attempt had to be abandoned; steam was all well and good for bringing the guns up the line of communication, but for the last mile or two into action, recourse was taken to the oxen once more.

(An interesting side note on military tradition — or conservatism — comes to light here. So as to attach the howitzers — designed, of course, for horse draught — to the traction engines, special linkages were designed and issued as 'Engine Draught Connectors'. In 1947 the term was still in use for the linkage which connected the 25pdr field gun limber to its towing vehicle.)

As the South African War drew to its untidy close, a blizzard of Commissions of Enquiry blew about the Army. The Dawkins Commission began investigating the War Office in January 1901, eventually reporting that the organisation was over-centralised and devoid of clear-cut definitions of responsibility for the various sections and lacking co-ordination between sections and between military and civilian staffs. The 'Royal Commission on the Conduct of the War', or Elgin Commission, began work late in 1902, and produced a voluminous report in the following year, castigating the Army for neglecting warnings by its own intelligence organisation, for inadequate preparations, for insufficient forces deployed at the opening stage of the war, for inefficient equipment, poor training and poor leadership. The Norfolk Commission looked into the performance of the Militia and other auxiliary forces, deciding they were inadequately trained, poorly equipped and badly organised. The Esher Committee of 1903 was charged with proposing changes in the structure and organisation of the War Office. All appeared to agree that the private soldier was in good heart but that those set above him were failing in their duties in a variety of ways.

Some of the recommendations were acted on with surprising speed. The Esher Committee proposed the abolition of the post of Commander-in-Chief, to be replaced by an Army Council, so that the duties of policy-making, administration and command would be separated and no longer concentrated in one man's person. Administration should be decentralised to district commands, and a General Staff should be set up. These main recommendations were accepted and on 8 February 1904 the historic post of Commander-in-Chief vanished, replaced by a seven-man Army Council. Eight generals were summarily retired, an Inspector-General of the Forces was appointed, and the Committee of Imperial Defence was reconstituted (it had been set up and abandoned some time previously since its deliberations were incompatible with a one-man Commander).

The setting up of a General Staff bogged down in procedural delays. The new Army Council debated every minor detail of the proposed Staff's pay, terms of service, responsibilities, duties, dress, composition and anything else they could find to procrastinate about. Although an Army Order formally set up the General Staff in January 1905, debate continued and by November nothing more than a memorandum of the Council's conclusions had appeared. In the following month the Conservative government fell, the Liberals took office, and Richard Haldane was appointed Secretary of State for War. He did not particularly covet the office; indeed, in a pre-election speech he said, 'A good deal of the time of the next ministry will be taken up with the reform of the army; I don't envy the man who has got that job'. But due to a political indiscretion (he backed the wrong man for Prime Minister) instead of being given the Lord Chancellorship he wanted, he got the War Office instead. It was the most fortunate mistake that ever came the British Army's way.

Haldane's brief was clear; the Liberals wanted to decrease military spending. The Army Estimates had spiralled from £18.15million in 1897 to £29.82million in 1906, and Campbell-Bannerman, the Prime Minister, was anxious to reduce the figures as quickly as possible so that the money could be used for domestic purposes. Whilst Haldane agreed entirely with this, he was, though, insistent that economy must go hand in hand with improved efficiency and he carefully pointed out to the Army that 'greater efficiency *might* mean less expenditure'.

Haldane first specified the principles which would govern the reform of the army; he contended that 'the country needs a highly organised and well equipped striking force which can be transported, with the least possible delay, to any part of the world where it is required', and he argued that for this it required a large

Left:
34 Battery, Royal Field Artillery and an observation balloon operated by Royal Engineers, during the advance on Johannesburg in 1900.

Above:
Infantry on the march in South Africa, 1900. The leading man is carrying a Lee-Metford carbine.

Above right:
The Royal Artillery began using indirect fire as a normal practice during the South African War. This unusual picture shows an observation party during training. The RHA Major has apparently 'acquired' a surveyor's alidade as an observing telescope; to the right is his assistant, carrying a gun-rule for calculating shrapnel fuze lengths; at the extreme left is the signaller, holding an early field telephone. *via Margaret Fall*

and equally well organised reserve force. This he proposed constructing from the existing Yeomanry and Volunteer forces, calling the new body the 'Territorial Army'. Since these would be principally concerned, in war, with protecting Britain, he further proposed a 'Special Reserve' formed from the existing Militia and so constituted that on the outbreak of war it could be instantly embodied into the regular army. In order to provide a source for the officers of both the regular and reserve forces he instituted the Officers Training Corps at public schools and universities. He proposed improvements in rations and the methods of provisioning, in the organisation of medical and nursing services, in transport and in training.

During the time that he was working out these and other ideas, there was an international crisis leading to strained Franco-German relations over Morocco, and there was a distinct possibility that the summer of 1906 might see France and Germany at war. If this occurred, popular feeling might demand British intervention on the French side, and if this happened then Haldane might well be asked what military assistance could be offered. He gave instructions for informal talks between the British Director of Military Operations and the French military attache in London, and he began an investigation into the army's ability to produce a force for use on the continent. To his horror he found that it would take two months to get 80,000 men into position in France.

This almost chance discovery gave Haldane's reforms an aim which was more coherent than his ideas on economy. He realised that in view of the political situation as it stood in 1906, sooner or later a British Army would have to fight on the continent, at the side of the French, and he now bent his efforts to developing the best organisation possible for this end. On the other hand he was practical enough to realise that if he postulated this in Parliament he would run into fierce opposition from his companions in the Liberal party. Fortunately his predecessors had made much play of the Imperial burden, particularly the need to hold sufficient reserves to reinforce India should Russia make a move toward it, the age-old bogey of the Russian Bear advancing through the Khyber Pass, and Haldane was able to use this as a smokescreen. In fact the Imperial commitments did not warrant a reserve of 160,000 men, but Liberal politicians were less liable to argue over this than they would be to argue over reinforcing the French in time of war.

Having made up his mind on the course to be followed, Haldane reorganised the army so as to replace the existing Army Corps organisation with a divisional organisation, producing six divisions which were complete with staffs and ancillary services such as transport, ordnance, supply, medical and veterinary services. The infantry battalion was changed from eight 'service companies' to four large companies each commanded by a major or senior captain, and each consisting of four platoons commanded by subalterns. By the time Haldane left the War Office in 1912 there were six infantry divisions and one cavalry division ready for war.

Organisation was a difficult matter, and Haldane literally fought every inch of the way against entrenched ideas and political enemies, but organising the army was only half the battle; arming it was the other half.

The South African War had shown serious deficiencies in armament; we have already seen that Sir Henry Brackenbury had to scour the continent to find sufficient guns to flesh out the augmented artillery and give them modern equipment. Before the war ended the Royal Artillery convened a Field Gun Committee to draw up specifications for new weapons for the Horse and Field batteries. The conditions it laid down were that for the Horse Artillery the selected gun had to be a quick-firer, with shield, weighing no more than 28cwt (31,361lb) behind the horse team, and that it had to be capable of

Above:
Mounted infantry, South Africa, fitting equipment to their saddles, with the horse lines behind them. *via Margaret Fall*

Top right:
A railway locomotive in South Africa draped in steel netting as a rudimentary form of armour protection against Boer snipers. *via Margaret Fall*

Above right:
A slight disaster during a crossing of the Tugela River in South Africa; the wagon has come off the bridge deck, and the horses have been unhooked, after which one has managed to fall into the river. *via Margaret Fall*

accurate shrapnel fire to 6,000yd with a 12.5lb shell. For Field Artillery the conditions were broadly the same except that the shell was to weigh not less than 18lb. These conditions were augmented by various technical points about sights and other details, and the specifications were supplied to gunmakers. Specimen guns were provided for test in 1902, and from these tests it seemed that whilst no one gun was suitable, there were a number of features of each which were desirable. So the Committee took the surprising step of inviting the representatives of Vickers, Armstrongs and Woolwich Arsenal and persuading them to agree to a composite design, embodying the Armstrong gun, the Vickers recoil system and the Woolwich carriage. Two guns were so constructed, one 13pdr for the Horse Artillery and one 18pdr for the Field Artillery, and a complete battery of each was built for trials in 1903.

At this juncture the suggestion was made that two guns were superfluous — that the 13pdr had shown itself to be somewhat superior to the 18pdr for accuracy, and one design would simplify manufacture and supply. This led to some acrimonious arguments and eventually, since there seemed to be a deadlock, the whole affair was dropped into the lap of the Prime Minister, Mr Balfour. He, being no artilleryman but a shrewd politician, decided to have both guns in service, as originally intended, and in 1904 the two designs were approved for manufacture and issue.

One minor point which arose (though it was not minor at the time) is illustrative of the dangers of bureaucracy ignored. All previous artillery had its ammunition issued in separate components — shell, fuze, cartridge, primer — all packed in separate packages and unpacked and assembled into rounds at the gun. But the South African War had shown the drawbacks of this system in a vast theatre of war, when guns were frequently issued with ammunition lacking one vital part. Therefore, and since the new guns used fixed rounds of ammunition, it was decided that henceforth the ammunition would be packed and issued in complete rounds. But when the manufacturers began to ship ammunition to military magazines, the railways refused to transport it, since a complete round infringed the bye-laws for transportation of explosives which had been laid on the railway companies by the Explosives Act. It took protracted negotiations with the Home Office and the Railway authorities before this impasse was resolved and the ammunition could be moved.

Another interesting feature of these equipments is that the time fuzes adopted for use with the shrapnel shells were designed and patented by Krupp, and a license fee was paid to Krupp for every fuze made. After World War 1 Krupp made a successful legal claim for the license fees unpaid during the war in respect of the fuzes which had been fired against Germany.

Heavier weapons were also required, and a 4.5in howitzer and a 5in 60pdr gun were developed and brought into service. These weapons were intended for heavy support and for destructive fire against structures — defensive works, fortifications, blockhouses — and thus they required a destructive shell, and the high explosive shell was introduced. Prior to this the 'common shell', filled with gunpowder, had been the only anti-materiel projectile, but the high explosive shell was filled with 'Lyddite' (molten and cast picric acid, named from the fact that the development experiments were performed on the artillery ranges at Lydd, in Kent) which had a far greater destructive capability.

With the artillery properly equipped, all that remained was to improve the infantry's prime weapon, the service rifle. The Lee-Enfield, using cordite smokeless cartridges, had been successful in South Africa but there had been complaints that it was somewhat too long and cumbersome, particularly when issued to mounted infantry. On

the other hand the shorter artillery and cavalry carbines were less robust and, by having three separate designs, meant that manufacture and supply were complicated. To rationalise this, a new 'short rifle' was designed; at 44.5in it was 5in shorter than the original Lee-Enfield and 5in longer than the carbines, so that it became a universal-issue rifle for all services.

Whilst the soldiers were happy with the 'Rifle, Short, Magazine, Lee-Enfield Mark 1' or SMLE as it came to be known, the theorists were far from satisfied. The long-range school of thought was loud in condemnation of the rifle as being incapable of accurate fire over long ranges and provided with a weak and inaccurate cartridge. Newspapers and technical journals were filled with argument; for example *Arms & Explosives* magazine, the journal of the gun trade, said in November 1908, 'The rifle was always bad, its defects notorious . . . and the propagation of badness will doubtless continue for several more generations to come'. Whether or not this campaign of calumny had any effect, the War Office began developing a rifle more in keeping with the critics' ideas of what a military weapon ought to be. The resulting rifle was based on the Mauser bolt action (which has theoretical advantages over the Lee bolt) and was in 7mm (0.276in) calibre. The cartridge was based on a design by Sir C. H. A. F. L. Ross, a noted designer of sporting rifles, and was extremely powerful. The rifles were approved for issue on a trial basis in 1913 as the 'Pattern 13', but the tests soon showed that it was a cumbersome weapon and the cartridge gave excessive muzzle flash and blast, barrel overheating, excessive wear of the barrel, irregular chamber pressures leading to inconsistent accuracy, and a violent recoil which the troops disliked. Fortunately the outbreak of war in 1914 put a stop to the trials and the 0.276 cartridge was never heard of again; the rifle, though, was to survive.

Above:
The original caption to this picture merely says 'Siege guns brought by relief to Kimberley'. They are, in fact, 6in Mk 7 coast defence guns which have been removed from their usual locations and temporarily placed on railway trucks. They no doubt worked, but the design was 'not perpetuated in service' as the old phrase had it. *via Margaret Fall*

Below:
Off-duty gunners in Nowcong, India, with their 30pdr field gun, 1909.

Below right:
The mechanism of the Lee-Enfield rifle; the bolt and removable magazine were Lee's contribution, the remainder of the design coming from the Royal Small Arms Factory at Enfield. The bolt locked by lugs towards its rear end, and the shaping of these lugs gave the Lee the smoothest and fastest action of any military bolt design.

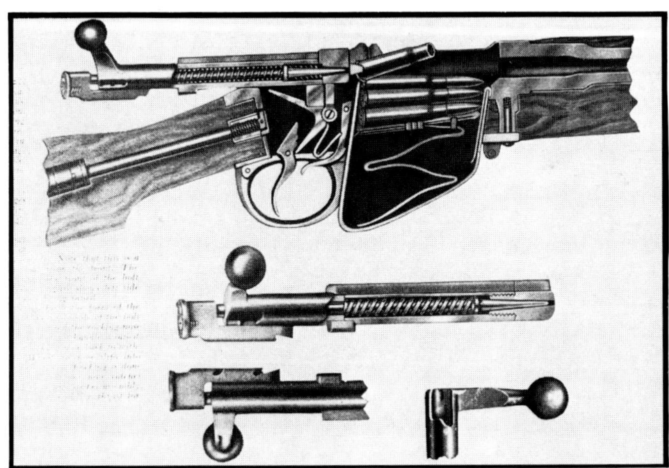

Medical

As much as anything else it was the lack of medical attention in the Crimean War which upset the lay public. Florence Nightingale caught the public fancy, although in fact she appears to have had rather less effect on military medicine than is popularly supposed. The greatest influence came from a Royal Commission in 1857 which discovered that the mortality rate from accidents and disease within the army was far greater than in the comparable civilian population. This led to immense efforts to improve sanitation and living conditions as well as facilities for medical treatment, with the result that from a mortality rate of 17.5 per thousand in 1857 the figure fell to 4.3 per thousand in 1899, while hospital admissions fell by 40%.

The Army Hospital Corps was founded in 1857 and was combined with the Army Medical Department to become the Royal Army Medical Corps in 1898, but hospitals during this period were classed either as 'general' or 'regimental', and since each regiment formed its own hospital there was wasteful duplication of basic amenities and a total lack of co-operation between them. In the 1860s the defects of the general hospitals led to two major establishments being built — Netley, near Southampton, and the Herbert Hospital at Woolwich. (Netley, being the first, was the subject of much argument between theorists; the result was something of a compromise, and its architectural features were such that for over a century the rank and file perpetuated the legend that it had actually been designed to be built in India but the builders got the plans mixed up and built it in England. The legend wasn't helped by the adoption of Netley as the army's lunatic asylum: Kings Regulations 1908 Para 1654: 'Lunatic Soldiers will be sent to Netley. Lunatic women will not be sent to Netley or any other military station. . . .')

The two Great Wars thoroughly exercised the medical system and introduced new blood in the shape of young doctors with modern ideas. By 1945 the chances of a wounded man surviving were immensely greater than they had been in the South African War, and wounds which would have meant certain death in the 1890s were now capable of being healed. The arrival of the rescue helicopter during the Korean War increased the wounded man's chances even more; it was heartening to know that if you were wounded in Korea you were likely to be tucked up in a hospital bed in Japan within five or six hours of being hit.

In the 1980s the problems of medical treatment have been aggravated by the need for precautions against Nuclear, Chemical and Biological (NBC) warfare; as can be seen from the photographs, medical staff, like the rest of the field army, must spend their working hours wrapped in NBC suits and with respirators close at hand, a form of dress which can do little for comfort inside an operating theatre.

Below:
A ward in Netley Hospital in the 1890s; the ambulant soldiers were expected to keep the wooden floor highly polished as part of their 'remedial therapy'.

Below right:
Reception area of a British field hospital during an exercise in Germany, 1980. The 'casualties' are actually healthy soldiers, detailed off to perform this role so as to exercise the medical system.

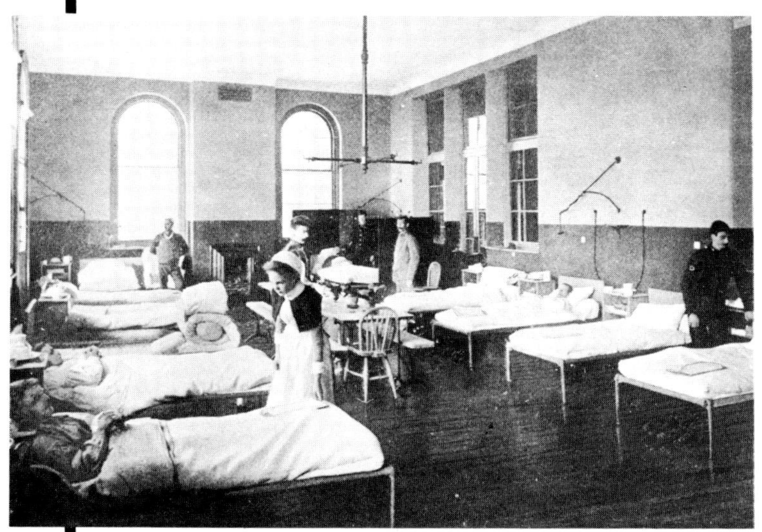

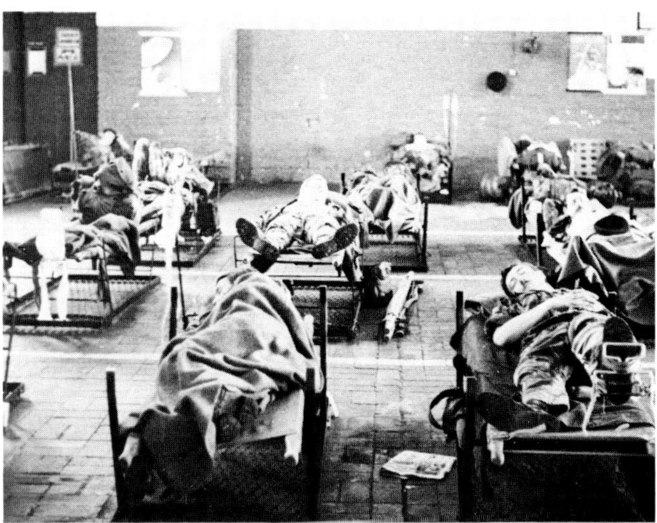

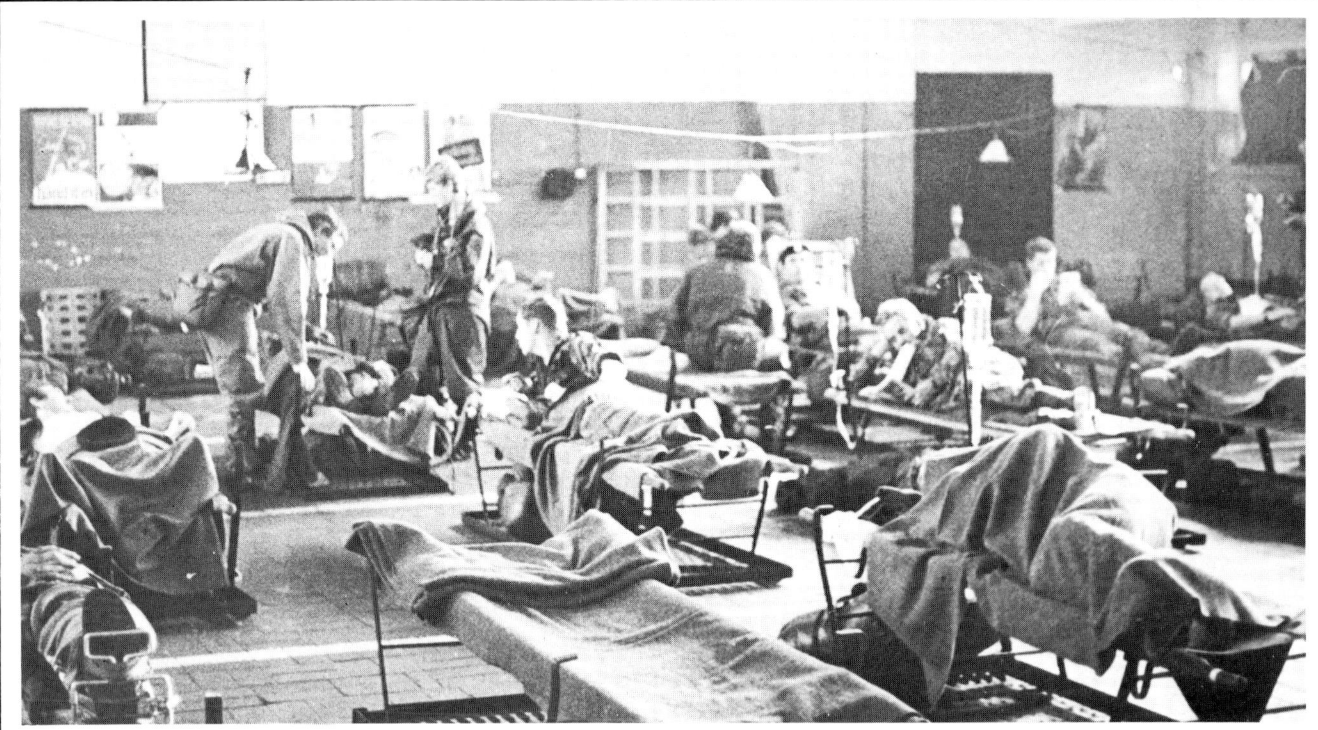

Above:
Another part of the field hospital 'ward', a converted garage inside a military barrack in the rear area. Note that the medical staff are wearing NBC clothing.

Right:
Evacuation of wounded from the front line — the advent of the helicopter meant that casualties could be moved to hospitals in safe areas very much quicker than hitherto.

Below:
The operating theatre of 219 Field Hospital, Germany, 1980. This is a Territorial Army unit which mobilises to reinforce the Army in Germany. Again, the staff are all wearing NBC clothing, some with hospital smocks on top.

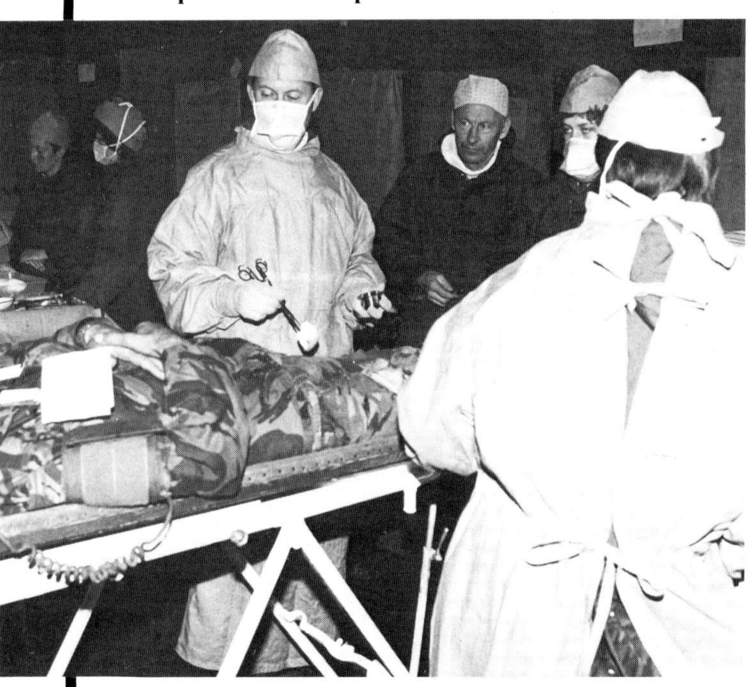

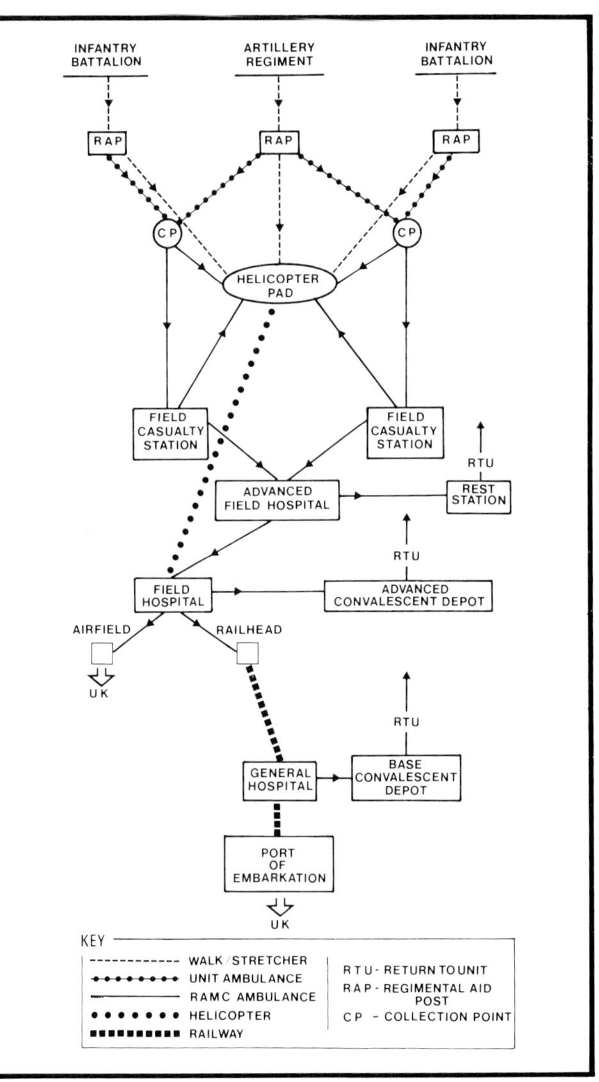

4 In Flanders Fields

In spite of the theorists who maintained that long range rifle fire would save the world, the fact remained that the British Army's principal defect was in medium-range rifle fire; the average soldier could hit what he aimed at at 100yd, and, taking his time, could make good practice at 1,000yd, but analysis showed that the shooting at 200-400yd left a lot to be desired, and it was this range zone which was critical in stopping the enemy's assault. Moreover the long fields of fire of the African veldt were rarely encountered in Europe, which was considered likely to be the next theatre of war.

Fortunately, the Chief Instructor at the Army's Musketry School at Hythe, in Kent, was Lt-Col McMahon DSO, of the Royal Fusiliers, a man with firm ideas on the subject of infantry firepower. He was a considerable enthusiast for the machine gun, but the proposal to change the rifle calibre to 7mm had caused a suspension of machine gun manufacture until this was settled, and therefore the Maxim machine gun was issued on a scale of two per infantry battalion and there was little chance of this figure being increased. A new gun, the Vickers, which used the Maxim principle but was a great deal lighter, had been designed but it was not to appear until the eve of World War 1.

McMahon therefore decided that musketry had to fill the gap, and he began to stress rapid firing of the rifle. He admitted that such rapid fire would not produce pin-point accuracy, but the object in view was to drench the oncoming assault with bullets, so that the law of averages would ensure sufficient of them found a mark to cause a severe casualty rate. It was known that German infantry manuals prescribed a slow and steady advance by men in close order, and with this sort of target precise aiming was not required; provided the bullet hit somewhere, it would suffice to drop the man and put him out of the assault.

The training schedule worked out for the infantryman in about 1908 began with his recruit's course, which gave him the fundamentals of handling his rifle. Then he passed to the 'Trained Soldier' course which covered grouping (placing all his shots into as close a group as possible, irrespective of their location on the target) at 100yd, followed by 'application' (shooting for the bull's-eye), 'snap' (shooting at small fleetingly-exposed targets) and rapid-fire practice at ranges up to 600yd. The most highly stressed was the rapid fire at 300yd, known as the 'mad minute', in which the man had to fire at least 15 shots in the minute and get them on target. The general standard was such that almost every infantryman could place his 15 shots inside a two-foot circle, and the more skilled men could get off 30 shots in the minute with the same degree of accuracy. Once range practice had been mastered, the soldier went on to perform 'field firing' in which he fired from trenches, from behind cover, and generally attempted to simulate combat conditions. 250 cartridges per man were allowed each year, and since this allocation

Above right:
9 August 1914 and the Grenadier Guards march past their sovereign en route to France. In the background can be seen King George V (with raised hat), and to the right Queen Mary, Edward Prince of Wales, Princess Mary, Prince Arthur of Connaught and Queen Alexandra (widow of King Edward VII).
via Margaret Fall

Right:
After the march past; the Grenadier Guards 'marching at ease' through the streets of London on their way to Victoria station. Note the diversity of styles of carrying a rifle and also that the men are not equipped with bayonets. *via Margaret Fall*

included various non-effective personnel, it usually meant that each man had about 300 rounds to perfect his skills and keep them practised every year.

It might be added that there was a considerable tactical advantage in this sytem of rapid rifle firing; a machine gun could put forth as many bullets, but they came from a single, identifiable, point, so that retaliation was relatively easy and the single weapon could be neutralised. But a storm of bullets from 30 or 40 men spread across the front was impossible to pin-point, and retaliatory fire against any one point made relatively little difference to the volume of fire.

Scarcely had the South African War ended than the Russo-Japanese War began on the other side of the world, and, as was the practice in those days, officers from non-belligerent armies soon made their way to the theatre of war and attached themselves as 'observers' to one or other side. This proved to be fortunate; had the lessons of the South African War been allowed to stand alone they would have led to a doctrine unsuited to warfare in Europe, but these lessons were now to be leavened with reports from Manchuria, where two major armies, with modern equipment and training, were in headlong collision. This war introduced such novelties as barbed wire, trench lines, artillery in concealed positions, hand grenades, machine guns and quick-firing artillery. It soon became apparent that in the face of machine guns and quick-firing artillery the leisurely infantry advance to contact, short rushes towards the enemy, and then the final assault were all doomed; unfortunately it did not become apparent to everyone. Even so, there were sufficient officers impressed by the reports from Manchuria to begin re-examining their tactical ideas, and this was particularly so in the Royal Artillery. They found themselves faced with several problems; how to disperse and conceal artillery and yet keep it under centralised control; how to find the enemy's concealed guns and neutralise them; the need for movement, occupation of gun positions and engagement of targets at night; and the problems of observation against an enemy who no longer walked upright in full view but concealed himself in trenches.

One of the greatest lessons to come out of Manchuria appears to have been the need for cooperation between artillery and infantry. In Napoleonic days this had been automatic, since the two fought side by side, but as the range of artillery had lengthened, and as concealment became necessary, the two arms had drifted apart. As one unknown officer (quoted by Headlam) wrote, 'We each of us look upon the other arms with mild toleration; we dine with them, play polo with them, and affect a polite interest in each other: but as for combining to practise our joint work — it is not the custom of the army'. In 1907 artillery brigades were affiliated to infantry brigades, a step which brought about considerable mutual benefits and which was further helped by the formation of the army into divisions. This brought about the quartering together of infantry, artillery and cavalry, so that at last the officers and men began to mix; it was followed by annual exercises in which the three arms co-operated in manoeuvre, and in practice camps of each arm at which officers of the other arms would attend.

This gave some social mixing, and it also introduced officers to the problems and techniques of their partner

Top:
A 2.75in mountain gun being brought into action at Salonika, 1916. This was one of several designs of 'screw-gun' in which, for convenient animal carriage, the barrel came in two parts; the junction can be seen just in front of the gun shield.
via Margaret Fall

Above:
A 60pdr gun being moved up in France, probably in 1915. Note that a 12-horse team is needed to move it on what passed for a first-class road in that area; across shell-torn country it would be almost impossible to move. *via Margaret Fall*

Below:
Some interesting minor details can be seen in this picture of an intelligence officer examining papers taken from a wounded German prisoner. The hand-cart and stretcher was officially an 'Ambulance'; the wearing of steel helmets (one with a sacking camouflage cover) puts the date after mid-1915, but the kilt of the stretcher-bearer (note his armband) indicates that mustard gas had not yet appeared. The lance-corporal appears to be wearing shorts. *via Margaret Fall*

arms. But it did very little to produce actual battlefield co-operation, since this produced a conflict; the infantry wanted the guns alongside them, but the artillery now knew that their only chance of survival, and hence of being able to give effective support, was to be concealed behind the line of contact. And if they were there, how could they know what the infantry wanted? The proposal was to adopt an idea seen in the latter stages of the Manchurian War when Japanese artillery officers went forward with the infantry carrying telephones and paying out wire, so that they could pass orders back to the supporting guns.

This brought about immediate objections; it might be very nice for the infantry company commander being accompanied to have artillery on tap, but the higher artillery commander was incensed at the prospect of losing command of some of his guns at what might be a critical moment in the battle. As usual, compromise won the day; the artillery officer would be an 'observer' without command function. The practice season of 1909 saw the first 'Forward Observing Officers' deployed with infantry; their task was to report back what was happening; the higher authority at the rear would then decide what action to take. This is an interesting sidelight; the artillery's eyes are still 'Forward Observing Officers', but the construction placed on the term today is 'observation' of the enemy and action thereupon, not mere 'observations' on what is happening at the front.

However, the assimilation of these lessons was but a part of the turmoil which the army was going through as the first decade of the century drew to its close. Following in the wake of the Wright Brothers' historic flight, the armies of the world began to take a closer look at aviation and ask what it could do for them and, perhaps more important, what could be done to prevent an enemy taking advantage of aviation. In 1909 the Frankfurt International Exhibition had shown a variety of aeroplanes, and, more significantly had produced a number of 'anti-balloon guns' from Krupp and Ehrhardt, both towed and self-propelled. This display stimulated action in other countries; in Britain, Vickers, Son & Maxim produced a 3pdr high angle gun, while the French solution was to adapt their by now famous 75mm quick-firer on a De Dion Bouton chassis. The Army Balloon School at Aldershot, developed to investigate the use of balloons for observation and the repository of such aviation knowledge as there was in the army, concluded that the prime function was indeed observation and that hostile fire might possibly scare an observer away and interfere with his task. The gunners disagreed; a Capt Sargeaunt proposed attacking the aircraft with shrapnel fire 'in order to hit the pilot or mechanism' or with high explosive shells 'to upset the stability of the aircraft' and concluded his proposals with the prophetic observation:

'It will not be sufficient to rely on our own air fleet, even if numerically stronger than the enemy . . . it might, through a series of misfortunes, be made impotent, or one or two of the hostile airships might evade it and do incalculable damage. . . .'

An even more prophetic suggestion came from a Maj Hawkins, writing in the Proceedings of the Royal Artillery Institute in 1912:

Above:
A 4.7in gun being lined up with its emplacement in East Africa, c1915. This is one of a small batch of ex-Naval guns which were fitted with locally-designed carriages in South Africa during the Boer War and subsequently retained by the Army. *via Margaret Fall*

Below:
A Royal Engineers despatch rider confers with a companion over a map in Salonika, 1915. Both are wearing the 'PH Helmet' gasmask, a flannelette bag soaked in chemicals and fitted with eyepieces and a simple exhaust valve. *via Margaret Fall*

'. . . had we kept our proper place in the van of scientific progress by judicious expenditure in the last few years, we might well have mobile aerial torpedoes worked by wireless currents which would make the approaches to our dockyards as dangerous to dirigibles at night as the three-mile limit is to hostile ships of war. . . .'

All this agitation (and much more) caused the Admiralty to express fears for the safety of some of its installations, particularly its enormous ammunition magazines at Chattenden and Lodge Hill, north of Chatham and well within range of an airship from the continent. By this time both the army and the navy were developing anti-aircraft guns, but since these were still in the paper stage, in 1913 four 6in howitzers were solemnly mounted on their 'siege beds' around Chattenden. Inappropriate as they may appear to have been, the fact was that these were the only weapons the army had which could be elevated to a high enough angle to reach an aircraft, and firing a 118lb shrapnel shell they would undoubtedly have punished any aircraft they were lucky enough to hit. Though in the absence of any sort of air target sight or fire control system, such a chance would seem to have been remote in the extreme. Eventually the purpose-built anti-aircraft gun, the '3in 20cwt High Angle' appeared in the following year; by August four were in existence — two at Chattenden (replacing the howitzers), one at the Royal Gunpowder Factory at Waltham Abbey, and one protecting the Army's powder magazines at Purfleet.

The other side of the coin was the positive use of aviation, and this had begun as early as 1910 when two aeroplanes were employed in the annual manoeuvres. Contemporary reports indicate that 'they were regarded by the troops and the spectators as an interesting curiosity' but were of no practical use. In the 1912 manoeuvres however, aviation played a useful part in reporting movements of troops, and a series of extensive trials carried out in 1912 and 1913 led to the publishing of instructions for co-operation between aircraft and artillery; these included the location of targets, observation and correction of fire, and the steps to be taken to conceal guns and equipment from aerial observation.

Mechanisation was also beginning to take effect on the ground. The experiments with drawing guns by steam engines which had begun in South Africa continued, but it was generally agreed that the smoke and noise were far too obvious and the speed was insufficient. On the other hand the motor truck and car were now reaching a degree of reliability; the West Riding of Yorkshire Territorial Artillery made headline news in July 1914 when it used

Above:
An ingenious way of moving a 6in howitzer, some time in 1916. The trail end is supported on a small flatcar running on a stretch of Decauville railway track; these light railways were easily laid and uprooted, to keep supplies flowing to as near the trenches as possible. An 18pdr field gun is passing behind. Note, too, the 'Boydell Footed Wheel' attachments, preventing the narrow gun wheel sinking into the soft ground; these wheels were originally used in the Crimea. *via Margaret Fall*

Below:
A most unusual photograph, of unknown provenance, which appears to have been taken from an observation balloon somewhere on the Western front. The dress indicates that the men are of the Royal Flying Corps; the truck is the winch wagon controlling the balloon. The prominent knotted ropes, right and left, are the ground-handling ropes by which the ground crew would control and manoeuvre the inflated balloon prior to ascent. *via Margaret Fall*

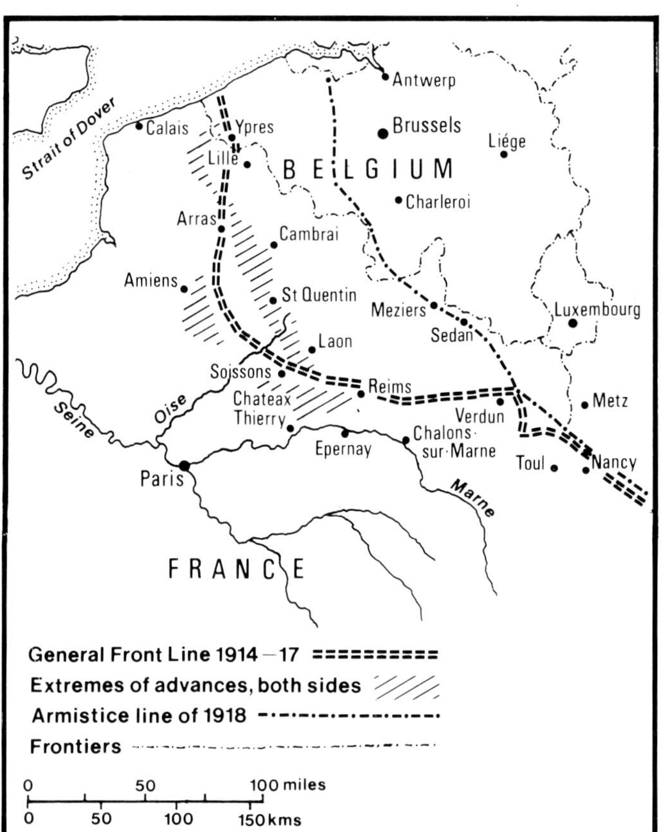

Above left:
Waiting for the breakthrough that never came; Indian cavalry behind the lines in Flanders. *via Margaret Fall*

Above:
Old habits die hard; a battery of field artillery in action in the open in France, 1916.

Left:
World War 1 front lines — after the race to the sea the front lines remained fairly static until 1918.

Below:
Mud. The memory of four years of this sort of endeavour influenced the design and development of gun tractors and military equipment in the 1920s.

30hp Sheffield-Simplex touring cars to tow its 15pdr Erhardt guns over a 120-mile route at an average speed of 21mph, but this was private enterprise rather than official policy and nothing came of it. Trucks were studied for supply purposes and a number were purchased. Another purchase was of a small number of Holt tractors; these were an American device, driven by petrol, and using an endless articulated steel 'track' which passed around a number of idler wheels and was driven by a sprocket geared to the engine. These gave rather good performance across country and might possibly be of use in towing guns, it was thought. But the bulk of the army still relied on the horse. A single battery of field artillery required 168 horses to move it, horses pulled the wagons which carried the infantryman's equipment, horses carried officers in every service, horses delivered rations, coal, fuel, spare parts, horses were everywhere. Since the army operates on two 'establishments', the 'War Establishment' and the 'Peace Establishment', the latter being reduced in strength, the number of horses required in war almost doubled overnight, and to cope with this the Army Horse Reserve existed, which marked down suitable horses, paid their owners a retainer of £4 a year, inspected the animals every six months, and called them into service on 48 hours' notice. The artillery section alone had 10,000 horses earmarked, and they were all scooped up on 4 August 1914.

On that August day the British Army, still twitching from the overhauls which had followed the South African War, marched into a continental war, confident that it would all be over by Christmas and that its experience in such diverse places as South Africa, the Sudan, China and the North-West Frontier of India would see it through. Strangely enough, it did, but it took rather longer than most people had expected.

This is not the place to rehearse the long course of the war in any detail; our brief is to look at weapons technology and its effects, and the strategy of the war has been well enough dissected in many volumes. Technology, though, moves in two ways; it either responds to events — attempts to solve a tactical impasse by developing a new weapon — or it precipitates events — the impact of a new weapon causes changes in tactics. But in either case somebody has to realise that the existing system has run out of answers; a soldier has to say that the tactic doesn't work and demands a new device, or a scientist, seeing an impasse, produces a possible solution and leaves it to the soldier to work out a method of applying it in battle. There were to be numerous examples of both approaches in the four years to come.

The opening phase of the war was one of movement, enough to justify the general belief that this was to be a re-run of 1870 with the result reversed and that the tactics which had been developed from study of the 1870 war would satisfy the needs. But towards the end of 1914 the famous 'Race to the Sea' was run; in truth this was no race, it was simply the outcome of the minor-unit tactics employed. Skirmishers and scouts on both sides went forward, met opposition, called up the infantry; the two forces, more or less evenly balanced went to ground; a flanking movement developed, both sides making the same move and thus meeting each other and going to ground once more; more flanking . . . and so it went on until the final flankers found themselves with their feet in the English Channel or brushing the Swiss border. Both sides then dug in, built field fortifications according to their pioneer textbooks, strung barbed wire, and the trench line was established.

Entrenchment was nothing new in itself; what was new was the length of time the opposing armies were going to stay locked together in this way, and as the days lengthened into weeks and months both sides began to consider specialised methods of attack which might help to break up the deadlock. The German Army, ever innovative, had already developed a short howitzer

Above:
13pdr anti-aircraft guns mounted on Peerless motor lorries acted as the basic air defence for the army in France.

Below:
The assembly shop of Foster's works in Lincoln, with a batch of Mk I tanks under construction. Engines, transmission parts and a steering wheel, dragged behind the tank, can be seen about the shop.

Above right:
'Mother', the prototype Mk 1 tank, on her first trial, 20 January 1916. The trial was conducted in Burton Park, Lincoln, and the tank is crawling out of an artificial shell-hole.

Right:
A 'Male, Mk I' tank, armed with 6pdr guns in the sponsons and with trailing wheel steering apparatus, crossing a trench in 1916.

capable of being manhandled into place in a trench and which fired a bomb on a high trajectory to drop into the opposing trench; the German word for a low-velocity howitzer being 'Morser', this soon translated into 'mortar', a word of antiquity, and the British troops were soon demanding something similar with which they could hit back.

The quickest solution was to send a captured German 'minenwerfer' to Woolwich Arsenal and have 100 copies made, and these were completed and sent to Flanders by Christmas 1914. After that the gunmakers and engineering companies were informed of the requirement, and the army waited to see what would turn up. The result was the most peculiar collection of weapons ever seen on a battlefield. Impressed by the need to make the new weapons as cheaply as possible, some inventors went too far and produced designs of grotesque primitiveness. To supplement these, storekeepers in France dug into corners and managed to exhume some old cast-iron and bronze mortars dating from the start of the 19th century, together with a stock of bombs, and these were presented to the British to form the initial armament of the 'Trench Mortar Service'. This was less formally known as the 'Suicide Club'.

These various extemporised designs managed to fill the requirement until a properly designed weapon appeared. Early in 1915 Mr (later Sir Wilfred) Stokes, managing director of an engineering company, designed a robust but simple weapon consisting simply of a smoothbored steel tube with its base resting on a steel baseplate and its muzzle supported by a bipod with screw elevating gear. The rear end of the barrel was closed by a removeable cap which held a fixed firing pin. The projectile was a simple cylinder with a perforated cartridge holder at its rear end which held a 12-bore shotgun cartridge loaded with 'Ballistite' smokeless powder. On the front was a simple fuze derived from the fuze of the Mills hand grenade.

When ready to fire the mortar-man dropped the bomb tail-first down the barrel; the shotgun cartridge struck the fixed firing pin, the Ballistite exploded, generating gas which blew the bomb out of the tube. As it did so a spring-loaded pin released the firing lever of the fuze which lit a short length of powder and thus exploded the bomb at the end of its flight.

Having perfected his design, Stokes offered it to the army, but by this time there were so many eccentric mortar designs being offered to the Trench Warfare Department that the assessors decided to take a very close look at this design before approving it. They objected to the fact that the bomb turned end-over-end in flight, even though Stokes showed that this made no difference to the accuracy; to placate the objectors he designed a new bomb with a finned tail so that it landed on its nose. Then the fixed firing pin was objected to for various reasons, and Stokes designed one which could be withdrawn to a safe position when required. Eventually, after these and some smaller points had been cleared up, the 3in Stokes Mortar was given official approval and entered service in August 1915.

It would be as well, here, to dispose of the oft-told tale of how the Army ignored the Stokes mortar and how only the personal agitation of Lloyd George, the newly-appointed Minister of Munitions, got the weapon accepted. The facts are laid out in full in the Minutes of

the Ordnance Board for 1915 and the army were aware of the Stokes mortar and had already instigated some of the improvements before Lloyd George ever got to the Ministry. The delay was simply due to the army's insistence that this one, at least, would be right before it was issued, since confidence in mortars was rapidly evaporating in the wake of some of the more primitive designs which had reached the front. In the event they were proved correct, since with little further modification Stokes' original design served throughout the war and well after and formed the prototype for almost every mortar which has come along since then.

The other trench weapon was the grenade, and in this case the British Army was ahead of the field. The officers who had gone to Manchuria to report on the Russo-Japanese War had noted the reappearance of the hand grenade (a weapon which had dropped out of sight in the early 19th century) and the British Army developed a model of their own in 1908, the 'Grenade, Hand, Mark 1'. It consisted of a brass tube filled with explosive and carrying a serrated cast-iron ring to provide fragments, mounted on a 16in cane handle. The fuzing mechanism was simple in the extreme; a mining detonator was inserted in a hole at the top of the brass tube, and a loose cap carrying a firing pin clipped on top. It was thrown by the cane handle, and this also gave it stability and ensured that it landed head-first so that the cap was driven in and the pin struck the detonator. Unfortunately the grenade had been designed for more spacious warfare than obtained in Flanders; there it was found that when the thrower grasped the handle and swung the grenade back, ready to throw it, the head usually struck the rear wall of the trench, blowing the thrower and his

Top left:
Tank C-19, 'Clan Leslie', with a crowd of admirers in 1916. The wire framework on the roof was a defence against hand grenades and explosive charges which, lobbed on to the flat roof, could penetrate the thin boiler-plate armour.

Above left:
A typical pontoon bridge crossing a Belgian canal, c1918.

Above:
An early experiment in mechanised bridge-laying was this 'Royal Engineer Tank' of 1918. A handful were built and proved useful test-beds for ideas which were to see fruition in the next war.

Below:
The network of railways laid behind the lines in France encouraged the use of railway guns, which could be rapidly moved from place to place to give long range support to attacks. A 9.2in Mk 13 gun which fired a 380lb shell to 22,600yd range.

companions to pieces. As might be imagined, it took few of these accidents before the word passed around that the Grenade, Hand, Mark 1 was best left in its box. In its place came a number of local inventions, usually consisting of jam tins or beer bottles filled with blasting powder and with a short length of safety fuze stuck in.

In 1915, though, another inventor immortalised his name by inventing something for the army. A Mr Mills of Birmingham patented his hand grenade, a cast-iron oval casing with a striker inside held off its detonator by a lever, which in turn was locked securely in place by a pin. The thrower grasped the grenade so that he held the lever against the body, pulled the pin, and threw the grenade like a ball. As it left his hand so the lever flew off, and the striker fired a detonator which lit a short length of fuze and exploded the grenade 5sec later. Officially introduced as the 'Grenade, Hand, No 5' in May 1915, it has ever since been known as the 'Mills Bomb' and in its final form, the 'Grenade, Hand, No 36M', it was to remain in British service until the 1960s.

The next innovative weapon to appear was poison gas, and in this case the British were given the problem of defending against it before they could think about using it themselves. It is generally believed that the initial use of gas was at Ypres, on 22 April 1915, but this is incorrect. There is evidence to show that the Germans first used lachrymatory (tear) gas filling in some shrapnel shells fired against the British at Neuve Chapelle on 27 October 1914, but it failed to have any effect — indeed it was not even noticed by the British — due to a combination of bad design and faulty tactical application. They then used another form of tear gas against the Russians on the Eastern Front on 1 February 1915, but here the temperature was so low that the gas mixture failed to vaporise so that no tactical effect was achieved. Even so, the Russians realised what was happening and began taking steps to prepare protective masks, but they entirely failed to advise their Allies about the affair, so that the subsequent use of gas on the Western Front came as a surprise.

But whilst these new inventions were being developed and put to use, the traditional weapons were being demanded in greater and greater quantities and bigger and better versions. The British Army went to France in August 1914 with the 13pdr and 18pdr field guns, the 4.5in howitzer, and a handful of 6in howitzers. There was also one single 9.2in siege howitzer which had completed its acceptance trials a few days before the outbreak of war, a handful of 4.7in guns which had been used in the South African War, and some elderly 5in howitzers. In August 1914 the artillery strength in the Expeditionary Force was six batteries of 13pdr, 54 of 18pdr, 18 of 4.5in howitzer, and nine batteries of heavy artillery, containing the various 4.7in, 5in and 6in weapons. There were another seven batteries of 13pdr and 15 of 18pdr and obsolescent 15pdr field guns in the Home Defence organisation and 12 field batteries in the Reserve. All this added up to about 650 pieces of artillery, and as the war increased in scope so the demand for more guns soon made itself heard.

Allied to this, of course, was a demand for more ammunition. The prewar scale of ammunition relied largely upon shrapnel shell for field guns and high explosive for howitzers, but the Flanders method of warfare placed a premiumn on high explosive since it was far more effective against entrenched troops. Consequently, field batteries began demanding high explosive to a higher proportion than had been allotted in peacetime. The supply system was geared to the production of replacement ammunition at the rate of eight shells per gun per day, but by early 1915 the demand was reaching 100 rounds per gun per day even when things were quiet and the supply organisation fell apart under the strain.

Even the most rabid quick-firing enthusiast had never envisaged ammunition expenditure at this rate, but as soon as the signs appeared, the army took steps to rectify the situation. Maj-Gen von Donop, Master-General of the Ordnance, vastly increased the ammunition contracts and canvassed commercial engineering companies to bring them into shell production, but all this took time to develop. Moreover peacetime civilian habits died hard; workers were disinclined to work night shifts, so for half the time the factories stood idle. Endeavours to recruit more workers ran into trade union opposition to the 'dilution' of labour by unskilled workers, and the skilled

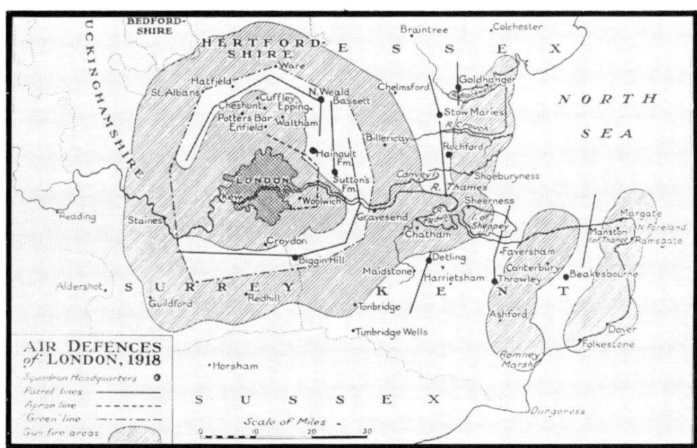

Above left:
The London Air Defences of 1918, showing the gun areas and the fighter aircraft patrol lines. All had gone in less than two years from the Armistice.

Left:
The start of it all; the first practical anti-aircraft gun was this German 'Erhardt Motor Balloon Gun' of 1909.

workers clung to every time-hallowed restrictive practice so as to safeguard their skilled status. There seemed no way out of the impasse; to the civilians the war was a long way off, and the army had no powers to do anything.

Eventually the shortage of ammunition was revealed by the press and rapidly assumed the proportions of a scandal, though in fact the fault lay not with the military but with the commercial concerns who had failed to honour their contracts. In May 1915 it led to a Coalition Government and the appointment of Lloyd George as Minister of Munitions, with a mandate to produce the goods. Sweeping powers were sought and obtained, powers to outlaw strikes and lockouts, organise shift work, draft labour forces, take over premises and control profits. But even with these powers it was still a slow business. Lloyd George discovered what people in France and Germany were also discovering — that munitions cannot be called into existence by a stroke of a pen. The machinery has to be coaxed into motion and allowed to run before it begins producing, and in this case it was Gen von Donop's contracts which began to show their results first. Gradually the situation was brought under control but it was to be the middle of 1916 before ammunition supply could be said to be adequate.

At the same time guns had to be provided to outfit the expanding army and, of course, replace those which were being lost in action. Moreover new designs of guns were demanded; the nature of the war asked for a greater number of heavy howitzers to bombard entrenched positions, long range guns to reach behind the German lines and shell supply dumps, communications and headquarters, anti-aircraft guns to deal with the increased number of enemy aircraft. These had firstly to be designed, then built in prototype and tested and finally put into production, so it was not until 1916 that artillery began to appear in large quantities in the front line.

Some of the demand was met in peculiar ways; although the Ministry of Munitions had a tight control over production there was still room for companies to develop private designs and offer them as possible service equipments. Moreover the major gunmakers — Vickers, Armstrongs and the Coventry Ordnance Works — had tooling set up for designs which had been sold on the export market in prewar days and some of these could be adopted for British use. Some weapons arrived by extremely circuitous routes; the Coventry Ordnance Works had developed the service 9.2in howitzer in 1914, and once that had been delivered to the Army for trial they set about developing a similar design but in 15in calibre, purely as a private venture. Having built and privately tested it, the next problem was to get the Army interested. One of the company's directors was Admiral Bacon, retired from Naval Service, and he passed the word to some friends in the Admiralty, expecting them to tell somebody in the army. Instead of this Mr Winston Churchill, First Lord of the Admiralty, decided that here was a way of getting the Navy into action. Things were relatively quiet on the sea at that time, and Churchill liked to have the Royal Navy well in the public eye. So the Admiralty accepted delivery of the 15in howitzer, ordered 11 more, and sent them to France manned by Royal Marines. Admiral Bacon, by some unrevealed leger-demain, managed to become a Marine colonel and commanded them in action. In 1916, with the Navy having more and better things to do, they were handed over to the Army.

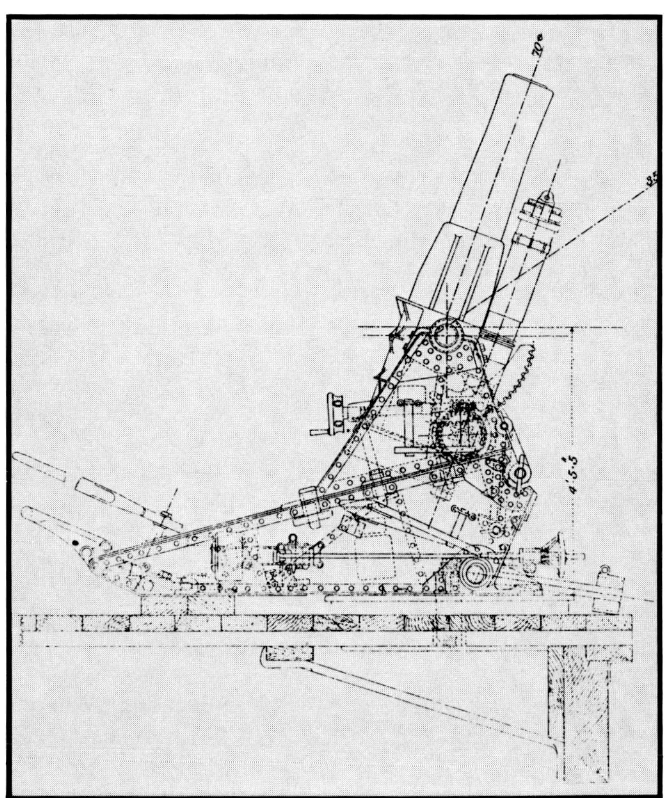

Above:
The 6in 30cwt howitzer, on its siege bed, installed at the Royal Naval Magazines, Chattenden, in 1914 as an anti-aircraft gun, simply because it was the only movable gun in the army capable of elevating to the desired high angle.

Also in 1915 the Admiralty ordered two 12in guns from HMS *Cornwallis* to be mounted on railway trucks and handed over to the Army; they had the guns built by Vickers and tested at Vickers' private proof range before informing the army that they were ready. Just what lay behind this manoeuvre is a mystery, but the Army accepted them and sent them to France. They proved to be useful and two more were then built, to a better design. This stimulated Armstrong's Elswick Ordnance Company to drop a line to the Army to say that they just happened to have two 14in naval guns, built for Japan and not delivered, lying about their yards and how would the army like them railway-mounted? These, too, were accepted and went into action early in 1918. Finally, the Army decided that if anything else was needed it would make its own mind up and set about designing an 18in howitzer to be mounted on a railway unit; this took longer to build than had been expected and it did not appear until 1920. It was to be the last of the railway-mounted monsters.

Railway mountings were also developed for 9.2in and 12in howitzers in some numbers; these were rather more useful in day-to-day firing than the large-calibre long-range guns. Due to the static front line, a vast network of railway track had been developed in the rear, and it was possible to shunt railway guns into place to cover almost any likely target area, and this system was a good deal more reliable than the prospect of trying to drag a road-mobile howitzer, in pieces, through the mud.

The need for air defence guns led to some hurried improvisation. The 'official' anti-aircraft gun was the 3in 20cwt, introduced in 1914, but it was a complex equipment and production was slow. To fill the gap a number of 13pdr field guns were taken from the Royal Horse Artillery; the guns were removed from their field carriages and mounted in simple pedestals, which were then installed on motor chassis. Improbable as this conversion sounds, it proved to be very successful, since the shell was of good ballistic shape and carried a respectable shrapnel charge, ideal for damaging the aircraft of the day.

The installation on motor truck chassis is of interest, since it reflects the contemporary anti-aircraft tactical doctrine. In the early stages of the war the principal target to be expected was the Zeppelin or the observation aircraft, neither of which was very fast, particularly if flying into a head wind. Since it was impractical to defend every acre of ground with a gun, it was decided to 'stable' these self-propelled equipments at suitably central points and, upon the warning of an aircraft, turn them out like fire engines to drive off into the path of the approaching target and open fire. Should they miss, it was possible for them to pack up and drive off to another position to get another shot or two in.

Since the 13pdr proved to be a highly successful anti-aircraft weapon, it seemed logical to convert the 18pdr field gun in the same way, but this turned out to be a failure. The shell of the 18pdr was not well suited to vertical firing, for various complicated ballistic reasons. So in August 1915 it was suggested that it might be a good idea to put a liner inside the 18pdr barrel to reduce the calibre from 3.3in to 3.0in and fire the 13pdr shell, using the 18pdr cartridge to obtain more velocity and thus more vertical range. This combination proved to be another success, but since calling it an 18pdr would have confused the issue even more, it became the '13pdr of 9cwt'.

With these two equipments, plus an increasing number of 3in guns, plus a heterogenous collection put together from various guns which the gunmaking companies had in stock, air defence began to take shape. But there were some technical problems to be overcome before it became efficient. The first major drawback was the question of ammunition. Shrapnel shells were the standard projectiles for all these guns, but experience showed that they were not the optimum for shooting down aircraft. The original presumption was the lead balls would do sufficient damage to bring down the stick-and string machines of the day or put sufficient holes into a Zeppelin gas-bag to cause it to descend, but practice failed to bear this out. The French were using high explosive shells in their 75mm guns used for air defence and these gave better results; the burst area was multi-directional, whereas shrapnel discharged its bullets forward in a cone, and the detonation of the explosive added an incendiary effect to the blast which would ignite aircraft fuel or Zeppelin hydrogen gas.

Another reason for discarding shrapnel as a ground-to-air projectile was that after the shell had functioned and discharged its bullets, the empty shell body fell back to earth; this was of little concern in the war zones, close behind the front line in France, but it began to cause problems when air raids began in England and houses were bombarded by a rain of empty shrapnel shells. A high explosive shell shattered into fragments; these rained down as well but they were less likely to do serious damage when they landed.

The provision of high explosive shells, as we have already seen, was slow, due to their relative novelty in 1914-15, but a more serious problem lay in the provision of fuzes. For anti-aircraft fire it was necessary to provide time fuzes which would burst the shell in the air at a pre-set time, calculated to coincide with the arrival of the shell close to the target aircraft. At that time, such fuzes were used exclusively with shrapnel shell and would not physically fit a high explosive shell; moreover, existing time fuzes, being used with 'low explosive' shells, were not provided with safety devices to prevent accidental premature action in the gun barrel, a thing which had to be rigorously avoided with high explosive loadings. It was necessary to design and put into manufacture a totally new fuze, a slow process.

For some reason or other the subject of anti-aircraft ammunition fascinated the general public and particularly the lunatic fringe of inventors. To study the records of the Munitions Invention Departments, the Ordnance Board and the Patent Office for the wartime years is to conclude that practically every man, womand and child in Britain had invented a new kind of anti-aircraft projectile. Towards the end of 1915 the Secretary of the Ministry of Munitions — which had only been in existence for a few months — informed the War Office that he had over 200 designs of shell which had been submitted by the public, and could the War Office kindly provide the services of an 'expert artillerist' to review them? He added that he had a similar number of suggestions for shells to destroy wire entanglements, and did the army have any interest in them?

The War Office replied that it, too, had desks full of designs, and proceeded to categorise them: firstly there were shells which contained bullets or segments joined together, to be expelled by an explosive charge and then scythe their way through the air and anything else they met. Then came shells filled with boomerangs or discs, also expelled by explosives to fill the air with flying sub-missiles. Next were shells built in pieces, joined by chain or wire, which would be blown apart to cut through targets. There were shells built in pieces but unconnected, shells filled with lengths of chain, with loose rods, with chains having grappling hooks on the ends. And finally, the most common entrant, shells with knife-like blades which would spring out in flight and carve their way through the target. All these had been proposed, and many of them tried, but the majority of inventors had little or no idea of the forces involved or the conditions to which a shell was subject when fired, so many of the ideas were hopelessly impractical. And the vital point overlooked by most of the inventors was that their shells demanded a direct hit on the target — particularly the expanding-knife variety — and if this minor requirement could be met, then a house-brick would probably have proved lethal to the aircraft of the day.

Even with gun and ammunition perfected there was still the basic question of finding the aircraft in the first place and then aiming at it. Detection at first was entirely by eye, using ground observers, but the aircraft of the time were small and easily missed in the sky. The only other detectable attribute was the noise made by the engine, and so sound detection came to be the principal 'early warning' system. This, though, brought problems of its own. The aircraft of the day had an average speed of about 100km/hr; sound travels at about 330m/sec or 1,188km/hr. Supposing an aircraft to be heard when it was 6km from the gun; it would take the sound 16sec to reach the hearer, by which time the aircraft would actually be 5,550m away, and this sort of time lag would persist throughout the subsequent engagement. If the gun crew were alerted at this point, and suppose it took them 30sec to prepare and fire the first shot, by that time the aircraft would be 4,700m away — though the crew still thought it to be 6,000m. Add, now, the 20sec it would take for the shell to reach the assumed position, and the plane is now 4,100m distant.

By devising various plotting instruments which incorporated corrections, sound location was eventually made to yield results, so that a very reasonable approximation of the target's position could be arrived at. The next task was to point the gun correctly; since the target was moving, as we have seen in the example just given it would move a considerable distance during the time the shell was in flight toward it. This, though, was a familiar problem to anyone conversant with gunnery — coast defence artillery were used to shooting at moving ships — but the scale of the correction was un-nerving at first; it seemed peculiar to be aiming and shooting in totally different directions. Indeed, the gunnery problem now resolved itself into three components; firstly to locate the target in space; secondly to calculate how long the shell would take to reach it; and thirdly calculate where the target would be by the time the shell arrived at the original position. Having calculated all these, equations two and three had then to be juggled until they both produced the same answer, and shell and target appeared in the same place at the same time.

This sort of calculation cannot be done mentally, nor on the fingers, and many and various were the tables, graphs, slide-rules and patent sights which were invented to try and produce a solution before the enemy flew out of range. Moreover, due to the tactical system of deploying the guns individually, the arithmetic had to be done by every gun, leading to more and more complicated sights, to incorporate the various corrections, and more and more men clustered around the gun setting the sights, adjusting them, making corrections, setting fuze-lengths, and generally getting in the way of the handful of men who were trying desperately to get off a few shots from time to time. Eventually it occurred to someone that life would be made simpler if all the mathematicians were concentrated in one spot to do their sums and the answers simply passed to the guns; it would at least economise on mathematicians, who were in short supply.

After several false starts, a French invention, the 'Brocq Tachymeter' or 'Central Post Instrument' appeared, which changed the face of the gun position and gave coherence to defensive shooting. The tactical basis was changed; no longer were the guns to turn out like fire engines, they would be permanently deployed in suitable places ringing some point or town which had to be defended. Having placed four guns in position, the Tachymeter sat in the middle, operated by two men. Each had a telescope, and each tracked the target by turning a handwheel which moved his telescope; one man tracked the course and the other the height. Their handwheels also actuated electrical generators which produced current proportional to the speed and tracking, so that target speed and height were accurately reproduced on dials. By inserting an electrical resistance, proportional to the shell's time of flight, an artificial answer appeared which was the 'future position'. This was now converted into gun bearing and elevation and fuze length and ordered to the four guns. Provided the target flew straight and level and maintained a constant speed, there was a fair chance that the shells would arrive in his general area. And, allowing for improved instruments and guns, this was to remain the broad outline of air defence technique until the missile era.

If we turn now to the actual scene on the ground in France and Flanders, we can see just how all this proliferation of weaponry had taken effect. The two belligerents faced each other across a stretch of ground — No Man's Land — which could be as little as 50m or as much as a kilometre wide; the only firm rule was that it ought to be wider than a man could throw a grenade, but otherwise it was generally dictated by the lie of the land. Each line of trenches would be protected by barbed wire, and here it would be as well to appreciate what barbed

wire means in a World War 1 context. It does not mean the homely three or four strands of wire found in farmland; it means a dense thicket of steel barbs as thick and long as a man's thumb, perhaps 10-20m wide and 3-4m high, rusted, decorated with debris and rotting flesh, and a truly monstrous obstacle to confront a man on foot. The remainder of the space between trenches would probably be pocked with shell holes, filled with stagnant water, and the whole area was assiduously watched by sharp-eyed men with rifles and machine guns ready to shoot anything which moved.

Behind the trench lines, out of range of casual mortar bombs and short-range artillery, would be the main concentration of artillery. It had a number of tasks; firstly to shoot in support of infantry attacks; then to shoot in defensive fire to prevent an enemy infantry attack reaching their own trenches; to bombard enemy artillery from time to time in order to harass them, or to bombard them prior to an attack to put them out of action; to bombard enemy supply points and headquarters to destroy stores and paralyse command functions; and to bombard the wire in front of the enemy's trenches so as to blow holes in it which the infantry could pass through during an attack.

All this massive array meant that when an attack was decided upon, it had little scope for clever tactics; there was no point in talking about flanking movements when there were no flanks to be seen. The only possible method of attack was simply to bombard the enemy with guns until his position was battered and his senses reeling, and then get the infantry out of their trenches and across No Man's Land to make a hand-to-hand assault on the enemy trench line with grenades, rifles and bayonets. This brutal fact was patently obvious to the soldiers from late 1914, but some people never did appreciate it, which is why the generals of the period were later reviled as butchers of men. True, some generals were less than perceptive about many aspects of the war; too many, for example, were obsessed with territorial gains, overlooking the basic fact that the culmination of war is to bring the enemy to battle and destroy his army. It matters little whether you do this on one piece of ground or another, since if the battle is successful all the ground will be yours anyway, and if it is not, then it matters not at all. But on the whole it was unfair to criticise generals for making frontal attacks when no other form of attack was possible; the alternative was simply to sit and wait for the enemy to attack, and if both sides took that attitude the war would go on for a very long time indeed. The fault generally lay in failure to maintain the momentum, failure to provide the attack with sufficient strength (usually the case until 1916 since neither side was sufficiently well provided with munitions), or failure to follow up the attack with reserves, often because the attack's success came as a surprise.

One of the prime causes of failure was simply that once an attack had begun, fine control was virtually impossible. The artillery carried out its preliminary bombardment, often planned with considerable skill and fired over a period of days to destroy wire and pulverise rear areas so as to prevent reserves from getting up to the front. The infantry clambered from their trenches and went forward into the smoke and gas . . . and from then on the generals in charge usually lost control, since they knew practically nothing of what was going on. Occasional runners would get back bringing information of this or that unit's location and progress, but by the time they had run and crawled back across No Man's Land — if they survived the trip — the information was out of date. The artillery were paralysed; all they could do was continue firing programmed tasks in the hope that the infantry were conforming to the pre-arranged plan. If, as often happened, a lone machine gunner held up the infantry for 10min, then the artillery barrage would gradually work its

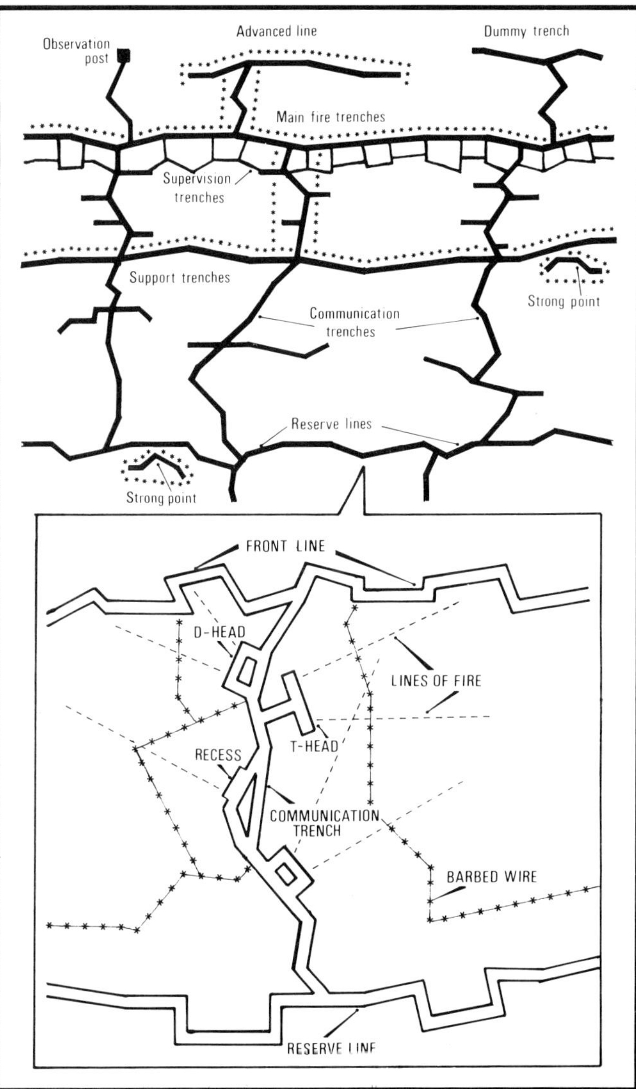

Far left:
One of the earliest trench mortars, the Vickers 1.57in was, for obvious reasons, better known to the troops as the 'Toffee Apple Mortar'. It was copied from a prewar German design by Krupp.

Left:
Sir Wilfred Stokes with his original mortar and a selection of bombs. The bomb in front of his right leg is fitted with the original 'pistol' time fuze, based on the fuze of the Mills Bomb hand grenade.

Right:
Trench warfare — lack of mobility and dominance of artillery and the machine gun led to the preparation of miles of trenches in which the static battles of World War 1 were fought.

Above:
A Vickers medium machine gun in action, 1917. These weapons had legendary reliability and could keep up continuous long range fire for hours in order to deny areas to the enemy.

Right:
The answer to trench warfare was the tank and at Cambrai, on 20 November 1917, it was used to great effect for the first time.

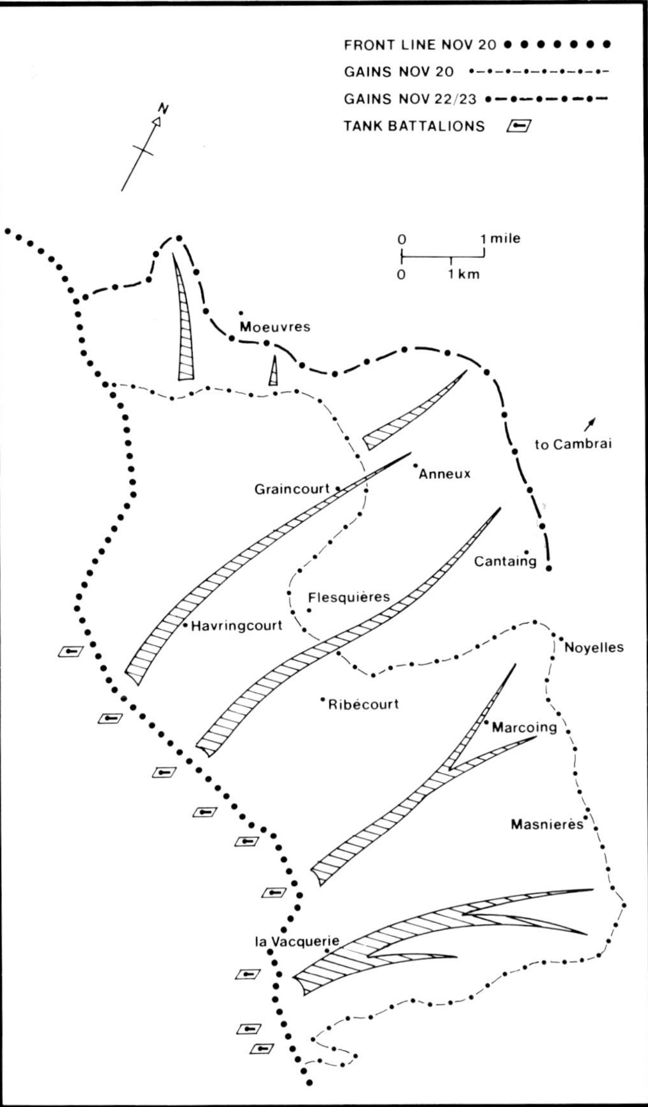

way forward, leaving the infantry behind; and once that happened the defenders could come out of their holes, set up their machine guns, and proceed to decimate the infantry. If the advance went more or less smoothly and the infantry got well ahead, then they went beyond the range of their close support artillery; these should, in theory, have been able to move forward and take up fresh positions from which they could support the advance, but in fact they were prevented from moving by the shell-torn ground, and in any case they had no idea where the infantry were, no reason to think that a move was desirable, and no forward observers to tell them where there might be targets or what the advance was doing. In short, the problem of World War 1 was *communications*; the absence of valid and timely information about what was going on at the line of contact was fundamental to most of the failures of the period.

But even if this fundamental defect was appreciated, there was very little that could be done about it. Wireless was in existence but was insufficiently portable, robust or reliable to allow it to be used in a tactical role. So until some miracle occurred, the soldiers simply had to put up with the defect and attempt to operate as best they could without communications.

What was more obvious were the physical problems facing the attacking soldiers, and the most staring obstacles were the wire and the machine gun; the two in combination virtually rendered movement on the battlefield impossible. This fact was becoming apparent even by the end of 1914, and in those early days neither was as big a problem as it was to become in later years. But it was sufficient to set at least one British officer thinking about a possible solution as he drove back to England in October 1914. Lt-Col Ernest Swinton, a Royal Engineer officer, was the official 'War Correspondent', an officer detailed by the War Office to visit units and tour the front and produce stories for the home press. No vulgar reporters were going to be allowed into the theatre of war; look at the trouble that chap in the Crimea had caused. Let's have it all under control. The idea failed to last, of course, and Swinton went on to more important work. But as he drove back across France his mind was on the wire and machine gun problem, and he recalled seeing a Holt caterpillar tractor pulling some stores. What was needed, he decided, was 'a power-driven, bullet-proof, armed engine capable of destroying machine guns, of crossing country and trenches, of breaking through entanglements and of climbing earthworks . . .' A Holt tractor, with an armour-plated body and one or two machine guns might very well provide what he envisaged.

It would take far too long to detail all the twists and turns which followed Swinton's inspiration, many of which were outrageous coincidences or pieces of outright luck. Briefly, Swinton's ideas found their way to Winston Churchill, and the Royal Navy were already operating armoured cars in Belgium so Churchill felt that there was some affinity. Eventually an 'Admiralty Landships Committee' was formed, but when Churchill was removed from office in the wake of the Dardanelles disaster the Admiralty rapidly attempted to disencumber themselves of his less nautical additions such as the 15in howitzers, the armoured cars and the Landships Committee. They succeeded in all but the latter, which Asquith, the Prime

Ceremonial links the present with the past and reinforces the soldier's identity with his regiment. These two scenes of British Army parades show: *(above)* the King's Troop Royal Horse Artillery passing the saluting dais on Horse Guards Parade during the 1983 Royal Tournament Preview Parade; and *(below)* the band of the Royal Irish Rangers at the Allied Forces Army Parade, Berlin 1980. *D. F. Ashby; Martin Horseman*

A Chieftain armoured recovery vehicle of the Royal Scots Dragoon Guards hastens to rescue a stranded tank during an exercise in Germany. *Simon Forty*

A Challenger main battle tank of the Royal Hussars on 'Lionheart 84'. *Robin Adshead*

Below:
Soldiers of 5 Parachute Brigade Pathfinder Team making for their rendezvous after a HALO (high altitude, low opening) descent. *Robin Adshead*

Far right:
The airborne packhorse: a member of 2 Para with his 'equipment and necessaries' after a practice drop on Salisbury Plain. *Robin Adshead*

Left:
A Saxon armoured personnel carrier of the Royal Anglian Regiment during Exercise 'Lionheart 84'. *Robin Adshead*

Below left:
The MCV80 infantry fighting vehicle under test by the Irish Guards during 'Lionheart 84'. *Ian V. Hogg*

Right:
A Military Policeman of the Berlin Garrison with the Wall visible behind him. *Martin Horseman*

Below:
A Chieftain crossing the River Weser by an M2 bridge system during Exercise 'Lionheart 84'. *Robin Adshead*

Scorpion CVR(T) on the beach at Arishmell, near Lulworth Cove, having just landed during an amphibious exercise.
Martin Horseman

The Carbine, Cavalry, Magazine, Lee-Enfield, Mk I of 1896, a shortened version of the standard rifle for carrying in saddle buckets by mounted troops. Both the long rifle and the short carbine were superseded by the 'Short Magazine Rifle' in 1903, which pioneered the use of one standard rifle throughout the army.

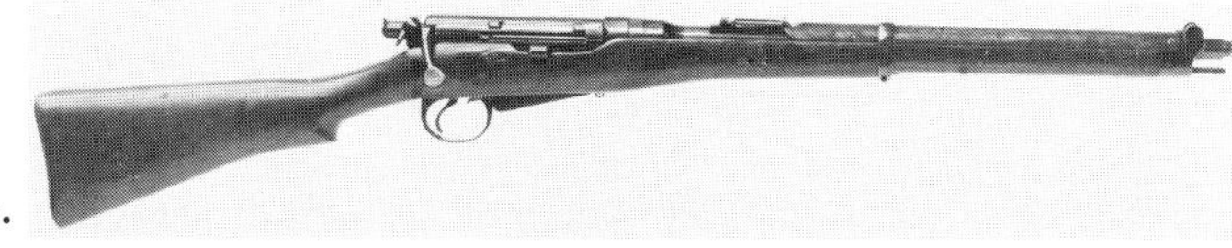

The Farquhar-Hill automatic rifle, one of many designs put forward to replace the Lee-Enfield magazine rifle. Trials of this weapon lasted from 1912 to 1926, but it was not considered suitable for service use.

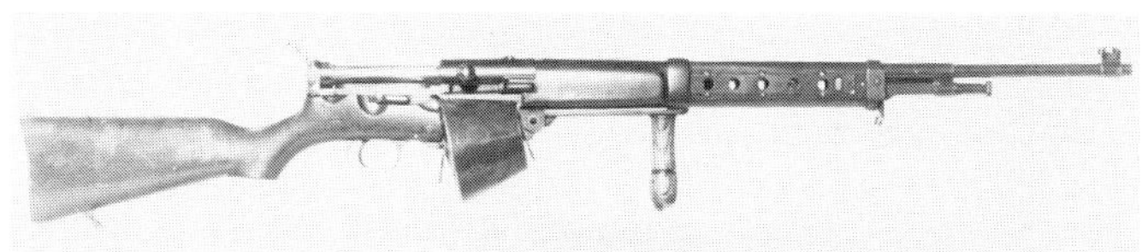

Rifle, Magazine, Lee-Enfield, Mk I of 1895, the 'Long Lee-Enfield' designed for infantry use. Note that it carried a cleaning rod beneath the barrel; this was soon abandoned in favour of a cord 'pull-through' for cleaning the bore.

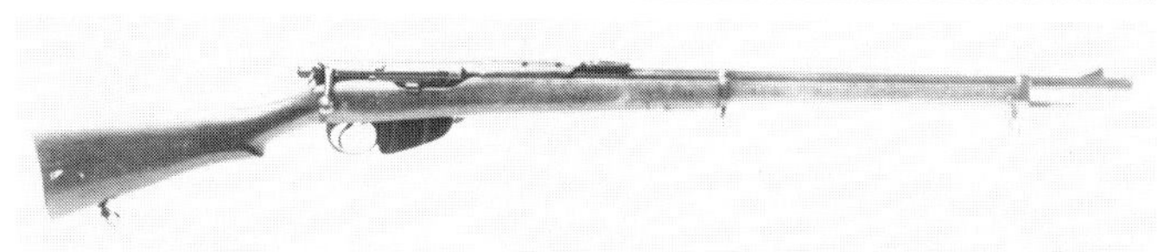

Minister, viewed with some favour. But in the summer of 1915, the Army, who were still being prodded by Swinton, discovered the Committee and placed some representatives on it. Then the Ministry of Munitions appeared, and in August 1915 there was a three-party conference of the Ministry, the Admiralty and the Army at which each told what they had done, what they hoped to do, and what they hoped the other parties might do. As a result it was agreed that the Admiralty, whilst easing itself gracefully out of the picture, should continue to develop a suitable machine since it already had several irons in the fire, but that the actual specification would be laid down by the War Office on the grounds that the soldiers were in the best positon to know precisely what was wanted. The Ministry of Munitions would give aid in supplying materials and equipment but would otherwise merely hold a watching brief until development was complete, whereupon it would step in and organise production.

The specification finally drawn up demanded a machine which would cross a 2.4m trench and climb a 1.5m parapet, and the designers, (Lt W. G. Wilson RN, an engineer who had been with the armoured cars in France, and Sir William Tritton, a director of Foster's of Lincoln, agricultural machinery manufacturers) decided that the only way to achieve this was to design a machine in which the caterpillar track ran around the entire body, and the body had an upward-swept front section such that the curve of the track approximated to an arc of an imaginary huge wheel big enough to defeat the required obstacles. And in this manner the lozenge-shaped tank was born. 'Centipede' (as the first tank was originally known) made

Below:
The Lewis light machine gun was cooled by air passing through the jacket around the barrel. Though American in origin, it was almost totally ignored by them and was made in huge numbers in Britain and Belgium

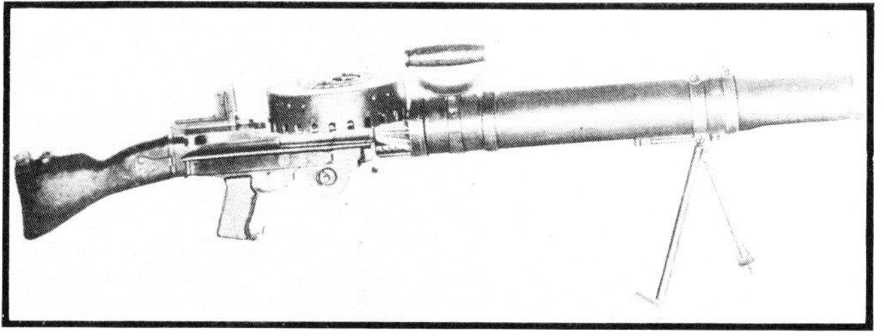

its first run on 12 January 1916. But 'Centipede' was Foster's registered trade name for their heavy agricultural tractors and it was thought wise to abandon that name for the sake of security. Faced with the problem of finding a suitable cover name, Swinton recalled that when the vehicle was being built in Foster's works, it had been represented to the work force as a water-carrying vehicle for use in Mesopotamia; as a result of which the workers began to refer to it as 'that tank thing'. So Swinton called it a 'tank' and that was that.

The gestation of the tank had been a long one, but Swinton had not wasted his time during this process; he had drawn up a far sighted paper called 'The Necessity for Machine Gun destroyers' which laid down, in considerable detail, how he thought these devices should be built, transported, and used in both offensive and defensive actions. One of the notable points about this paper is that Swinton confined himself to the matter in hand — the problem of breaking through the wire and overcoming the machine gun. He resisted any temptation to flights of fancy; there were no demands for 1,000 machines, no suggestion of invincibility, no requests for excessive armament, no forecasts of grand fleets manoeuvring on the battlefield. Such elements would have immediately labelled his paper 'visionary' and 'impractical' and would have consigned it to the wastepaper basket. By keeping his plans down to 50 machines operating on a three-mile front, Swinton avoided the pitfall into which many advocates, before and since, have fallen to their destruction.

One remarkable aspect of the tank development programme was that GHQ in France knew nothing whatever about it until a very late stage. Once again, Winston Churchill was the catalyst; after his removal from political office he had gone to France in his yeomanry rank of Major and was attached to the Grenadier Guards. What he saw there, together with what he had been privy to in England, moved him to sit down and write a paper entitled 'Variants of the Offensive', expounding various methods of breaking the deadlock of the trenches and also describing the possible use of tanks. The paper was forwarded to Sir Douglas Haig who was surprised to read that 'about 70 machines are nearing completion' and who immediately despatched a staff officer to London to find out what was going on. By this time 'Centipede' was being built.

Once the first tank (now christened 'Mother') had passed its trials, an order for no more than 40 was given. Swinton argued that training vehicles and replacements would be needed, and the order was raised to 100. Swinton then had another inspiration; the prototype was armed with a 6pdr ex-Naval gun on each side and four machine guns, and if it was attacked by infantry Swinton thought the 6pdr might be of little use. He therefore suggested that a second type should be built, armed only with six machine guns. This, too, was accepted, the 6pdr tanks being classed as 'male' and the machine gun tanks as 'female', and the contract was increased to 75 of each.

General Haig, having now learned what tanks were and having read Swinton's tactical ideas, asked for tanks to be made available for his forthcoming attack on the Somme, beginning on 1 June 1916. Since it was now March, considering that construction had only been authorised some six weeks before, and considering that the minimum time to train a recruit into a moderately competent infantryman was six months, Haig was being a trifle unrealistic in thinking he could have a trained tank force available to him in 3½ months. In reply, Swinton said that it was probable that 75 could be ready by August.

In the event the Somme battle was delayed and began on 1 July, and, as is well known, ran into difficulties. Before the month was out tanks were being demanded, but it was not until 13 August that the first ones arrived in France. A Tank Training School was set up with the intention of allowing the crews time to complete their training and allow the mechanics time to complete the final adjustments. But this laudable aim was ruined by GHQ's insistence that the tanks should 'perform' at set times for crowds of visitors. The surprising thing is that even with scores of officers and men visiting the school to see the circus, no word of the new machines crossed the line.

Eventually, on 15 September, the tanks were sent into action for the first time. Swinton's guidelines were almost entirely ignored by GHQ and instead of the new machines being used en masse, they were split into 'penny packets' and distributed across the front. At the end of the day the few surviving tanks had managed to perform some useful work alongside the infantry, they had boosted British and undermined German morale, and the general opinion was favourable — at least, General Haig was generous in his praise, and that was all that counted. He demanded a further 1,000 forthwith, but this order was countermanded, cancelled, reinstated and changed until it resulted in a contract for a further 100 and a promise that an improved model would be coming and the balance would be made up from these.

Perhaps the best summing up was one which was written some time afterwards by Maj-Gen J. F. C. Fuller. He observed that the tank was, in principle, sound and merely needed mechanical improvement; that it had not been put into battle on favourable ground; that because of the secrecy surrounding it, commanders had little or no idea of its potential and no chance to train with it; that the crews had insufficient training; and that much had to be learned about reconnaissance, preparation and logistics in connection with tank operations. It was an eminently fair summary of what the first limited use of tanks had disclosed.

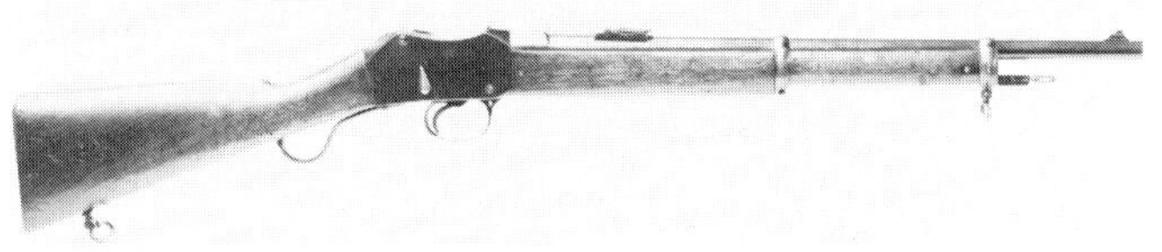

The Martini-Metford Cavalry Carbine of 1892, a conversion of the Martini-Henry .45in carbine to .303in calibre.

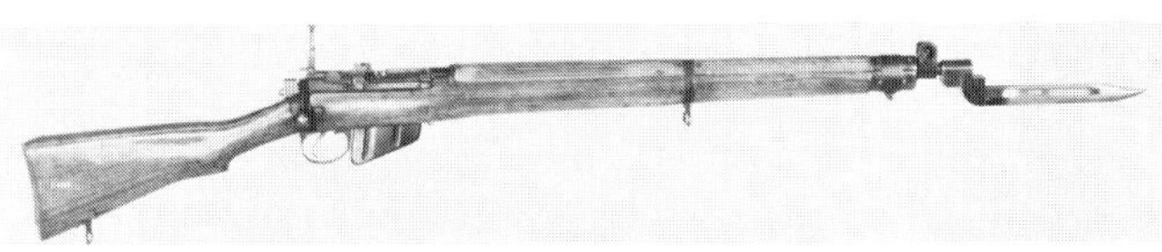

Rifle No 4 Mk 1, introduced in 1939, was the Lee-Enfield adapted to mass-production.

The De Lisle .45in calibre Silent Carbine, developed in 1943 for use by Commando and Airborne forces, used a Lee-Enfield bolt action attached to a Thompson submachine gun barrel surrounded by a complex silencer and fired American .45in automatic pistol cartridges in almost complete silence.

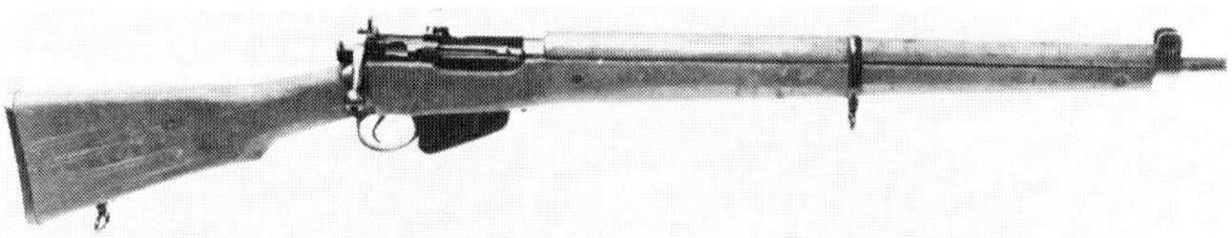

A wartime experiment to try and speed production was this No 4 rifle with an all-steel stock instead of the customary wood. It proved a failure, the recoil being violent and the shooting inaccurate.

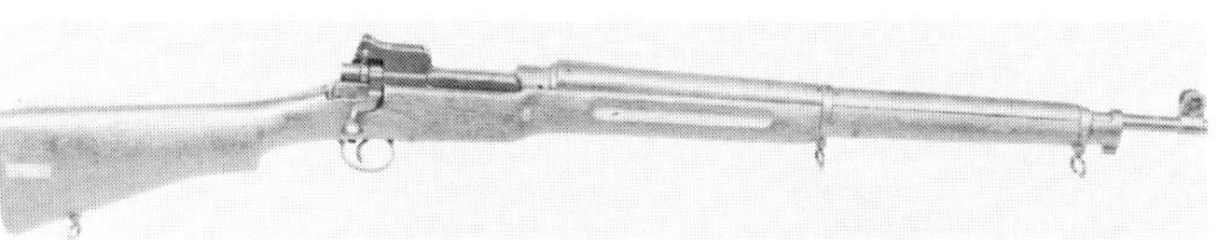

The Rifle, .276in, Pattern '14 was a modified Mauser design intended to overcome the theoretical shortcomings of the Lee-Enfield. Designed by a group of target shooters it proved to be a fine target rifle but an impractical service weapon and was never introduced in this form.

The Rifle No 5 or 'Jungle Carbine' of 1944. Developed as a light and short rifle for use in difficult country, it was popular enough with the troops until they discovered that it failed to 'hold its zero' and soon became inaccurate in constant use.

Above:
The Webley Mk 1 British service revolver, introduced in 1887.

Eventually the mechanical improvements came, the tanks were given the chance to perform on good ground, problems of command and supply were partially mastered, and by the time the war ended the tank was an accepted piece of equipment. Suitable tactics had been devised — based largely upon Swinton's original paper drawn up before any tank existed — so that the machine was used in tight conjunction with the infantry to carry firepower forward, smash down obstacles and protect the infantryman during the assault. At Cambrai, in November 1917, tanks used in accordance with these tactics, and operating on unbroken ground, made a formidable incursion into the German lines. But the operation came to naught when the promised reserves never appeared; the reserves which should have been available had, in fact, been wasted away in the Third Ypres battle and what was available was a force largely composed of shattered remnants hurriedly grouped together and evincing a colossal lack of interest in the whole affair. Within a fortnight the British Army had been evicted from its gains and the stalemate persisted.

Haig, for all the criticisms that have been levelled at him in subsequent years, was a shrewd judge of the strategic situation, and by the end of the summer of 1918 he appreciated that the exhaustion on both sides — both among troops and among home population — was such that the side which made the biggest effort would win, and win rapidly. He had successfully drawn the sting of the two German offensives earlier in the year and now reckoned that a sharp assault would do the trick.

Unfortunately, he had made similar prognostications before, and the politicians disbelieved him. Nevertheless, he was right; he began the Second Battle of the Somme on 8 August 1918, and he brought back the war of movement, with tanks and infantry advancing together. The British armies punched through the thin crust of German resistance, first in one sector then in another. At the end of September the much-feared Hindenburg Line was smashed; in October the Belgian coast was cleared; on 11 November the Armistice was signed and the war was over.

The 'Hundred Days' of 1918 was the British Army's greatest achievement; most of the fighting was done by the British; they took over 188,000 prisoners, compared with 196,000 by the French, Belgians and Americans together, and took 2,840 guns against 3,775 by the other Allies. And yet in postwar years few people ever heard about that part of the campaign; all the writers and politicians could talk about was the losses at Paschendaele and on the Somme, the mud, the misery, and poor generalship. And in the wake of the Armistice the French began seeking reparations, the Americans told everybody how they'd won the war and the British Army just went home.

Table 4: Weapons of the First World War

	Title	*Calibre*	*Length* (in)	*Weight* lb/oz	*Capacity*	*Bullet Weight* (gr)	*Muzzle Velocity* (ft/sec)	*Muzzle Energy* (ft/lb)	*Effective Range* (yd)	*Remarks*
Small Arms										
1888	Rifle, Lee-Metford Mk 1	.303	49.5	9/8	8	215	2,200	2,308	600	First magazine rifle
1895	Rifle, Lee-Enfield Mk 1	.303	49.5	9/4	10	215	2,200	2,308	600	Cordite adopted
1907	Rifle, Lee-Enfield Mk III	.303	44.5	8/10	10	215	2,060	2,028	600	Short Lee-Enfield
1916	Rifle, Enfield Pattern '14	.303	46.3	8/11	5	174	2,785	3,005	600	Made in USA on contract
1912	Vickers Mk 1 MG	.303	45.5	39.9	250 belt	215	2,444	2,855	2,000	450rd/min
1914	Lewis Mk 1 MG	.303	50.5	26.0	47 drum	215	2,444	2,855	600	550rd/min
1916	Hotchkiss Mk 1 MG	.303	46.7	27.0	30 strip	215	2,424	2,808	600	500rd/min
1915	Pistol, Webley Mk 6	.455	11.2	2.4	6-cyl	265	655	252	15	

Title	*Class*	*Calibre* (inc)	*Barrel Length* (calibres)	*Shell Weight* (lb)	*Charge Weight* (lb)	*Muzzle Velocity* (ft/sec)	*Mounting*	*Weight in Action* (tons)	*Max Range* (yd)	*Remarks*
Breech-Loading (BL) and Quick-Firing (QF) Artillery										
12pr BL	Horse	3.0	22	12.5	12oz C	1,585	2-wheel	0.75	6,000	
13pr QF	Horse	3.0	23	12.5	1.25 C	1,675	2-wheel	0.95	5.900	
18pr QF	Field	3.3	28	18.5	1.45 C	1,615	2-wheel	1.25	6,525	
4.5in QF Howitzer	Field	4.5	13.4	35	1.0 C	1,010	2-wheel	1.35	7,300	
60pr BL Gun	Siege	5.0	32	60	9.75 C	2,080	2-wheel	4.4	12,300	
9.2in BL Howitzer 1	Siege	9.2	13.2	290	10.9 C	1,187	Siege	13.35	10,060	
12pr of 12cwt QF	Coast	3.0	40	12.5	2.0 C	2,258	Pedestal	4.1	8,000	
4.7in QF Mk 2	Coast	4.72	40	45	5.5 C	2,150	Pedestal	Various	11,800	
6in BL Mk 7	Coast	6.0	45	100	11.5 C	2,493	Barbette	16.1	12,000	
9.2in BL Mk 10	Coast	9.2	46.5	380	120 C	2,643	Barbette	157	29,200	
QF 3in of 20cwt HA	AA	3.0	45	16	2.5 C	2,500	Pedestal	5.9	23,500ft maximum ceiling	

Note that all these were breech-loaders; the notation BL or QF signified the use of bagged or brass-cased charges respectively. 'HA' in the terminology of the 3in 20cwt gun meant 'High Angle' in 1914 — the term 'anti-aircraft' came later. Note also that 'C' in the cartridge column indicates the universal adoption of Cordite as a propellant, in place of gunpowder.

Transport

Above:
The baggage cart of the Royal Scots regiment on the march in 1890. Not the least interesting feature of this picture is the revelation that the soldiers actually wore those enormous hats in day-to-day work.

Below:
An elephant battery in India, pulling a 40pdr siege gun.

Bottom:
Holt's tracked tractor pulling 8in howitzers in France, 1918. The tractor had been developed in England but found no backers in the early 1900s and the patents were sold to the USA, from whence the tractors had to be bought in 1914.

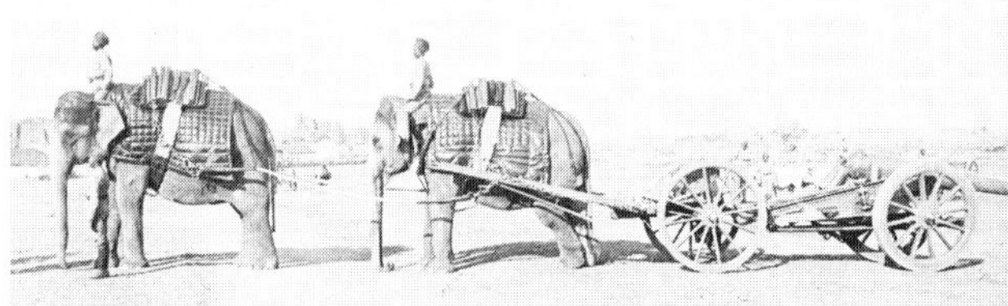

In spite of its long love affair with the horse, the army has never been reluctant to try other methods of moving its equipment. Every type of indigenous domestic animal has been adopted at some time or other, and the difficulty of moving loads through the mud of the Crimean peninsula led to the provision of a steam traction engine. In 1858 a Bray steam engine was delivered to the Royal Artillery for trial as a gun tractor, though without subsequent effect. In the 1870s and 1880s numerous steam traction engines, almost all of English make, were bought by continental armies and put to use, and in 1899 15 engines were sent to South Africa for traction purposes, together with two steam ploughs intended for the rapid excavation of breastworks. At least one such engine was used for the 'Fowler Armoured Road Train', being protected by armour plate and used to tow a number of similarly-protected wagons carrying troops and guns.

The petrol engine was adopted for military service by various armies in the 1890s in small numbers, and these grew rapidly in the early years of the new century. On the outbreak of war in 1914 the British Army had an estimated 1,000 motor trucks and cars, many of which had been impressed from civil owners, and this number increased rapidly as the war progressed. The most appealing feature of motor vehicles was that, in contrast to horses, they did not require feeding when they were not actually working; the least appealing feature was their demand for specialised operators and mechanics, of which there was a scarcity in those days. But perhaps the most vital fact facing the army was that due to the gradual adoption of motor vehicles by the civil population, the supply of horses was falling in proportion, and unless the army mechanised it would have to go into the horse-breeding business in order to keep itself supplied.

The interwar years saw the adoption of the motor vehicle for almost every aspect of military transportation, from the delivery of rations and coal to the moving of heavy artillery, and by 1939 the British Army was, without doubt, the most completely mechanised army in the world.

The economic problem facing armies is the question of whether to adapt commercial vehicles to military use or to design and construct purely military vehicles which are better-suited to their particular tasks. Both solutions have been adopted in the past, but today, with a few exceptions, military transport vehicles are largely of commercial pattern, since the modern commercial vehicle is closer to the military specification than it ever was in the past.

Above:
A 'gun tank' designed to carry a 60pdr medium gun through the Flanders mud and deliver it to its firing position; the gun's wheels had to be removed and hung on the side of the tank during transport. France, 1917.

Above right:
The American 4×4 Willys Jeep became as commonplace in the British Army as it was in the American; 13 (Martinique) Field Battery, RA, Korea, 1952.

Right:
The Bedford 'QL' 3-ton truck was a universal provider for the British throughout World War 2 and afterwards; this one has been adapted as an artillery command post in Korea, 1952.

Below:
A modern commercial design adapted to military use with minimal change, the Foden 8×4 'Low Mobility Unit' using a Rolls-Royce engine. *Foden*

Above:
Special transport for speciai terrain; the Swedish Volvo Bv206 over-snow tractor, here seen in use towing a 105mm light gun in Norway. Thc forward unit contains the engine, and a flexible coupling drives the track of both units.

Right:
High-speed delivery in difficult country is now generally done by RAF helicopters. Here a Puma helicopter delivers rations to a unit in Norway during NATO exercises, 1980.

Below:
More specialisation: a heavy tractor belonging to the Commando Engineeer Squadron towing a Land Rover ashore during a landing exercise in Scotland, 1979.

5 Real Soldiering

The army which came home from France in 1918 was a far different army to that which had gone out in 1914. The 1914 army was a compact group of professionals; the 1918 army was a sprawling mass of conscripts leavened by a handful of professional survivors. Most of the soldiers considered themselves civilians in uniform and were merely concerned with getting back to civil life, and the remains of the regular army would not be sorry to see them go, so that they could then turn back to what was commonly called 'real soldiering' once more. In spite of the fact that impressed civilians had brought unexpected talents into the army, had fought well, made good soldiers, and formed an extremely useful reservoir of technical talent which enabled the army to put the wartime developments to good use, the fact remained that they were, with few exceptions, little interested in anything but getting the war over as quickly as possible. And once that had been done they wanted no part of the organisation which had been running their lives for the past few years.

But the mass conscription which had been necessary to fuel the army brought one slight consolation in its wake; it awoke the nation to the fact that they had an army, and it gave the man in the street some inside knowledge of what a soldier's life was like, so that in postwar years the regular soldier was no longer the social pariah he had been before 1914. Even so, the rapid dissolution of the major part of the army, bringing the force back to prewar manning strengths, meant that, once more, the army virtually disappeared behind the gates of its barracks and garrison towns, and within 10 years the soldier was a rarity. I first saw a soldier on an omnibus in Durham, in 1932, and this man, in his peculiar dress with brass buttons and a peaked cap, was so strange a sight that every child on the 'bus clustered round him, asking what he was, what he did, where he came from. He was to be the last soldier I saw until 1938.

With the prospect of unemployment outside the barrack gates, there were some of the wartime entrants who, finding they liked soldiering, volunteered to stay on and enter the regular army. So far as the rank and file went this was welcomed, and the army appears to have had very little trouble in settling at its maximum permitted manpower figure. With the officer corps it was a little more difficult; many men who had attained commissioned rank during the war were not of the class or quality who would have been accepted as officers before 1914, and applicants for regular commissions were carefully screened before being accepted. Regimental colonels, who still had the final word on whom they would accept as officers in their regiments, were, for the most part, elderly and conservative gentlemen and they were making quite sure that the regiment got back to 1914 standards just as quickly as it could.

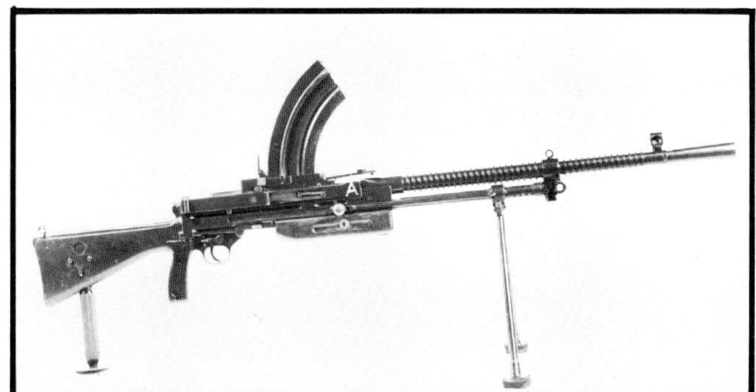

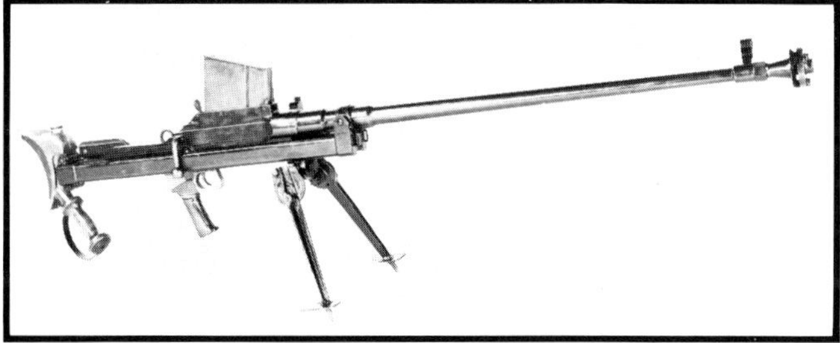

Top:
The Vickers-Berthier light machine gun was adopted by the Indian Army in the 1930s, but the British Army preferred the Bren.

Centre:
The Bren light machine gun, designed in Czechoslovakia and manufactured at Enfield, replaced the Lewis and Hotchkiss guns and has remained the British standard since 1933.

Above:
The Boys anti-tank rifle, calibre .55in, was a simple but powerful bolt-action weapon which could defeat the thin armour of prewar tanks but was rapidly outclassed by improved wartime armour.

'Getting back to peacetime soldiering' meant, for them, returning to an ordered life in barracks — hunting three days a week, regimental soirees and balls in season, the

training year culminating in the annual exercise, and forgetting all that stuff about trenches and gas and tanks and making sure that the soldiers were drilled and well turned-out for the annual administrative inspection. It meant getting back to India, Bermuda, Singapore, Egypt, Mauritius and the score or more of Empire stations. For a few it meant Cologne and the Army of Occupation, but even this soon turned into British barrack life in the normal manner. Not to put too fine a point on it, for 80% of the army it meant a gentle drift back into apathy, a sort of reaction against the frantic hurly-burly of the war. Lessons learned in blood in Flanders were rapidly forgotten, except by a handful of officers and men, a situation which was encouraged by the adoption, by the Cabinet, of the 'Ten Year Rule'. This rule simply said that the Army (and the Royal Navy and Royal Air Force) should make their plans on the assumption that there would be no war for 10 years, and it was conveniently restated annually, so that the 10 years never diminished.

All this was not entirely the army's fault, it was simply that in a massive sigh of relief at seeing the war over, the nation lost interest in military affairs. The government pared the defence budget to the barest minimum and appeared to take a delight in demolishing military structures. General Ashmore, who had commanded the London anti-aircraft defences, tells how the defences shrank from a strength of 286 guns in November 1918, to 164 by January 1919, to 42 by June 1919, to eight by December 1919. 'The finale . . . came in 1920 when a reporter happened on a gun station near London with a real gun and real soldiers (two caretakers). The subsequent outcry was too much for the authorities; the few remains of the London Air Defence Area were hurried away and hidden near Aldershot.'

It was against this background that a handful of officers tried to record the lessons of the war and tried to develop some tactical doctrines which incorporated these lessons and reflected the changes in equipment which had taken place. Maj-Gen J. F. C. Fuller, Capt (later Sir) Basil Liddell Hart, Percy Hobart, Gifford Martel, Lt-Col Alan Brooke were among this number and became perhaps the best-known names, but they were merely the tip of a small iceberg.

What appears to have fascinated most of the more vociferous thinkers was the advent of the tank and the promise of new tactics which it brought. But even while these people were having their first thoughts on the matter, the tank itself nearly vanished down the same path as air defence. The first tanks had been operated by the Heavy Branch of the Machine Gun Corps, a regiment raised in October 1915 and disbanded in 1921. In July 1917 the Tank Corps was formed and took over from the MGC. At the end of the war the Tank Corps, being very much the junior corps of the army, was in a vulnerable position, the more so because of a widespread belief that the tank had merely been an ad hoc solution to a peculiar problem — that of beating the trench/wire combination — and that in a properly conducted war there would be no

Left:
One of the first 3.7in anti-aircraft guns, seen in the Royal Ordnance Factory in 1936. The complexity and expense of the design is apparent.

Above:
A 3in 20cwt anti-aircraft gun on a Peerless lorry mounting in position on Westminster Bridge, London, during the Munich crisis of 1938.

place for such devices. This opinion was summed up by Maj-Gen Sir Louis Jackson, a former Director of Trench Warfare, at a lecture given in 1919, when he said 'The tank proper was a freak. The circumstances which called it into existence were exceptional and are not likely to recur. If they do, they can be dealt with by other means'. Considering that the tank had come into existence because every 'other means' had failed, this was a peculiar statement, but such was his seniority that it was never questioned and his lead was taken and rapidly exploited. Innumerable schemes were proposed for the future of the Tank Corps, from retaining it as it stood, to seconding personnel to it, to splitting it into independent and infantry-supporting branches, to making it part of the Royal Engineers . . . eventually, late in 1922 it was agreed to retain it as a separate corps of the army, established at a strength of four battalions. By that time, of course, demobilisation had taken its toll and even meeting this reduced establishment meant raising two new battalions and recruiting large numbers of officers and men.

But if the flesh was weak, the spirit was more than willing, and the theorists on tank warfare were not going to permit the relative dearth of tanks to stand in their way, largely because they were of the opinion that the wartime designs were mechanical pioneers and would soon be replaced by improved models. This was a correct assumption so far as it went, but in fact there was to be little replacement, for simple reasons of finance.

What had gripped the fancy of the theorists was Fuller's 'Plan 1919' (as it came to be commonly known), which had been drawn up in 1918 as a postulated strategy for the 1919 offensive-to-be. Fuller, basing his ideas on a new design of 'Medium D' tank then on the drawing board, argued that the tank could be used as an independent striking force to cut through the enemy lines, ignore the immediate defences, and strike deeply into the rear area so as to cut communications, destroy dumps and headquarters, and generally 'paralyse the nervous system' of the opposing force. Fuller's plan, first broached in May 1918, assumed that by the spring of 1919 there would be a force of some 2,500 heavy and 2,400 Medium D tanks available to perform this manoeuvre, but in fact in November 1918 only two Medium D tanks existed and in the following two years it proved to be a mechanical disaster.

Nevertheless, the audacity and dash of the Plan captured the imagination of many students and was the genesis of wide-ranging theories of tank employment which were put forward during the 1920s by several persuasive authors. Fuller himself was the foremost of these; in the *Cavalry Journal* he forecast the demise of the horse, pointing out that 'either the cavalryman has to become impervious to bullets or a new weapon has to be invented which will prevent bullets being thrown at him'. In the *Royal Artillery Journal* he argued that artillery was to be the principal arm of the future, but then qualified this by pointing out that of course, the guns would have to be mounted in tanks. He continued to play on his 'Plan

1919' theme that the modern method of warfare was not to kill infantrymen and occupy ground but to make a decisive strike at the enemy's 'nervous system' paralysing the 'brain' (the headquarters/communications complex) and thus rendering it incapable of controlling the 'body' (the troops in the field). Given this assumption, it naturally followed that the ideal instrument for this purpose was the tank, and Fuller then developed this from merely having gun tanks as a spearhead to proposing that the entire force should be on tracks — gun tanks, man-carrying tanks and artillery-carrying tanks. This, unfortunately, led him to suggest (doubtless in an unguarded moment) the formation of 'Royal Tank Marines' and 'Royal Tank Artillery'; this, as might be imagined, did not go down well with either the infantry or the Royal Artillery, who saw a threat to their independence and a promise of their being assimilated into a much junior corps, and there was a good deal of uproar in consequence.

'Plan 1919' postulated a pincer movement — attack on two flanks simultaneously — accompanied by a massive thrust in the centre; the flank attacks would head for the rear area on their 'brain-severing' task, while the central attack would take advantage of the ensuing dislocation and break through the line of resistance. Fuller now modified this into a fresh theory, that of 'Dual Penetration' which used the same three forces but modified their aim; the flanks would now be content to cut the main line of resistance, thus isolating the sector between. The two attacks would be successive; the first would draw a proportion of the enemy's reserve to it, the second would attract the remaining reserve from the sector, and then the main attack would be driven frontally against the now-weakened sector. The two flank attacks were merely to isolate and attract reserves; the central attack would do the damage.

The principal objection to this manoeuvre appears to be the difficulty of imposing restraint on the two flank attacks which, by the nature of the tactic, had to be of limited objective. Experience shows that attacks with limited objectives are pointless if they fail and not amenable to control if they succeed; when success is in sight the attackers usually forget their limited objectives and endeavour to push on and improve matters, which usually leads to disaster. Moreover the limited objective attack rarely allows for the whims of fortune; if, for some reason, the enemy sensationally collapses, the commander with a limited objective is often loath to seize the opportunity presented to him, and in any case is unlikely to have reserves sufficient to take advantage of his luck. World War 1 could show some prime examples of all these various possibilities, and Fuller appears to have forgotten them.

As Fuller was propounding his tank theories, another writer, Capt (later Sir) Basil Liddell Hart, was writing his proposals for infantry attacks and propounding his theory of the 'expanding torrent'. Here he advocated a 'forward body' which would probe ahead of the main force until it found a weak spot, whereupon it would break in and the main force or 'manoeuvre body' would follow up, breaking through the defences, widening the gap, and then spreading out on the other side — the expanding torrent.

Liddell Hart and Fuller met in 1920 and the latter soon pointed out that the expanding torrent theory was all very well when infantry met infantry, but that adding tanks to the equation would ruin it, since 'it is impossible to pit infantry against machines'. This led Liddell Hart to look more closely at the tank, and by 1922 he was writing of 'an army composed principally of tanks and aircraft, with a small force of siege artillery' and advocating a mixture of 'scout', 'cruiser', 'battle' and 'supply' tanks.

It was all very well for the theorists to talk gaily of these various types of tank and their employment, but the soldiers of the time were trying to learn the basics of their trade on leftovers from the war. The Ministry of Munitions having been dissolved, the official tank design teams had shrunk to a mere handful of men and their budget had been pared to the bone, and in an endeavour to obtain tanks without undergoing the expense of developing them 'in house', the army had turned to private enterprise. This had been more or less forced on them, also, by the peculiar financial system. With the reduction on strength of the design team there was no possibility of any manufacturing, but in 1921 the War Office had half a million pounds allotted for tanks, and unless it was spent during the current financial year it would be lost for ever. So rather than forego the money, a contract was given to Vickers to supply a medium tank, and this set the pattern for the British Army's tanks until 1938. The design which Vickers produced was originally known as a 'light' tank since, by comparison with the wartime models it was light — 11 tons as against 30 — and it had a rotating turret armed with a 3pdr gun and four Hotchkiss machine guns, two Vickers machine guns in the sides, and an air-cooled engine giving it a speed of 15mph. Although its armour was thin — too thin to resist small arms fire at first — it nevertheless represented a considerable technological step forward, and it also had the virtue of mechanical reliability.

Below:
Firing of a 9.2in coast defence gun at Nodes Point Battery, Isle of Wight, during an annual practice camp in the 1930s. The magazines are buried beneath the emplacement and supplied ammunition by means of lifts beneath the flat 'shell-pit shield' forming a floor around the gun. From there the shells and cartridge went up by lifts to the gun breech.

With about 100 of these Vickers tanks, plus the leftovers from the war, the Tank Corps set about building up their own tactical theories; at the same time they demonstrated their ability to build a tank around a theory by setting out specifications for an 'independent' tank. The official doctrine of the period said that tanks were to operate in support of infantry — the task for which they had been designed in 1915-16. But there was a growing body of opinion, fuelled by reading Fuller and Liddell Hart, which thought that an armoured force should be an independent force, driving through the enemy's outposts to rove behind the lines and destroy worthwhile targets. Such a force would require a well-armed, well-protected and fast tank with a wide radius of action, and from a specification based on this premise, drawn up by the Tank Corps, Vickers developed its 'Independent' tank.

Weighing 32 tons it could move at 20mph, had 29mm of armour, and had no less than five turrets. The main turret carried a 47mm gun, while the four lesser turrets, virtually at each corner of the hull, each had a single machine gun; in theory any target could be engaged by two machine gun turrets and the main gun. But it was an expensive machine, and it arrived when disarmament was in the air, so that it remained the only one of its kind. There has never been any shortage of people who regretted this and who have held out all sorts of tempting prospects for the British Army had the 'Independent' been adopted in quantity. The result would probably have been disastrous; several countries copied the 'Independent' and were far from satisfied with the results. The principal drawback of these multi-turret designs is that of ensuring adequate control. The tank had an eight-man crew — commander, driver, gunner, loader and four machine-gunners. The commander, in his cupola at the rear of the main turret, had to control the activities of his crew, indicate targets to four turrets, navigate, signal, direct the driver, take tactical decisions and, in the expressive term, 'fight his tank'. Everyone who tried the multi-turret tank soon found that all this was far too much for one man.

While the tank soldiers and tank theorists made their predictions about warfare, there were other sections of the army equally interested in forecasting. The Royal Artillery looked at the multitude of guns with which they finished the war — everything from the Horse Artillery 13pdr to an 18in howitzer on a railway mounting — and wondered if it might not be possible to reduce the number of types and introduce a measure of rationalisation. For example, the divisional artillery used three basic weapons — the 13pdr and 18pdr guns and the 4.5in howitzer — and surely it might be possible to reduce this. The 13pdr was no longer practical; the shell was too light and the range too small, and it survived merely as an exercise, training and ceremonial weapon. (Indeed, some of the many anti-aircraft 13pdr guns were removed from their air defence mountings, remounted on their horse artillery carriages, and are still in service today as ceremonial weapons.) The 18pdr high explosive shell was too light to be effective, while the 4.5in howitzer had a good shell but had limited range. Moreover neither gun was easily adaptable to dealing with fast-moving targets, which meant that the Royal Artillery were already looking at the tank as a possible target in future wars and needed a gun capable of rapid changes of direction. What was needed

Left:
A remarkable idea of the 1920s was this two-barrelled gun; fitted (as here) with a small-calibre barrel it was a high velocity anti-tank gun. By changing to the large-calibre barrel (carried alongside the trail) it became a low-velocity infantry support gun. The idea worked but was not pursued.

Below:
Another offering from the gunmakers of the 1920s was this 2.5in infantry support gun. The infantry didn't want it.

was a sort of 'half-way house' weapon, more nimble than the 4.5in but with a better weight of shell than the 18pdr.

It would be tedious to tabulate the many designs which were contemplated during the 15 years following the Armistice, but one or two significant points can be mentioned. In 1924 the Director of Artillery asked for '. . . a range of 15,000yd . . . with a super-charge' and suggested a 3in gun firing a 16lb shell. Since this was asking for a shell lighter than the existing 18pdr it was not followed up, but it is noteworthy as the birth of the 15,000yd demand which was to form part of every field artillery gun specification for many years afterwards.

The next proposal was for a 105mm howitzer firing a 33lb shell with a range of 12,000yd. By 1926 this had progressed to the point where it had been designed as a bagged-charge weapon and to be drawn by mechanical means; this latter was a significant step forward since it automatically removed the old weight restriction of 30cwt (3,360lb), the maximum which could be drawn by a six-horse team. In order to encourage this design the maximum range demand was quietly lowered to 12,000yd and after several alternative paper designs had been examined, Vickers received a contract to produce a pilot model and an in-house design was begun in Woolwich Arsenal. Soon after this another design appeared, this time for a cartridge-case QF gun of 3.9in calibre firing a 30lb shell to 11,900yd but the 12,000yd rule defeated that idea.

By 1931 the 105mm howitzers had appeared and were subjected to various tests on Salisbury Plain. By this time the thinking had come around to demanding two weapons, the 105mm howitzer and an 84mm gun to range to 12,000yd, be capable of anti-tank firing, and be towed by a motor vehicle, and in June 1929 Vickers had been asked to produce a design of this latter weapon. But by the early 1930s it seemed unlikely that money would be forthcoming for two weapons when the avowed intention of the development programme had been to replace two

Left:
The 'Hornet' or Medium Mark C is generally thought to be the best tank design to come out of World War 1. Designed by Foster's as a result of interviewing tank crews, 450 were ordered and begun in September 1918. The end of the war terminated the contract when only 48 had been made, and these formed the major equipment of the Tank Corps until the Vickers medium design arrived.

Below left:
50th Field Battery RA showing off their new Morris-Commercial tractor and 18/25pdr gun in 1937, after mechanisation. Note that the tractor carries civil license plates, as did most military vehicles until 1939.

Below:
The Light Tank Mk IV built in 1934 was the first British light tank to use the hull as a chassis. It was armed with a .50in Vickers machine gun.

Bottom:
The Matilda Mk II infantry tank was heavily armoured but poorly armed, using the universal 2pdr gun which lacked an effective high explosive shell for supporting infantry.

with one. And since nobody could decide which of the two proposed weapons seemed the more attractive, a new theory arose of a 'dual-purpose' gun or 'gun-howitzer' which would, by having a high enough range of elevation and a number of alternative propelling charges, have the velocity of a gun or the high trajectory of a howitzer as required. In late 1933 the General Staff discussed various suggestions and finally agreed on a 3.7in (94mm) gun-howitzer firing a 25lb shell. In September 1934 a pilot model was ordered.

At this juncture finance raised its head once more; the only way to assure sufficient funds for a worthwhile re-equipment programme was to adopt a design which used as much existing equipment as possible. So the proposed 3.7in calibre was reduced to 3.45in (87mm) since with this dimension it would be possible to build a loose gun barrel which could then be slipped into the jacket of the existing 18pdr carriages, have the 18pdr breech attached, and thus provide a new weapon without having to pay for a new carriage as well. Whilst this idea was accepted, the Director Royal Artillery, Maj-Gen H. A. Lewis, set his designers to work on a completely new weapon, with new barrel and carriage, to be ready when the inevitable finally happened.

In a similar mood of economy, in 1933 a proposal was made to replace the 60pdr (5in) medium gun, a cumbersome relic of the 1900s. Instead of making a clean sweep, the same course was adopted, of designing a 4.5in (114mm) barrel to slide into the jacket of the 60pdr, so obtaining a better performance in range (though at the expense of shell weight) without having to pay for a new carriage. In a remarkable example of short-sightedness the design was accepted, production begun, and only then was it found that there were only 76 serviceable 60pdr guns in existence, far short of the number required to outfit an expanding army. So Gen Lewis took responsibility once more and authorised development of a completely new design of gun which would fit the carriage of another weapon then at the design stage, a 5.5in (140mm) gun.

The Royal Artillery had also looked at Fuller's 'Tank Artillery' proposal in the 1920s and found it had some merit, and went on to design a self-propelled gun based on the chassis of the Vickers medium tank. This became known as the 'Birch Gun', after the then Master-General of Ordnance Gen Sir Noel Birch who sponsored its development. Unfortunately there was, at that time, a fixation with dual purpose weapons, field guns capable of anti-aircraft fire, and thus the design called for mounting an 18pdr gun so that it could elevate to 90deg for air defence, traverse 360deg, and have double sets of sights for air and ground firing, all of which led to a very complicated piece of machinery. Moreover it had the gun and its crew sitting naked on top of the vehicle hull. After this came a second design in which the air defence requirement was dropped and the gun placed inside an armoured turret, but this now had insufficient elevation to reach its maximum range and was too heavy for the engine. Finally came a third design which dispensed with both turret and air defence but shielded the crew from fire. Six of these were built and deployed in the experimental armoured formations tried in the 1920s. But eventually the experimental armoured formations were broken up without arriving at any significant conclusions, and the Birch Guns were scrapped in 1931. There has been argument ever since as to why they were abandoned; some say it was the fundamental objection that if the vehicle broke down the gun became useless; others argue personality clashes; still others suggest that the Tank Corps were not in favour of accompanying artillery support. Whatever the reason, it was the last anyone heard of self-propelled guns for the next 10 years.

When the infantryman went to war in 1914 he had little more than a rifle and a shovel and possibly a Vickers machine gun to master. When he emerged in 1918 he had added the Hotchkiss and Lewis machine guns, four or five varieties of trench mortar and a score or more of hand and rifle-fired grenades to his inventory and a host of new tactical manoeuvres to his repertoire. With the coming of peacetime soldiering much of this equipment — particularly the more nervous hand grenades and trench mortars — was abandoned, and so too was much of the tactical skill; such exercises as trench-clearing and bombing, the bread-and-butter of trench life, were soon forgotten and training reverted to the classical open warfare manoeuvres, though admittedly tempered by the lessons of the war. It was no longer thought disgraceful to go to ground when shot at, for example.

The equipment which was discarded went not because it was irrelevant to the infantry's task but because it was the result, in the main, of hurried wartime improvisation. The first technical task therefore was to replace some of this equipment with improved models. The war had shown that hand grenades and light machine guns were essential even in a war of movement, so the first task was to produce a reliable grenade which could be either thrown by hand or launched from a rifle. The Mills grenade, which had metamorphosed through three changes of design to emerge as the 'Grenade 36M' had what were thought to be fundamental defects, notably a tendency to throw large and lethal fragments for erratic distances, and a detonating system which was eccentric to the main body of the explosive and therefore not conducive to efficient fragmentation. Another complaint was that the time fuze mechanism was so designed that if a man were to be shot in the act of throwing, and drop the grenade, so releasing the safety lever, then it would go off and kill him and his companions. Finally the 36M was so heavy that firing it from a discharger cup on the end of a rifle placed an enormous strain on the rifle and ruined it for accurate shooting thereafter.

Out of all this came a list of desirable characteristics of a grenade which read like a child's Christmas letter to Santa Claus in its starry-eyed specification, and from that came the 'Grenade, Hand and Rifle, No 54'. This was small enough to be convenient for throwing to useful distances, and had two machined bands on the body which fitted a 2in diameter cup discharger. This device could be clamped to the muzzle of the service rifle and a blank cartridge then used as a propelling charge to launch the grenade to a range of about 150yd. But the crowning glory of the 54 grenade was its 'all-ways fuze', so-called because it would operate on impact irrespective of the attitude in which the grenade struck the ground. The heart of the device was a lead ball between two conical faces, one of which was movable and carried a firing pin; whichever way the grenade landed, the momentum of the ball would cause movement of the coned faces and thrust the firing pin into

Top:
The Vickers Medium Mk I tank of 1924, developed as a cheap and reliable tank to 'fill in' until the government-sponsored designs appeared. They failed to appear, and the Vickers, with occasional improvements, remained the principal tank until the late 1930s.

Above:
The Carden-Loyd Mk VI machine gun carrier, one of several two-man ultra-light tanks designed in the late 1920s. Though out of service before war broke out they were valuable forerunners of the Bren carrier and influenced light tank design.

Below:
The Valentine Infantry Tank Mk III was ordered 'off the drawing board' in 1938 and was the most successful of prewar designs, over 8,000 being made.

a detonator. To make the fuze safe, a pin passed through one of the conical parts and was secured by a tape wrapped around the fuze, terminating in a lead weight. When thrown or projected the weight would drag the tape off the grenade, eventually pulling out the pin somewhere in flight and 'arming' the grenade, or making it ready to operate on impact.

Development of the 54 began somewhere in the early 1920s and continued until 1939, but when war broke out it was the 36M grenade which the infantryman carried; lack of finance and a somewhat desultory approach to research meant that the 54 was never brought to the state of perfection in which it could have been issued for service.

The light machine gun fared rather better. The Lewis, an American invention developed in Belgium and eventually manufactured principally in Britain, was a good enough weapon but suffered from over-complication in design and a rotating drum magazine which often jammed and equally often stopped due to breakage of its driving mechanism. Something simpler and lighter was desirable, and several prospective designs were put forward. Among the foremost contenders was the Vickers-Berthier, a Belgian design which had been adopted and improved by Vickers and which was taken into service by the Indian Army. It was a very smooth-working gun and very reliable, but being supported by Indian Army opinion did it little good in the corridors of Whitehall. Another weapon tested was the Danish Madsen gun, another design of considerable complexity but one which had been in successful use all round the world since the Russo-Japanese War of 1904. A native design was the Beardmore-Farquhar, an unusual but simple design which was extremely light and had first been put forward as an observer's gun for use by the Royal Air Force.

The general opinion was to the adoption of the Vickers-Berthier, but at the eleventh hour the British Military Attache in Czechoslovakia sent in a report on a new design developed by the Zbrojovka Brno (Brno Arms Works) called the ZB26. He was fulsome in his praise, and, surprisingly, Whitehall took notice and purchased some guns for test. A series of extensive and exhaustive tests proved everything the Attache had said: the ZB26 was outstanding in simplicity, reliability and accuracy. The only trouble was that it was chambered for the Mauser 7.92mm cartridge, while the British Army used the 0.303 Enfield round; the 7.92 was rimless, and the 0.303 was rimmed, so some fairly comprehensive redesign had to be done in order to get the gun to work with the British cartridge. Nevertheless, with the prospect of an order to re-equip the British Army in front of them, the Czechs laboured mightily and within a month had delivered three 0.303 guns, designated ZGB33, for test. These proved to be as good as the 7.92mm version, and the decision was taken to adopt the ZGB33. The first few were purchased from Czechoslovakia, but a license agreement was reached and manufacture was begun at the Royal Small Arms Factory, Enfield Lock. The drawings arrived in January 1935; these had to be dimensioned in inches instead of the Continental millimetre, tools had to be set up, gauges and testing equipment made, and it was September 1937 before the first gun came off the production line. By July 1938 production had reached 400 guns a week, and the weapon had a new name; the Bren gun, from the BR of Brno and the EN of Enfield.

Looking back, there is room for saying that the adoption of the Bren saw the missing of a great opporunity — that of getting rid of the 0.303 cartridge. The British Army (and the Commonwealth and Empire forces) and the Russian Army were the only major armies in the world still using a rimmed cartridge, every other force having changed to a rimless design years before. The advantages of a rimless design were several and well known; feed from magazines was often thwarted by cartridge rims jamming against each other, and the British Army hammered a strict drill into its recruits in the matter of loading rifle and machine gun magazines to avoid this type of stoppage; feed in machine gun belts was complicated since the mechanism had to withdraw the cartridge from the belt before feeding it forward; with a rimless cartridge the round could simply be pushed straight through. There were other advantages in production and packaging too, but feed was the principal question. Had the opportunity been taken, with the adoption of the ZB design, to turn over to 7.92mm, much of this would have been avoided in the forthcoming war; there was, in fact, an experimental design of rifle in 7.92mm calibre which could easily have gone into production. The full story is unlikely ever to be known, but it is probably the same story as obtained in Germany at much the same time. In the German Army a commission had determined that the adoption of a shorter 7mm cartridge would have several technical advantages, but the fact that there were several milliard cartridges in store was an economic fact which could not be ignored; nobody wanted to be the man who stood up and suggested scrapping them. Similarly, it is believed that Treasury objection to scrapping the massive stocks of 0.303 ammunition and converting vast numbers of weapons throughout the three services, was enough to bury the idea.

With the adoption of the Bren gun came a reorganisation of the infantry. The Vickers medium machine gun was now segregated into 10 special battalions, each with 48 guns, and the infantry now took one Bren gun for each rifle section, three to a platoon. This simplified training by having only one gun for the average infantryman to learn. The medium machine gun battalions were grouped under corps or army control and allotted to wherever their presence was required for heavy support. Each infantry battalion was given one platoon of 3in mortars, and each company had some 2in mortars (a Spanish design purchased in 1937) which were little more than grenade-dischargers capable of firing smoke or explosive bombs. Then came a platoon of 'Bren Carriers', light tracked vehicles with minimal armour protection intended to carry the Bren gun across bullet-swept ground to its tactical position. Finally, and somewhat to their surprise, the infantry battalion received a platoon of 2pdr anti-tank guns.

The question of defence against tanks had been receiving desultory attention ever since the middle 1920s. The Germans had given a useful pointer in 1918 when they introduced a powerful 'anti-tank rifle' of 13mm calibre, little more, in fact, than an over-sized conventional bolt-action Mauser rifle, but capable of piercing any tank then in existence. At the end of the war a 0.60in rifle

had been developed in Britain but this was abandoned after the Armistice and nothing much was done until the late 1920s when two designs were toyed with; the Elswick 0.80in rifle, a design from the Armstrong works, and the Swiss Oerlikon 20mm cannon, a weapon being adopted in several foreign countries for anti-tank shooting. Neither particularly appealed to the War Office and the Royal Small Arms Factory set about developing a design of their own; code-named 'Stanchion', this emerged as a 0.55in calibre bolt-action magazine rifle of considerable weight and recoil force. Just as it was about to be adopted the leader of the design team, a Capt Boys, unfortunately died, and the weapon was promptly renamed the 'Boys Rifle' in his honour. It came into service in 1937 as the basic infantry weapon, and was doubtless capable of piercing the skin of the current light tanks, but something heavier was obviously needed, if only to allow the infantry to engage targets at greater ranges than the 100yd or so recommended for the Boys.

The search for an anti-tank gun had been going on since the late 1920s and the result, the 2pdr gun, was undoubtedly the best of its kind in the world on the day of its introduction, New Year's Day 1936. It was towed on two wheels, rapidly brought into action on a three-legged platform, could traverse extremely rapidly through a full circle so that tracking a moving target was no problem, and fired a potent solid shot which could penetrate 42mm of armour at 1,000yd range when striking at an oblique angle of 30°. A semi-automatic breech gave a high rate of fire, and an excellent telescope sight made certain of accurate shooting in poor light. Unfortunately, all this meant a weapon which was expensive to produce and which weighed twice as much as any of its contemporaries in other armies.

It can be seen from the previous tally of the weapons now issued to the infantry that the battalion was now almost converted into a self-sufficient force with its own 'armour' and 'artillery', but attempting to produce the men for all this armament was too much of a strain and the infantry, looking for something to discard, decided that the elegant 2pdr gun was obviously an artillery weapon rather than an infantry weapon. So they rapidly pulled some strings and got rid of the gun to the Royal Artillery. Fortunately, the infantry adoption of mortars had rendered some artillery units redundant; these were the

Above left:
The Birch self-propelled gun of 1928, showing the 18pdr gun elevated for the air defence role.

Above:
Anti-gas drill; 20 Company of the Royal Army Service Corps prepares for a short training drive in respirators, 1938.

Below:
Boredom on a troopship; a mess-deck on the HT (Hired Transport) 'Lancashire'. The drafts of soldiers ate at these tables and slept in hammocks above them. These men were lucky; the presence of portholes shows that their messdeck was above the waterline. In the tropics a messdeck below the waterline was an ante-room to hell.

Below right:
The Universal Carrier; derived from the Carden-Lloyd 'tankettes' (right) these lightly armoured vehicles became maids-of-all-work, carrying machine guns or mortars, stretchers or artillery observers, laying telephone lines or mounting flame-throwers. They were, in some respects, forerunners of the armoured personnel carrier.

'light brigades' which had been developed in the 1920s to give close support to infantry, and were armed with 3.7in howitzers. Once the infantry had their mortars, the artillery were glad to back away from this infantry-accompanying role and use the men so saved to man the anti-tank guns which they had suddenly acquired.

To detail the twists and turns of tank design and construction in the period 1930-39 would demand an entire book on its own, and indeed many have been written on the subject. And it would be rather pointless since the brutal fact is that the British Army did not have a really battle-worthy tank of British design until the 1939-45 war was three-quarters over. The reasons for this are manifold and involved but can be summarised as follows; firstly, a lack of direction by the higher command in deciding what sort of tanks were needed; secondly, a reluctance to invest money in suitable manufacturing facilities until it was almost too late; thirdly, an uncoordinated design programme which meant that effort in design was spread across several 'possibles' instead of being concentrated on a few 'probables'; fourthly, the lack of a really powerful and compact engine, again due to parsimony in research and design; and, fifthly, a lack of mechanical reliability, due principally to lack of adequate testing and development in the rush to get designs into production.

Tank designs really began to stir in Britain in about 1935, with the realisation that Germany was rearming and that a threat was in process of taking shape. Moreover, in 1935 the Tank Corps and the War Office managed to get some degree of agreement on the shape the armoured force should take. The 'Mobile Division' had been created, bringing the cavalry, mechanised, into the armour fold and giving them the role of strategic reconnaissance. Support for the infantry would be performed by the Army Tank Brigades, each of three battalions which would be parcelled out on attachment to infantry formations as had been done in 1916-18. The Mobile Division consisted of about 600 tanks, mainly light models, two artillery brigades and two motorised infantry battalions. It was a bad balance being too much weighted toward the tank element and with far too many light tanks, and after testing in exercises a new formation was evolved — the Armoured Division. This consisted of a Light Brigade with three regiments of light or 'cruiser' tanks, and a Heavy Brigade with three regiments of cruisers, a total of 213 cruiser and 108 light tanks. Then came the Support Group, with a motorised infantry battalion, a motorised artillery brigade and a company of Royal Engineers. This arrangement was little better than the previous one; while the tank strength had been sensibly adjusted, the infantry and artillery strength had been halved. Nevertheless, this was the final word on the matter and this was the armoured formation which went to war in 1939. The light tanks were based on a Vickers design which had seen several improvements over the years, while the 'Cruiser Tank Mk 1', which began to be issued in 1938, was another Vickers design mounting a 2pdr gun in its main turret, with two smaller machine gun turrets at the front of the hull and a six-man crew. The Army Tank Brigades were equipped with the 'Infantry Tank Mark 1 Matilda' (which was christened after 'Matilda the Comical Duck', a cartoon character, and not 'Waltzing Matilda' as many Australians thought) with the 'Mk 2' entering production. The distinction between 'cruiser' and 'infantry' tanks was the result of the long arguments over the two roles of the tank, one of independent 'cruising' around the battlefield, and the other of slow support for marching infantry. As a result the Matildas were slow, poorly armed, but well armoured so as to resist whatever defences the infantry were attacking. And in spite of what happened in 1940, the division persisted for most of the war years, wasting untold hours of design and manufacturing effort, when every other combatant had given up such fine distinctions and had developed what might be called 'general purpose tanks'.

Ammunition

Right:
The Stokes 4in trench mortar of 1916, together with its bomb, a primitive cylinder of cast iron with a simple fuze and no stabilising fins. In spite of this it was remarkably accurate.

Below right:
'Bombing-up' a tank with fin-stabilised armour piercing discarding sabot ammunition. The ammunition is in a pre-packed delivery unit, and each cartridge has a short-circuiting clip attached to the base to prevent accidental ignition of the electric primer.

Bottom:
The Grenade, Hand, L2A2 exhibits a smooth metal surface, but this conceals a coil of hardened and notched wire which, when the grenade detonates, breaks up into several thousand dangerous fragments.

Below centre:
By contrast, probably the most complicated fuze ever devised, the 'Fuze Time 731' for the 3in anti-aircraft rocket, 1944. It was designed to be set by electro-magnets as it was fired from the launcher, so reducing the potential timing error by giving the most up-to-date setting derived from the position of the aircraft target. This was the only fuze to have a 50-page handbook to itself.

Bottom right:
Boxer's design for a major-calibre RML gun shrapnel shell contained all the essentials; the expelling charge is at the bottom and is lit, from the fuze, by flame passing down the central tube. The explosion then ejects the balls forward, breaking away the thin nose cover.

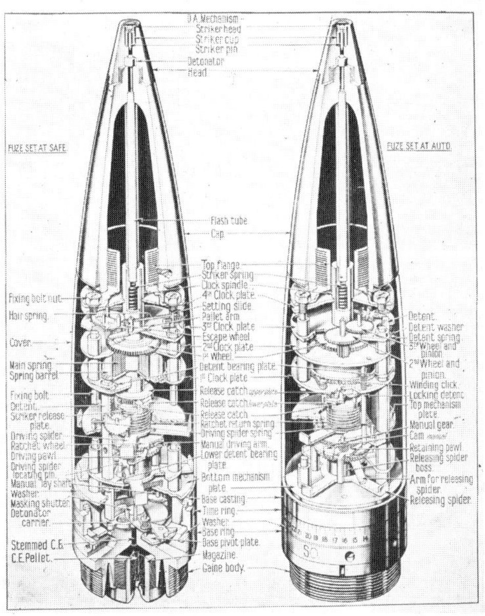

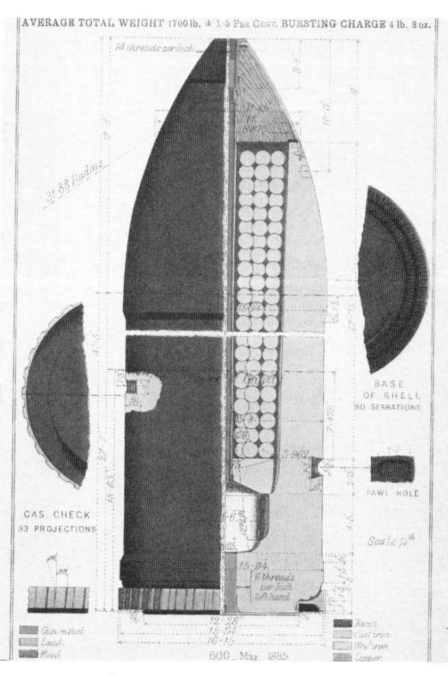

When all the manoeuvring and counter-marching stops, it is the ammunition fired by an army which decides the day, and whatever other shortcomings the British Army might have had, it has generally been in the forefront of ammunition design, partly due to military development agencies and partly to private enterprise.

The shrapnel shell dominated the 19th century so far as field warfare was concerned, since it was the prime man-killer against troops in the open — as troops usually were in that period. Henry Shrapnel's original 'Spherical Case Shot' was modified by Colonel Boxer in the smoothbore era and again to suit the new rifled ordnance, and the design he produced remained the pattern for the rest of shrapnel's service. (The last shrapnel appears to have been fired by British field artillery during the Burma campaign in 1942. It was retained slightly longer by anti-aircraft guns as a last-ditch defence against dive-bombers.)

Once troops began to vanish into the earth, the high explosive shell took over as the 'standard projectile' for field artillery, since it gave a combination of material and anti-personnel effect. Except for minor technical improvements, and the use of better explosives and steel, there is little difference between the HE shell of 1914 and that of 1945. Since then, though, ballistic improvements — better shaping, the adoption of a hollow base to reduce drag — have improved the flight characteristics.

The fuze fitted to the shell has passed through many stages of improvement, from the early powder-burning fuzes to the modern electronic proximity fuze which senses the presence of the target and detonates the shell in the most effective place.

The most modern munition currently being offered to the army is the 'smart' bomb for the 81mm mortar. This is fired like a conventional mortar bomb but uses millimetric wave radar to detect the presence of the target and then, by means of extending fins, steers the bomb to impact. The addition of this device to the infantry armoury will mean the ability to attack armour at ranges well beyond the present range of missiles or other anti-armour weapons.

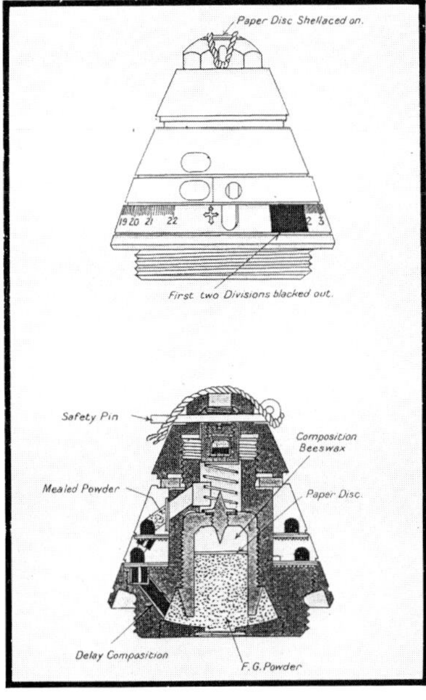

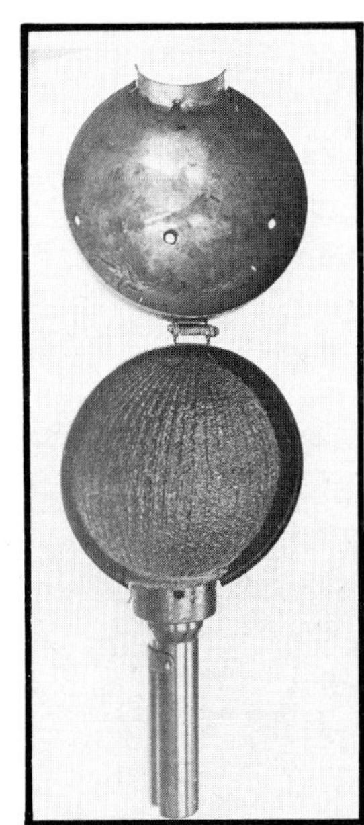

Above right:
The British Aerospace Merlin 'smart' 81mm mortar bomb uses a millimetric-wave radar to seek out its target and guide itself to impact at the end of the trajectory. It is under development (1985) for the top attack of tanks at long range.

Right:
A powder-burning time fuze of World War 1. By rotating the lower ring the time taken for the powder to burn could be varied, bursting the shell just as it approached the target so as to release the shrapnel balls in the most lethal position.

Far right:
The infamous 'Sticky Bomb' hand grenade of 1941. The bomb consisted of a glass sphere containing nitro-glycerine, enclosed in a stockinette bag coated with a powerful adhesive. It could be thrown or placed on a tank; the adhesive kept it in place and the nitro-glycerine wrought fearful damage. However, a careless swing by the thrower could result in the bomb sticking to his trousers, which could be embarrassing to say the least.

6 To the Siegfried Line

One lesson which the British Army had thoroughly absorbed during the 1914-18 war was that it was impossible to fight a continental war with two men and a dog; massive armies had to be raised and trained, and the recruiting of such armies had to be done in a sensible manner so that some of the worst horrors of the World War 1 system were not repeated. Then, in a reversion to Napoleonic times, individuals were permitted to raise formations, though not to command them, and this had led to some fearful mistakes. 'Sportsman's Battalions', 'Pals Battalions', 'City Battalions' and similar gatherings of kindred souls mustered into military formations merely led to the male populations of whole districts or sects being wiped out overnight as the battalion attacked. Voluntary recruitment was relied upon until January 1916, when compulsory service for unmarried men between 18 and 41 was introduced; in May 1916 it was extended to married men, though with many reservations and exceptions. In April 1917 a more rigorous Act was passed, removing many exemptions, and in March 1918 the age limit was raised to 50. But voluntary recruitment was allowed to run unchecked at the beginning of the war, and many men from skilled industries were permitted to enlist, thus causing a severe labour shortage in the munitions and engineering factories in 1914-15.

Below:
Showing a curious mixture of the new battledress and the old 'service dress', reinforcements mill around a dockside in France after arriving from Britain in 1939. A loaded Bofors light anti-aircraft gun is emplaced in the middle of all this activity.

All these things had been noted and resolve made that they were not to happen again. Conscription was planned as soon as the trend of events became clear and was put into effect in 1938 (though the word 'conscript' was studiously avoided — the draftees were called 'militiamen' instead).

At the same time there was a revolutionary change in the uniform for the soldier. Since 1850 the changes in dress had been part evolutionary and part cosmetic; headgear changed with bewildering rapidity in the latter half of the 19th century, but basically the uniform for the soldier was a jacket and trousers with equipment hung around him on crossbelts. Flapping trousers were a nuisance in some types of terrain and climate and gradually the use of puttees — long strips of cloth wound around the lower leg, covering the boot top and the trouser bottom — became standard. Service in India led to the adoption of dun-coloured 'Khaki' clothing, which was extended to South Africa during the war years there and to general service in the early 1900s. By 1914 the soldier wore a tight-collared tunic of khaki serge, trousers of similar material, studded leather short boots, puttees, and a stiff 'cheese-cutter' peaked cap, and in this he went to war in 1914. Subsequently the uniform changed little except for the adoption of steel helmets and the omnipresent gas mask. When peace returned the uniform remained the same, perhaps of a slightly better quality of material, neatly pressed and with brass buttons.

But in 1938 came 'battle-dress', which caused a sensation — and not just in the army but in the population at large as well. Gone were the brass buttons, the peaked cap, the puttees, the creased and folded trousers. In came a short 'bum-freezer' blouse, belted at the waist, with concealed buttons and two breast pockets; trousers with a huge pocket — reputedly for Bren gun magazines but actually for maps and papers — on the left thigh, and a small pocket for a first-aid dressing on the right, below the waist. Instead of puttees came gaiters, short canvas leggings with two straps which clamped around the boot top and confined the trouser bottoms — which were provided with buttons and tabs to strap around the ankle preparatory to fitting the gaiter. The headdress was a 'forage cap' — also called a 'fore-and-aft' and less complimentary names — which was capable of being unfolded into a rudimentary form of Balaclava helmet, protecting the ears in cold weather. This was worn cocked over the right ear in jaunty fashion, though light infantry regiments soon evolved a new 'tradition' and wore theirs perfectly central on the head. The basic cap was plain khaki and this remained the normal wear, but for 'walking out' when off duty, many corps and regiments devised 'Caps, Field Service, Coloured', which were of the same pattern but in the regimental colours. All of the old uniform which remained was the boots, still the same rock-hard leather boots with 13 steel studs on each sole. Even the overcoat changed, becoming longer and now called the 'greatcoat'.

Over this went a new issue of 'web equipment', the Pattern '38, which was to last until the 1950s. A thick waistbelt with brass buckles front and back acted as the foundation for a complex series of straps which could carry pouches big enough for Bren magazines or three or four grenades, a 'small pack' which held messtins, rations and waterproof cape, a 'large pack' which carried spare clothing and necessaries, a water bottle on the right hip and a bayonet on the left. With all this strapped on the man was in 'FSMO' or Field Service Marching Order,

Left, top to bottom:

The 7.92mm Besa machine gun was another Czech design and was used as a coaxial gun on most British tanks. Note the bag for catching empty cartridge cases, to prevent them falling into the tank and perhaps fouling the turret mechanism.

The Browning GP35 9mm automatic pistol; designed in Belgium, the drawings were sent to Canada where it went into production for the British, Canadian and Chinese armies. Used originally by airborne troops it was adopted as the standard service pistol after the war. This early model has a long-range backsight and a slot in the rear of the grip to carry a shoulder-stock.

The Webley Mk VI .455in revolver. Although officially superseded by a .38in design in 1933, several of these heavy pistols were retained by officers during World War 2.

The Sten machine carbine Mk II. At about £2.50 each, it was probably the cheapest weapon ever used by the British Army.

though in fact he rarely marched with it all; the large pack was usually lifted in unit transport and he marched in 'small pack order'. It was rounded off by a steel helmet, of the same pattern which had appeared in 1915, and a gas-mask or 'respirator' in official language, which, again, was merely an improved version of the design which was in use in 1918.

To go with the new dress came a new deal in accommodation. Mr Leslie Hore-Belisha was Minister of War at that time, and the barracks which were built as part of the rearmament programme have become known to two or three generations of soldiers as 'Hore-Belisha Barracks', so distinctive is their style. Two- or three-storied blocks, with barrack rooms on each side of a central stairwell and with 'ablutions' — washrooms and lavatories — in a short annex at the rear of the stairways. Each landing had two small rooms for NCOs who were in charge of the two barrack-rooms on that floor, and the whole was finished in brick and stone with composition flooring in the public areas and wooden floors in the barrack rooms which, in due course, acquired a blinding shine from the weekly application of pounds of wax polish. They were even connected to boiler-houses so that central heating and hot water was available, though many still had fireplaces in the barrack-rooms as well. A complex of these barrack blocks would be accompanied by a single-storied cookhouse and dining hall for the men, a single-storied sergeants' mess, a double-storied officers' mess and a series of single-storied office blocks and store rooms. After that the architectural aims slipped somewhat and the unit equipment — guns, tanks, carriers, trucks or whatever — would be housed in an unprepossessing series of green corrugated iron sheds around a vehicle park area. The whole assembly would surround the square, the undefilable stretch of asphalt upon which drills of every sort were carried out, parades took place, ceremonials were performed. And lying around the barrack area, separated from it by some small distance perhaps, would be rows of 'married quarters' — officers' in one direction, other ranks' in another — in which the married men lived with their families. Most of the quarters built in this period rank among the best ever built; even today they are avidly sought by soldiers since their standard of construction and finish was considerably better than the rash of quick building which appeared in the 1960s.

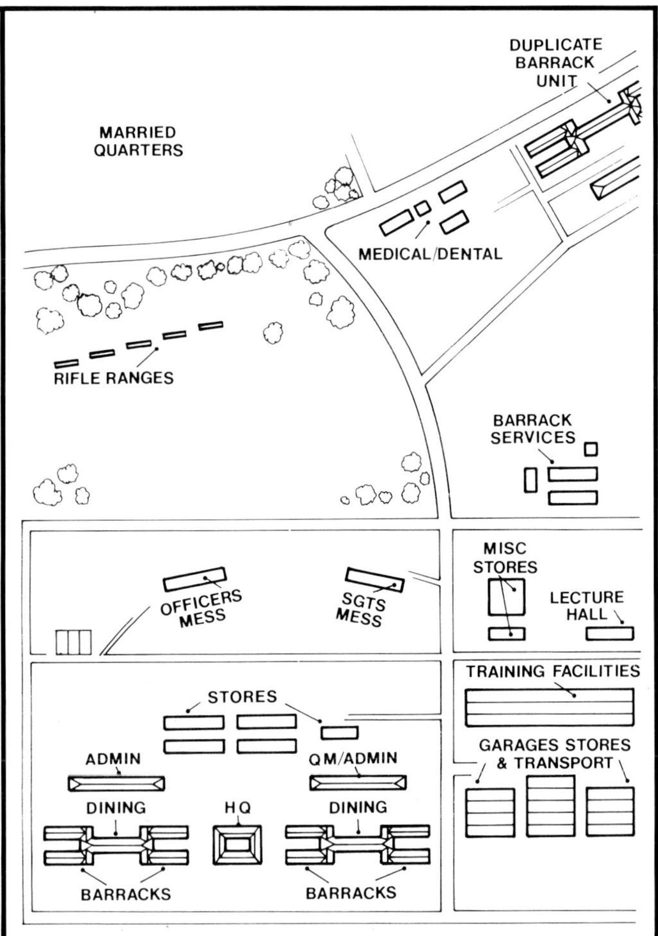

The Expeditionary Force was thus more or less ready for war, even if the quantity of equipment was lacking due to slow decisions and late production. The final piece to be placed on the board was the force for defending the United Kingdom while the Expeditionary Force went forth to war. Some infantry battalions were earmarked for 'Home Defence' but the most important part of home defence, in the eyes of most people, was air defence. Ever since Baldwin, in 1933, made his famous statement that 'the bomber will always get through', there had been concern about air defence, since the common prophecy about the next war always began with fleets of bombers appearing over the skies of England and dropping poison gas bombs on the defenceless population.

During the late 1920s and early 1930s various air defence 'schemes' had been put forward, but none got off the ground because there was neither the equipment nor the money to implement them. But in 1934 the existing scheme had been scrapped and the defensive plans were overhauled. The first requirement was to shift the emphasis of the system; it had orginally been based on the assumption that the only practicable direction of attack was from France. Now the balance of power, and of probabilities, had shifted to Germany and improvements in aircraft meant that bombers could fly from that direction, and the alignment of the defences shifted from the south of England to the east coast. A belt of artillery was planned to run from the Tees to the Solent, surrounding London, with 25 squadrons of RAF fighters to cover the area outside this zone. The artillery defences were to consist of 58 batteries of guns and 100 companies of searchlights; at that time a battery consisted of eight 3in guns and 12 Lewis machine guns for close defence, which meant a total of 464 3in guns and 2,400 lights. Since such numbers of guns and lights did not exist (there were only 120 searchlights in the entire army), and since no money was available, the plan would be tackled in stages: the first stage was to be 17 batteries and 42 searchlight companies by March 1940, and the plan was to be completed by 1946.

Left:
The Hore-Belisha barrack unit of c1938/9.

Below left:
The Mk III Bren Gun, a lightened and simplified version designed to speed up production.

Above:
Winston Churchill inspects a Thompson submachine gun. Purchased from the USA at considerable expense in 1939-40 they introduced the Army to the concept of the submachine gun. Though heavy, they were extremely reliable and well-liked.
IWM

Below:
Most of the Thompson submachine guns eventually found their way into the hands of Airborne (seen here) or Commando forces.
IWM

Assuming that the guns would eventually be available, the next problem was the old one of detecting the target. Sound was still the obvious choice and huge concrete 'sound mirrors' had been built in the Romney Marshes, oriented towards France. One of these was 200ft long and 36ft high, curved to reflect sound into microphones positioned at the focal point, while others were parabolic mirrors some 20 or 30ft across, with microphones similarly located. They are still there, mute reminders of the 'steam age' of air defence. The shift in emphasis made these mirrors redundant, and fresh sites were surveyed in the Thames Estuary, oriented towards Germany. In fact, the air exercises of 1934 showed that these mirrors were a failure, and the designers went back to try again.

Heat was another phenomenon associated with aircraft engines, and several inventors tried to perfect infra-red detectors which could take advantage of this. There was some powerful support for this theory, but the difficulties were enormous.

Finally, and at the eleventh hour, radar was discovered and perfected in sufficient time to develop an 'early warning' system which could alert guns and fighter aircraft to an approaching attack. Very soon after the first radar sets were made to work their application to the precise direction of guns on to targets was suggested and work began on gunlaying sets, but they were not to be ready for some time.

Although the defences had been predicated on the existing 3in guns, which, it will be recalled, were designed prior to World War 1, design of an improved air defence weapon had been slowly progressing since the late 1920s. In the early 1920s a 3.6in gun on a tracked trailer had appeared, but this still adhered to the policy of placing all the fire control equipment and sights on the gun and was therefore a complex piece of equipment which demanded five gunlayers to aim it while only two men loaded it. Giving five highly-trained men to every gun was grossly uneconomic in manpower, and a better system was sought. After examination of a variety of designs, in 1928 a 3.7in gun was decided on, while work also went forward on designing a 'predictor', a primitive type of computer which, if given the present position, height, speed and course of a target would calculate the firing data applicable to the position the aircraft would occupy when the shell reached it. All this, it should be emphasised, was performed mechanically in the predictor; a few factors, such as speed, lent themselves to being represented by varying electrical voltages, but many did not, and thus the device was filled with cams, gears, differentials and other mechanical methods of calculation. As a result predictors tended to weight and bulk — one model contained 35 differentials and 24 electric motors and weighed almost 1.5 tons, another model contained no less than 3,500 different components.

Once the predictor had arrived at a solution it was necessary to get this to the gun as rapidly as possible so that the information was still timely. The means adopted was to use electrical transmission to dials on the gun which informed the gunlayer of the pointing, elevation and fuze length required. These dials had two pointers: one was set by the information coming from the predictor, the other was coupled to the gun, so that the gunlayer, on seeing a dial reading, merely swung and elevated his gun until his pointer matched that of the predictor information.

This 'follow-the-pointer' system was incorporated into the new design of 3.7in gun which appeared in prototype for test in April 1937. It was a highly advanced weapon for its time, mounted on a heavy and luxurious carriage and much above the specified weight limit of eight tons. But its

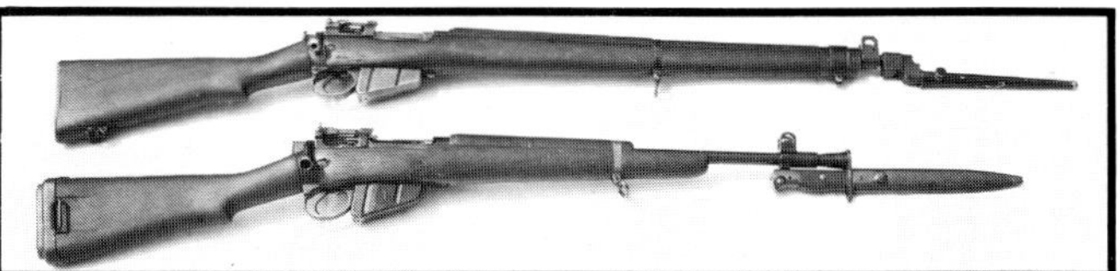

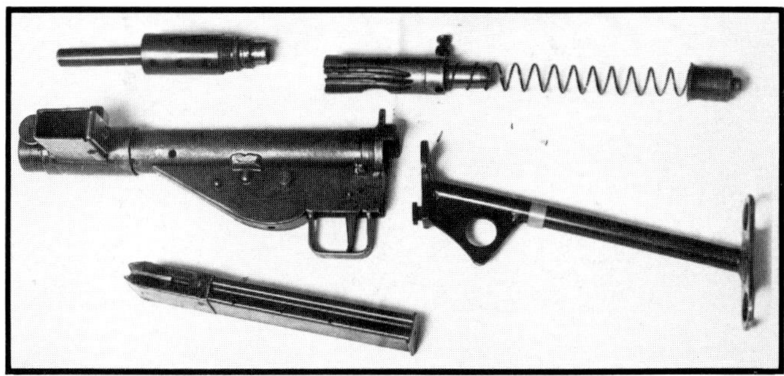

Top:
The Lee-Enfield Rifle No 4, designed for simple production, and the 'Jungle Carbine' Rifle No 5, showing their relative size.

Above:
A Sten Gun Mk II, the most common version, stripped to its component parts to show the simplicity of its construction.

Below:
The mule held its place into the 1960s, until the helicopter became more familiar. Here a mule column crosses a river in Burma during the 1944 campaign.

Above right:
Bren gun carriers moving an infantry company in Cyrenaica, 1941.

Right:
Air defence at its minimum; rifles and a Bren gun waiting for low-level raiders in Kent during the summer of 1940.

performance — it fired a 28lb shell to a maximum ceiling of 41,000ft at 10 shots a minute — was so far in advance of anything else in the world that its bulk was forgiven and the weapon was accepted for service. The lighter and handier 3in was still preferred for batteries accompanying the field armies, but for home defence the 3.7in, in static and mobile versions, was the more effective answer, though production was painfully slow at first.

A ceiling of 41,000ft — 7¾ miles straight up — sounds impressive, but is a deceptive figure. This is the 'maximum ceiling' to which a gun, if pointed perfectly vertically, would project a solid projectile of 28lb weight before the pull of gravity halted it and returned it to earth. But the workable ceiling of an air defence gun of that period was governed by the maximum operating time of the time fuze fitted to the shell, and in the case of the 3.7in this had a maximum time of 25sec. Moreover the gun could not elevate to a perfectly vertical position; its maximum angle was 80°. So the combination of 80° and 25sec flight actually brought the maximum ceiling down to 28,000ft. Even this is deceptive, since, obviously, it only applies to one spot in the sky; if the aircraft moved to a point where the elevation required was 70°, then the maximum fuze time would result in another ceiling figure. Therefore the performance of an anti-aircraft gun was measured by its 'practical ceiling', defined as that altitude at which the gun could engage a target for some worthwhile period of time; this period differed according to who was defining it, but in 1936 it was defined in Britain as the height at which the gun could engage an approaching target flying at 250mph for 20sec before the gun's elevation reached 70°. Under this criterion the ceiling now fell to 23,000ft, almost half the impressive 'maximum ceiling' value. It is only fair to say that in later years, with improved fuzes and fire control, the practical ceiling of the 3.7in gun increased to 32,5000ft.

For the moment, therefore, raiders operating over 23,000ft were safe, and since contemporary German bombers could fly higher than that it was considered necessary to have a heavier weapon with a higher practical ceiling. A 4.7in gun was proposed, but, as usual, finance came into it and the Army realised that asking for a 4.7in would jeopardise its chances of obtaining a useful number of 3.7in weapons. At this juncture the Royal Navy stepped in and suggested adopting its existing 4.5in gun; its performance was close to the predicted performance of the 4.7in design, it was tried and tested and in production, and since almost all the locations where the army was proposing to place these heavy guns were near naval installations, the supply of ammunition would present no problems. This made good sense, and the army adopted the 4.5in gun in 1938; it fired a 54lb shell to a practical ceiling of 26,500ft at a rate of eight rounds a minute and could reach above the flying height of any bomber of the period.

With the upper sky now controlled, it became necessary to look at the lower part and consider provision of a light gun to deal with low-flying ground attack aircraft. Once again time and money suggested finding a ready-made solution if possible, and after examining various ideas the Army once again turned to a naval weapon and adopted a twin 2pdr 'pom-pom' designed by Vickers. Designed for mounting on ships it was a cumbersome piece of static equipment but it was adequate for defending ports and other fixed points.

In 1936 the Swedish Bofors 40mm automatic gun had been brought to the army's attention, and at the same time as the 2pdr gun was accepted, an order for 100 of these guns was given to the Swedish company so that the field armies could be provided with a mobile light weapon. Experience with these guns soon showed that it was a far better equipment than the 2pdr, and thus the 2pdr order was cancelled after only 60 had been delivered, and a

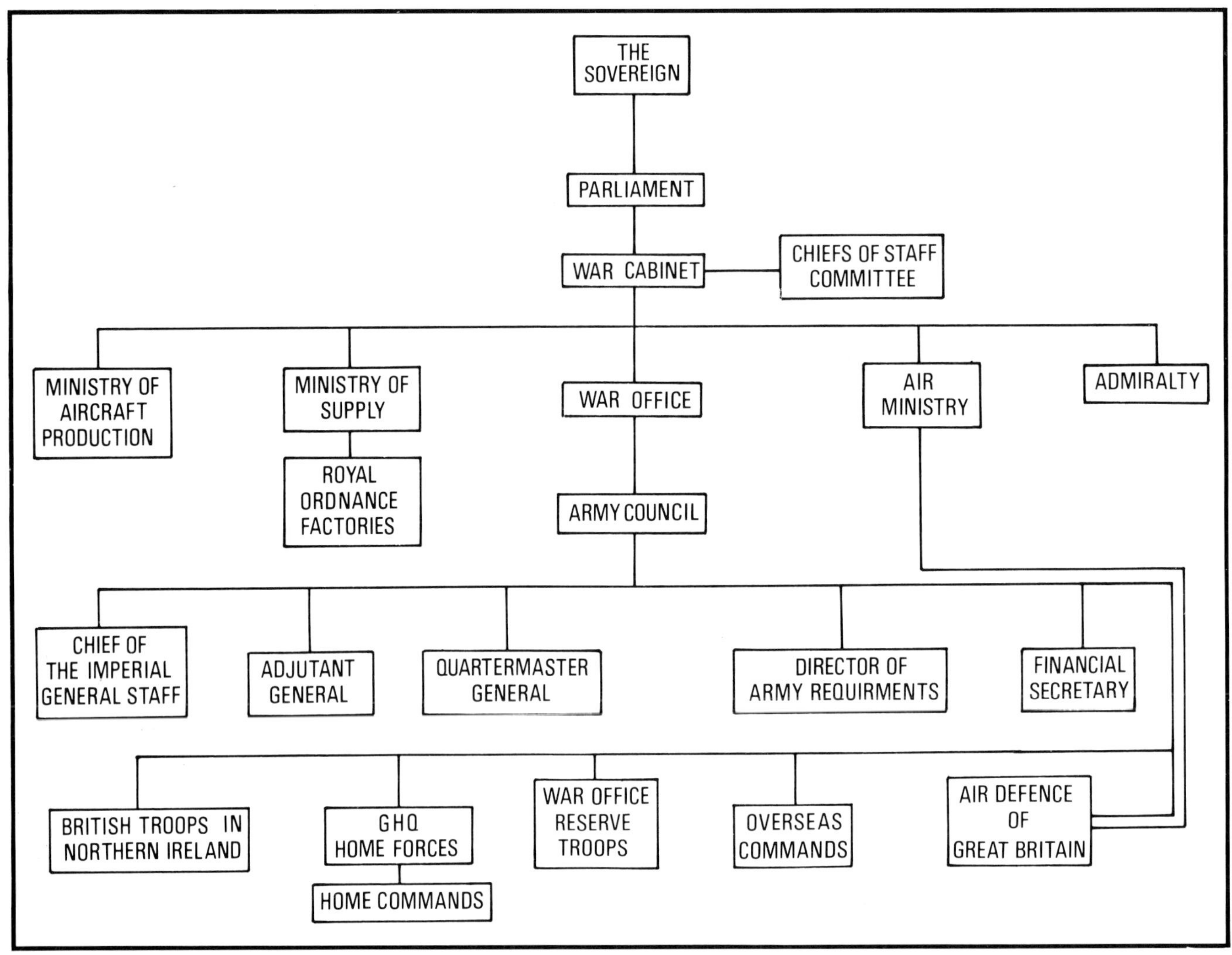

Above:
Organisation of the British Army in 1943.

licence obtained from Bofors to build the gun in Britain. In addition a large number were bought from Poland which had obtained a licence in 1935 and, after providing for its own services, was selling the guns in the export market.

By the middle of 1937 therefore, the situation on Home Defence was that an adequate selection of light, medium and heavy guns had been made, but production facilities were so poor that it would be some years before the planned gun strength was reached . . . and time was running short.

The War Office was aware of the likely shortfall in gun production, and in 1935 it had asked the Research Department of Woolwich Arsenal to look at the possibility of using rockets as a cheap anti-aircraft weapon. The advantage of the rocket was that the projecting mechanism could be considerably lighter, simpler and cheaper than a gun, while the rocket itself, once a design was perfected, would be little more expensive or complicated to make than a conventional round of ammunition. The only stipulation made by the War Office was that whatever was designed had to have a performance comparable with existing guns to a ceiling of 10,000ft.

Basing their design on the availability of cordite propellant, the Design Department arrived at two solutions, of 2in and 3in diameter. The rockets were simple steel tubes containing a solid stick of cordite electrically ignited and with a warhead on the front carrying a simple time fuze. By late 1937 the 3in model with an 18lb warhead was selected as the best air defence weapon and early in 1939 an extensive trial in Jamaica proved the design to be satisfactory. But now the War Office stepped in and insisted on a projector which launched the rocket from a closed tube, similar to a gun; this was quite useless since the blast, exiting from the muzzle at the same time as the rocket, upset its stability and led to erratic flight. The problem seemed insoluble, the General Staff was not satisfied, and in mid-1939 ruled that 'a requirement no longer existed' for rockets. The requirement certainly did exist, for the supply of guns was far from satisfying demand, but the formal expression permitted development to continue on a low priority to see if accuracy could be improved.

At roughly this point, war finally came and the British Expeditionary Force went to France, where it sat and waited and built field fortifications and pillboxes and patrolled the frontier while the Germans and Soviets carved up Poland. Almost everyone expected the war to be a continuation of 1918; people in Britain still spoke of 'going out to the trenches' as they had in the previous war,

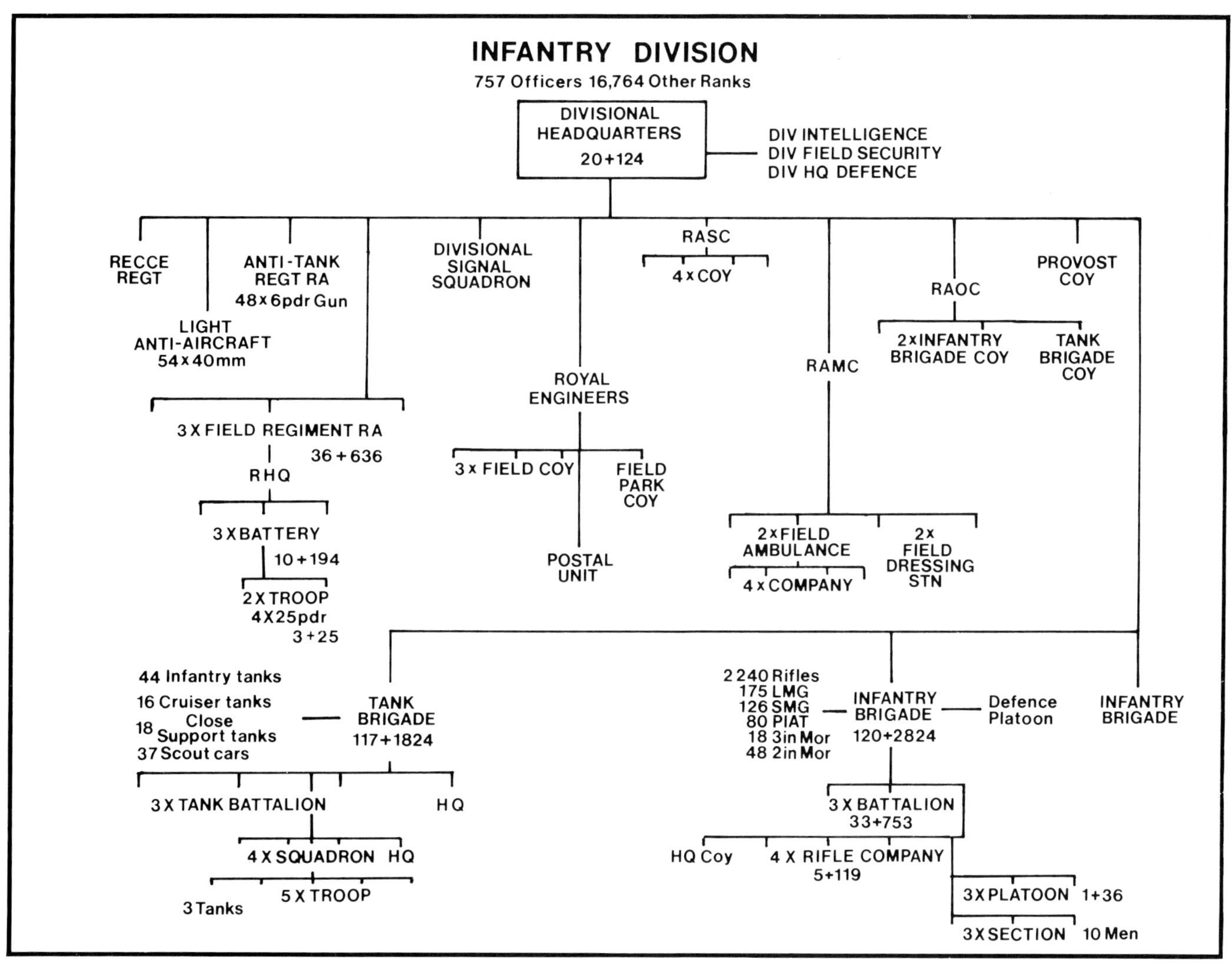

Above:
Organisation of a typical World War 2 infantry division. There were various options for divisional construction — this is one from 1942/3.

but the soldiers who went to France found things were not the same by any means.

The period between 1918 and 1939 had seen one immense change in the conduct of war — the ability to communicate. World War 1 is a remarkable anomaly in this respect; it was the one major war in which communication between commanders and commanded was virtually absent once a battle began, the only war in which the commander had no voice control of events. Prior to 1914 warfare had been on such a limited scale that a commander could position himself where he could oversee a battle and, by means of trumpeters, runners and liaison officers on horseback could communicate his commands to any part of the battlefield with adequate rapidity. But in 1914-18 this ability was lost, since after the infantry heaved themselves out of their trenches and advanced, the commander had little or no idea of what was was going on, could therefore not modify plans, and, even if he had, could not get any messages to the forward troops in time to do any good. It was this factor more than anything else which dictated the chaotic manner in which many a battle evolved. And 'commanding from the front' was no substitute; as one French general pointed out, 'If I go to the front all I can do is command one or two companies' and that is not what generals are paid for.

The one thing which changed all this was radio telephony (R/T) — the ability to speak to subordinates and receive information from them by radio. Wireless telegraphy (W/T) — Morse code — had been in use during World War 1 but its utility was stifled by the need to encode and decode, by the requirement for the operator to be trained in Morse, and by the slow process of transmitting letter by letter. Speech radio cured all this and brought voice control back to the commander.

In the British Army R/T had its greatest impetus from the Royal Tank Corps, seeking a way for a commander to control a squadron or regiment of tanks, and Maj Gen P. C. S. Hobart was probably the driving spirit in this development. By 1934 he had a practical R/T set for tank use, and the idea spread to other regiments, notably to the Royal Artillery who devised a 'regimental network' system which ensured a steady flow of information from the front and orders from the rear, together with communication between observers and guns for signalling target information.

Unfortunately, the one defect of radio communication is that it is dispersed into the atmosphere and is then available to be heard by anyone with an adequate receiving set. Thus the orders given for an operation can be heard by the enemy who can then devise his

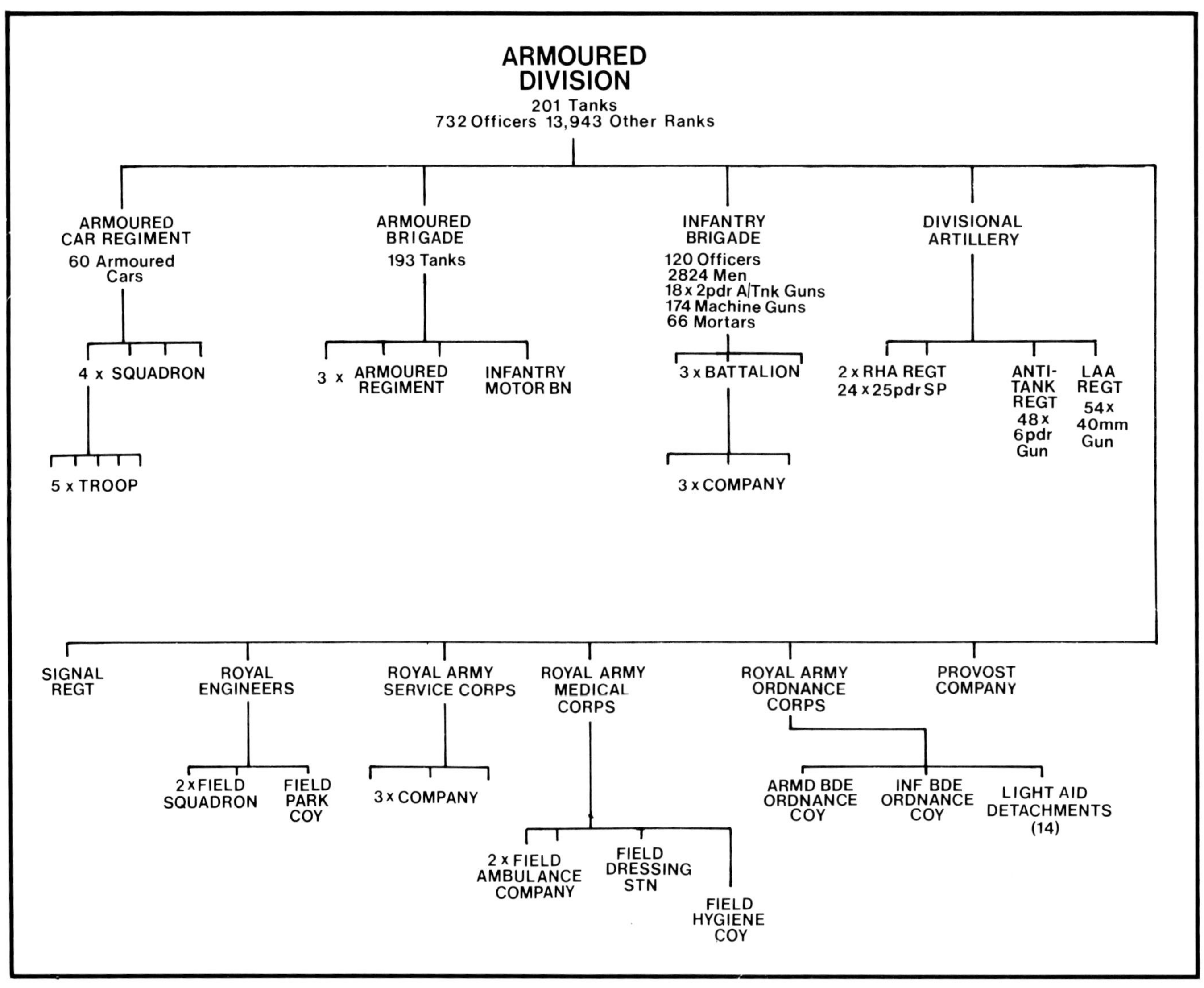

Above:
Organisation of a typical World War 2 armoured division.

counter-stroke. This can be countered by the use of codes, a slow procedure open to human error and, again, capable of being deciphered by an astute enemy. By and large communication therefore has to be graded — information which the enemy cannot make use of in time to counter it can be in 'clear' speech; all other information must have some degree of encipherment, the grade of code or cipher being selected so as to offer the amount of delay thought adequate. Thus information to be acted upon within the next 12 hours or so is adequately protected by a code which would probably take 24 hours to break, and so on. (This, of course, refers to the situation as it was in 1939; today, with the advent of computers which can rip through a message and decode it in a fraction of the time taken by a cipher officer of 1939 with a pencil, other measures are necessary.)

As a result of this, the BEF in France was forbidden the use of its radio communication systems so that information would not be disclosed to the enemy. This mattered little to the static troops in 1939, but when the Germans invaded in May 1940 the lack of practice in communication soon made itself apparent and many British units simply vanished into limbo as soon as they moved. Those few units who had defied the ban and kept their radio operators in practice found that it paid a handsome dividend in keeping their scattered formations together during the retreat.

The first demand for new equipment which arose from the war was as early as November 1939, when British infantry engaged in patrol action asked for submachine guns. The German and French armies both used these weapons, and the British saw that they had advantages in infantry patrolling. Although frequently castigated as 'gangster weapons' by some army spokesmen, in fact every available model of submachine gun had been tested before the war, and the Ordnance Board was ready with a recommendation. It suggested that the best model was the Finnish Suomi, but since Russia had just invaded Finland it felt there was little chance of obtaining any. The second choice was the American Thompson gun, the archetypal 'gangster weapon', although these were extremely expensive (about $275 each) a quantity was purchased and issued.

Before very much else happened to initiate new designs, the German war machine rumbled into life and rapidly overran Denmark, Norway, Belgium, Holland and France, resulting in the British Army evacuating the Continent and leaving behind much of its equipment.

Now Britain was alone in opposing Germany, and there was a very real threat of invasion, and this combination of circumstances acted as a powerful stimulant on design and development of an enormous variety of weapons and equipment.

The first priority, naturally enough, was to defend the country, after which it was necessary to re-equip all those troops who had left Dunkirk with little more than the clothes in which they stood and their rifles. After that would come the long haul of equipping the gradually expanding army. On top of all this was the need to develop new weapons when they were seen to be necessary, and put them into production; this frequently clashed with the first requirement, perhaps the most famous example being the case of the anti-tank guns.

Experience in France had shown that the 2pdr anti-tank gun had a marginal effect on the better German tanks; it could penetrate the thin Panzer I and II, but against the heavier Panzer III it was useless except at suicidally short ranges. The Director of Artillery had foreseen this as long ago as 1938 and had caused a new 57mm 6pdr gun to be designed and tested, the designs then being shelved ready

Above left:
A circular sound mirror, overlooking Romney Marsh and oriented towards France. The parabolic concrete face reflected the engine sound into a microphone to give some degree of early warning of an aircraft's approach.

Left:
After the German invasion began; British troops marching into a Belgian fort in 1940.

Below:
Girl convoy drivers of the Auxiliary Territorial Service, 1940. The exposed driving position was commonplace on military vehicles of the period.

Top:
A multiple 3in rocket launcher for air defence; the operator stood inside the armoured box to fire the rockets.

Above:
ATS girls of a mixed battery operating an anti-aircraft predictor during a snowstorm, 1942.

Above right:
An early gunlaying radar for anti-aircraft use. The chicken-wire laid on the ground provided an artificial reflecting plane for the radar signals.

for when they were required. In the summer of 1940 that time had arrived, but the dilemma which faced the army was one of priorities. Over 500 2pdr guns had been left behind in France, and anti-tank regiments in Britain were without guns. Starting production of the 6pdr would take several months, and when they were issued it would mean re-training these regiments on a new weapon before they could be considered effective; in other words if the 6pdr was selected, then the anti-tank strength of the army would be seriously impaired for almost a year — in the face of threatened invasion. On the other hand although the 2pdr was marginally good, it was better than no gun at all, and had the virtue of being in production and familiar to the troops. Therefore the decision was taken to keep the 2pdr in production until the army was completely equipped, after which the factories would turn over to 6pdr production. Although a contract for 400 6pdr guns was issued in June 1940 it had to wait until the demand for 2pdrs was satisfied and production capacity was available, and it was not until November 1941 that the first guns were made.

But the tank threat was assuming such proportions that even before the 6pdr went into service there was discussion on its successor. In November 1940 a decision was taken to develop a 3in gun firing a 17lb shot, and this appeared as the 17pdr gun in May 1942. Five months later the General Staff asked for work to begin on a replacement, to have at least a 25% increase in performance; the first solution was to take the barrel of the 4.5in AA gun and turn that into an anti-tank weapon, but this was abandoned as impractical and instead the 3.7in AA gun was taken as the starting point.

A little imagination here will show into what the army was now getting. The 3.7in AA gun barrel and breech weighed 3,900lb, and this had to be assembled on to a carriage suitable for anti-tank shooting. By comparison

to manhandle. The 32pdr gun was a prime example; it was capable of dealing with any tank in existence at that time, but it was impossible to get it into position without a large and powerful tractor. It might be said that the Germans and Americans faced the same problem; the Germans ended with a 128mm (5.04in) gun weighing exactly 10 tons, and the Americans with a 105mm (4.1in) weighing 7.15 tons.

It might be thought that the solution to this would be to put these monster guns on to self-propelled chassis, but in fact these were liable to produce a worse answer. The very nature of the weapon meant that it was to be used in the thick of the armoured battle, and so it needed extremely good armour protection in order to survive hits from ordinary tanks as it went about the business of destroying them. The SP version of the 32pdr gun was known as Tortoise and weighed 78 tons; it has been said that there was no landing ship or any bridge in Northwest Europe in 1945 capable of taking the weight. The SP version of the German weapon, the Jagdtiger, weighed 70 tons, and the American 105mm SP, the Gun Motor Carriage T95, weighed a staggering 85 tons. The laws governing gun construction are international, and every combatant came to realise that there was a practical limit to conventional anti-tank weapons.

The reason for all this activity in anti-tank guns was, of course, the progressive improvement in tanks, though in truth the Germans had more to worry about from the Russians than they did from the British. The outbreak of war had more or less coincided with a rash of production as various designs which had been in gestation began to arrive in the hands of troops. The Cruiser Mark III was one of these, and a design which introduced the Christie suspension into British service. This was a design using large wheels with long movement, developed by an American engineer, and which allowed tanks to travel at high speed without jarring the crew to pieces. It was widely adopted in Russia, and to a lesser extent in Britain, but here its advantages were lessened by the fact that

Above:
A 3.7in mobile anti-aircraft gun forming part of the London defences in November 1940.

Right:
One of many 4.5in heavy anti-aircraft guns deployed around the London docks in late 1940.

the 17pdr gun, complete with its carriage, weighed 4,600lb and was considered heavy. The ammunition to be developed for anti-tank use would be far more powerful than that used in the 3.7in AA gun, so there would be a more powerful recoil, which would necessitate a heavy and strong carriage. This all took time to design and the two pilot models were not completed before the war ended; they weighed almost six tons each.

The object of having an anti-tank gun is to stop a tank, obviously; but it also needs to be concealed and, usually, manhandled into position. By the end of the war these two demands were becoming incompatible. Tanks had become so thickly armoured that massive guns were necessary to penetrate them at useful ranges, but powerful guns demanded strong, heavy barrels and strong, heavy carriages, and this meant weights which were impossible

Above:
The 3in 20cwt mobile anti-aircraft gun had been in service since 1914 and was used in France in 1939/40. This photograph is unusual in showing the stowed rifles of the gun detachment; these were more usually left in the tractor.

Right:
A rush to man the 40mm Bofors guns of a South Coast battery during the flying bomb attacks of 1944.

Below right:
A 12pdr gun in a hurriedly-built emplacement, one of innumerable beach defence guns installed in 1940 during the invasion threat.

there was still no suitably powerful engine. Cruiser Mark IV was much the same tank but with thicker armour and with a 'Liberty' aero-engine; Cruiser Mark V, known as Covenanter had been designed by the London Midland & Scottish Railway Company works and was among the most eccentric and unreliable designs ever built; over 1,300 were made but it was used only as a training machine. It was later improved slightly into the Crusader but it inherited most of the mechanical faults and was never reliable.

For the tank brigades a new design of infantry tank appeared, the Valentine, which went into service in May 1940. This was a Vickers design and thus had some sound knowledge behind it; it went on to become the most prolific British tank, over 8,000 being built. It was well protected by 68mm of armour, carried the usual 2pdr gun, moved at 15mph and was trouble-free in service.

It was not until 1942 that tank design in Britain began to come right. In 1940 Harland & Wolff of Belfast was asked to design an infantry tank, presumably on the theory that since everyone else had tried, a shipbuilder was as good a

Above left:
Archer, a 17pdr self-propelled gun derived from the redundant Valentine tank. The gun faces rearward over the engine and had limited traverse, so that it was necessary to reverse into the firing position.

Above:
Firing a 6in 26cwt howitzer in the Western Desert, 1941.

bet as any. In the event its design was underpowered, and Vauxhall Motors was asked to develop a new engine, and, as an afterthought, to improve the whole tank. Vauxhall designed a flat-12 cylinder engine and the tank became the Churchill which, after a year of modification and adjustment, became a highly reliable design. In the cruiser family, the Crusader was improved into the Cavalier, inheriting all the Crusader's defects and inventing a few of its own, and the real breakthrough in cruiser tank design did not come until Leyland Motors suggested converting the Rolls-Royce Merlin aero-engine for tank applications. The first tank to use this engine was the Cromwell, designed by the Birmingham Railway Carriage & Wagon Company; the Cromwell appeared early in 1943. Armed with a 6pdr gun, with 63mm frontal armour, it was the first British tank to combine reasonable gunpower with mechanical reliability and it acquired a sound reputation in Northwest Europe.

Turning now to the infantry, they were in perhaps a less parlous state on their return from France in 1940 since much of their armament could be carried home, but the events in France had shown up some deficiencies in that armament. Moreover the problem of defence against invasion, the formation of the Home Guard and the expansion of the army meant that vast quantities of small arms and infantry weapons were demanded. Arms were procured in the USA: Enfield-pattern rifles and Browning and Lewis machine guns in 0.300 calibre were brought over and largely issued to the Home Guard, since the supply of 0.300 ammunition could then be channelled in one direction rather than confuse the regular army's supply system. (The Home Guard was also provided with grenades and mortars of eccentric design and manufacture which, thank goodness, are outside our terms of reference.) Two weapons, though, were in great demand: a good submachine gun and a good portable anti-tank weapon to replace the Boys rifle, now sadly deficient in its ability to penetrate tanks.

The quickest and simplest solution to the submachine gun problem, it seemed, was simply to take a good existing design and duplicate it. For some reason, which doubtless seemed good at the time, the design chosen to be copied was the Bergmann MP28, a German weapon dating from the middle 1920s. Why the far simpler MP38 was not chosen has never been explained. This was duly put into production as the Lanchester Carbine, but before this occurred a design appeared from the Royal Small Arms Factory at Enfield. Known simply as the 'N.O.T.40/1' it was simple and cheap, if repulsive to people conditioned to the better products of the gunsmith's art. After extensive testing it was adopted as the standard weapon for the army and RAF, and became known universally as the Sten Gun from the designers' initials and factory of origin — Shepherd, Turpin and Enfield.

The search for an anti-tank weapon capable of being carried by an infantryman was more difficult, but fortunately there had been something of a breakthrough in explosives technology just before the war, and this promised to aid in providing a solution. The accepted method of attacking a tank was to use kinetic energy — throw something hard as hard as possible with the aim of piercing the armour by sheer brute force. As we have seen in discussing anti-tank guns, as tanks grow stronger, so this method demands heavier and heavier weapons firing heavier and heavier projectiles at greater velocities, and this put the kinetic energy solution completely out of court in portable weapons.

In 1938 a pair of Swiss entrepreneurs had canvassed the various military attaches, announcing a 'new and powerful explosive' which would penetrate armour plate. In fact, when a demonstration was arranged, it appeared that there was nothing new about the explosive but that the two Swiss had revived and perfected an old phenomenon known as the 'Monroe Effect'. In the 1880s an American experimenter Monroe had found that if an explosive with a hollowed-out face was detonated against a steel plate, the shape of the hollow was reproduced in the plate. Later experiments in Germany had shown that if the hollow was line with metal the incision was deeper and occasionally cut through the plate. Now the Swiss had brought it to the point where it could be incorporated into a workable projectile which blew small holes through the armour. One of the British observers to the Swiss tests knew his

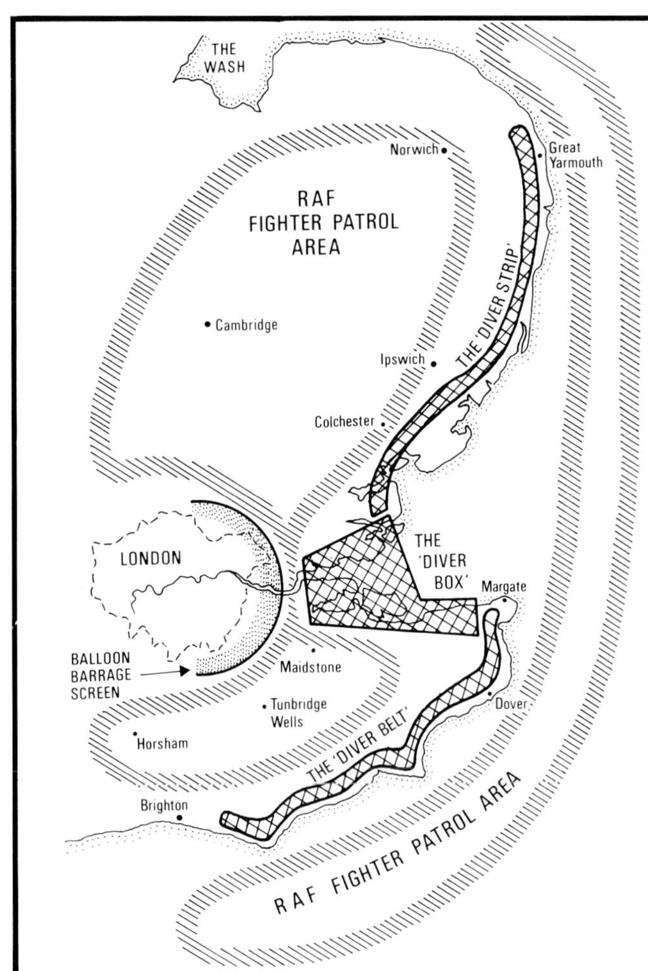

Left:
The 'Diver' defences against the flying bomb. **'Diver' was the codename for the V-1 flying bomb; the first planned defences were rings of guns around major cities, but when the attack began in June 1944 it was rapidly changed to the 'Diver Belt' of guns along the south coast, with RAF fighters patrolling over the sea and inland, catching what the guns missed. As a backstop there was a balloon barrage across the approaches to London. The 'Diver Belt' contained 412 heavy and 572 light AA guns, 28 multiple 20mm cannon and 200 rocket launchers manned by the Army and 584 light guns manned by the RAF Regiment.**

As the Allied troops advanced in France, the flying bombs were fired from more northerly sites, outflanking the 'Diver Belt', which led to the establishment of 'Diver Box' across the Thames Estuary. This held 208 heavy and 578 light AA guns. The final total for Belt and Box was 800 heavy, 1,800 light guns and 700 rocket launchers, with another 144 heavy guns in reserve.

The German attack moved farther north and included launchings from manned aircraft over the North Sea. To counter this, much of the 'Diver Belt' was moved to form 'Diver Strip' which ran from 'Diver Box' to Great Yarmouth. This contained 542 heavy and 503 light guns.

Had the attack been continued from even more northerly sites, 'Diver Fringe' was prepared, a gun belt running from Skegness to Whitby; some of these were deployed but saw little action.

explosive history, realised what he was seeing, and went back to Woolwich Arsenal determined that what he had seen he could duplicate. Now called 'shaped charge' or 'hollow charge', the Monroe Effect was harnessed by most combatants during the course of the war to provide an explosive means of piercing metal where kinetic methods were inapplicable. What was now required was a method of delivering a hollow charge projectile which could be man-carried.

A Lt-Col Blacker, of the Royal Artillery, had spent several years perfecting and promoting a novel design of mortar called a 'spigot mortar'. In this the weapon's barrel was replaced by a solid steel rod, and the bomb had a hollow tail which contained the propelling cartridge. The tail dropped over the steel rod, the cartridge fired, and the bomb was blown off the end of the rod; the whole thing was a reversal of the usual process of blowing the projectile out of the barrel, in that the 'barrel' was blown off the end of what was inside it. Blacker had submitted one of these to the British Army in 1937 as a possible small-calibre mortar, pointing out the great advantage was that no barrel had to be made, since the working part of the weapon was inside the bomb and instead of a barrel the launcher was a simple steel rod which anyone could make. He failed to impress the Ordnance Board and went back to work on more ideas.

In 1940 he reappeared with another 'bomb thrower' which could be fired from the shoulder on a flat trajectory. The basic mechanism was no more than another steel rod — or 'spigot' — and a powerful spring. The rod was pulled back against the spring and held, a hollow-tailed bomb placed in a trough at the front of the weapon, and the trigger pulled. The spigot shot out, entered the hollow tail, fired a cartridge, and the bomb blew itself off the spigot and, obligingly, blew the spigot back, so re-cocking it for the next shot. A heavy version of this weapon was accepted for the Home Guard; known as the 'Blacker Bombard' it hurled a huge 29lb high explosive bomb to a range of about 250yd and was employed as an anti-tank weapon. Blacker then evolved a smaller version with a hollow-charge bomb, but it was turned down by the Ordnance Board. He then went in by the back door, offering the device to MD1, a peculiar design agency which developed weapons for clandestine forces. MD1 took it, and Lt-Col Jefferis of that agency perfected it and eventually got the army interested. It was finally taken into service as the 'Projector, Infantry, Anti-tank' or PIAT (always called 'Pee-at') and it remained in use throughout the war. Although cumbersome it could penetrate any wartime tank, and if the operator took care in aiming at a sensitive spot, it would easily set the tank on fire into the bargain.

The Royal Artillery took its first steps into the unconventional when the rocket anti-aircraft weapon was revived. When the Army had rejected the original rocket designs in 1939 the Royal Navy had taken the 2in model and used it with a 'parachute-and-cable' device as a shipborne deterrent against dive bombers. The rocket was fired vertically from a simple open frame and ejected a parachute, a long wire, and an explosive mine. If a

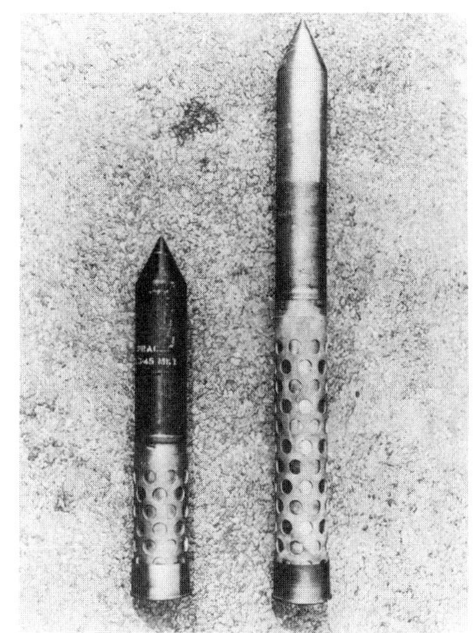

bomber struck the wire the dynamics of the arrangement ensured that the drag of the parachute pulled the mine to contact the wing where it would detonate and wreck the aircraft. The success of this device showed the Army that its requirement for a closed-breech launcher was unnecessary and that a simple open rail device would do equally well. By late 1940 production of a launcher had begun and eventually several thousand were deployed in fixed locations around cities, harbours and other sensitive targets. Their first deployment was against dive bombers, and for this purpose the rocket warheads were fitted with the first proximity fuzes. Until then, anti-aircraft projectiles used time fuzes, the time from firing to point of burst being determined as part of the prediction process, because the chances of a direct hit were minimal. The ideal would be a fuze which detected the proximity of the target and detonated the projectile at the optimum lethal point, and with the advances in electronics which had been ushered in by the radar era, this became possible with the 3in rocket.

The fuze operated on photo-electric principles, being 'tuned' to the normal intensity of daylight; if any shadow — as of a dive-bomber — reduced this light intensity the fuze would trigger the explosive payload of the warhead. In spite of a tendency to false alarms — cloud shadows or passing birds — it worked well enough until the Germans gave up daylight attacks and turned to night raiding, after which it was useless. Once this occurred the rocket projectors were grouped in massed batteries of 64 twin-launcher weapons and used to project barrages of 128 rockets into the sky in the path of the raiding aircraft. The only drawback to this was that some minutes later 128 empty rocket motors would rain down to earth. Therefore the siting of a rocket battery had to be done with some care so that the empty motors fell into empty space and not into a populated area.

The first proximity fuze was possible because of the relatively large space available and the low acceleration rate of the rocket warhead. Transferring the idea to a gun fuze was much more difficult; it was eventually solved, using radar techniques, placing a transmitter and receiver inside the fuze. Once the idea had been proven it was given to the USA, since no production facilities could be spared in Britain, and eventually American-made

Above left:
The 2pdr anti-tank gun was an elegant design but was rapidly outclassed by German improvements in the armouring of their tanks.

Above right:
Ammunition for the Burney recoilless guns with their characteristic perforated cartridge cases. Left, the 3.45in shoulder gun; right, the 3.7in anti-tank gun.

Below:
The PIAT (Projector, Infantry, Anti-Tank) used the 'spigot' principle. It was a formidable device to cock and fire, but was effective against most types of wartime tank.

Bottom:
The breech end of the 3.7in recoilless gun, showing the breech block opened and the six venturis through which gas was directed rearwards, so counteracting the recoil due to the firing of the shell.

Above:
An early Cromwell tank with 6pdr gun. The larger of the two holes in the front plate should carry a machine gun mounting; the other is the driver's vision port.

Right:
A Churchill Crocodile flamethrowing tank demonstrates its ability. The flamethrower was in the hull, a standard 6pdr gun being fitted in the turret.

Below right:
The Churchill tank; after a dubious start it went on to become the mainstay of British specialised armour. This is the Mk VII Close Support version, armed with a 95mm howitzer in the turret.

proximity fuzes returned to Britain to be fired by 3.7in guns against the flying bomb attacks of 1944.

One could go on for quite a long time outlining the various weapons which were developed under the pressure of war, but the point has been made. In spite of the last-minute rush to get the basic service weapons into service, only accomplished after war had actually broken out in many cases, the army's design and development system went on to perform extremely well. One authority once said that military design was like a savings bank; you paid in in peacetime and drew out in war. The penurious years of the 1920s and 1930s had a beneficial effect on British design teams, viewed in retrospect. Since money was short they were not permitted to run wild and build everything they thought of. Once a design was drawn up it was pulled apart, re-designed, criticised, modified and thoroughly wrung out until it was as near perfect as could be. Then it was shelved, and another project begun. All on paper, but all of it excellent exercise for the minds of

Right:
The 'Tetrarch' was the last British light tank and only survived in production because it could be air-lifted in the Hamilcar glider. Airborne troops used some during the Normandy invasion in 1944 and the Rhine crossing in 1945.

the designers. When the pressure of war appeared they were able to go back into their archives and into the recesses of their minds and recall something which had been done years before, bring it out, modify it, and put it to use.

The other significant feature of British wartime design was that so much of it emanated from military establishments. Apart from odd weapons developed for the Home Guard and for MD1, there were few private ventures in weaponry. No hand grenades designed by civilians, no engineering works developing a mortar of their own design, no home experimenters offering anti-aircraft shells, as had happened in World War 1. True, there were offers, but very few of them survived scrutiny by the Ordnance Board, since most duplicated work which had been done years before and could soon be demonstrated to be unworkable. Once more the work in the inter-war years paid dividends, since whenever an idea was put forward someone was able to say 'We tried it and this is why it didn't work; how do you propose to do it better?'

The culmination of all this design ability and talent came with the invasion of Europe, when specialised tanks swam through the surf, laid bridges and demolished obstacles, when the advancing troops crossed Bailey prefabricated bridges and walked behind tanks flailing the ground to explode mines harmlessly. When airborne troops descending from the sky with motorcycles and lightweight tanks, when Commandos swarmed ashore with silent submachine guns and plastic explosive. The savings bank had been drawn upon almost to the last penny by the time the war ended with the detonation of the biggest design effort of all.

Table 5: Weapons of the Second World War

	Title **Small Arms**	*Calibre*	*Length* (in)	*Weight* (lb/oz)	*Magazine Capacity*	*Bullet Weight* (gr)	*Muzzle Velocity* (ft/sec)	*Muzzle Energy* (ft/lb)	*Effective Range* (yd)	*Remarks*
1939	Rifle, Enfield No 4 Mk 1	.303	44.5	9/1	10	174	2,400	2,228	600	
1944	Rifle, Enfield No 5 Mk 1	.303	39.5	7/2	10	174	2,000	1,551	400	'Jungle Carbine'
1937	Bren Mk 1 MG	.303	45.3	22.4	30 box	174	2,400	2,400	600	500rd/min
1932	Pistol, Enfield No 2	.38	10.2	1.7	6-cyl	178	650	166	15	
1944	Pistol, Browning GP35	9mm	7.8	2.1	13 box	115	1,100	309	20	
1940	SMG Thompson M1928	.45	33.7	10.8	20 box	230	910	423	50	800rd/min
1941	SMG Sten Mk 2	9mm	35.7	7.7	32 box	115	1,000	256	30	450rd/min
1937	Rifle, A/Tk, Boys Mk 1	.55	63.5	35.9	5 box	735	3,250	17,261	300	Pierced 21mm of armour at 300yd

Note that submachine guns (SMGs) were originally known as 'machine carbines'. The Browning automatic pistol was not a general issue until the late 1950s, being restricted previously to airborne and Commando troops.

Title **Artillery Equipments**	*Class*	*Calibre* (in)	*Barrel Length* (calibres)	*Shell Weight* (lb)	*Charge Weight* (lb)	*Muzzle Velocity* (ft/sec)	*Mounting*	*Weight in Action* (tons)	*Maximum Range* (yd)	*Remarks*
25pr Gun-Howitzer	Field	3.45	26.7	25	1.75 C	1,700	2-wheel	1.77	13,400	
3.7in Mountain How	Field	3.7	11.7	20	9oz C	973	2-wh split	0.82	6,000	
4.5in BL Gun	Medium	4.5	41	55	9 C	2,250	2-wh split	5.75	20,500	
5.5in BL Gun	Medium	5.5	30	100	9.2 C	1,675	2-wh split	6.09	16,200	
7.2in BL How Mk 4	Heavy	7.2	22.4	200	19.8 C	1,700	2-wheel	10.16	16,900	
9.2in BL How Mk 1	S/Heavy	9.2	17.3	290	28 C	1,600	Siege	16.2	13,935	
12in BL How Mk 3	S/Heavy	12.0	17.3	750	48 C	1,468	Rail truck	76	14,350	
13in BL Gun	S/Heavy	13.5	45	1,250	293 C	2,550	Rail truck	240	40,000	
18in BL Howitzer	S/Heavy	18.0	35	2,500	282 C	1,880	Rail truck	250	22,300	
6in BL Mk 24	Coast	6.0	45	102	31 C	2,825	Pedestal		24,500	
9.2in BL Mk 10	Coast	9.2	46.7	380	53.5 C	2,700	Barbette	125	36,700	
15in BL Mk 2	Coast	15.0	42.4	1938	432 C	2,680	Barbette	373	42,000	Dover & Singapore only
40mm Bofors	AA	1.57	56.2	2.0	9oz C	2,700	4-wh pedestal	1.95	10,800 and 5,000ft ceiling	
3.7in QF Mk 3	AA	3.7	50	28	8.5 C	2,600	4-wh pedestal	9.2	20,600 and 32,000ft ceiling	
4.5in QF Mk 2	AA	4.5	45	54	14 C	2,400	4-wh pedestal	14.75	22,800 and 34,500ft ceiling	
6pr of 7cwt	A/Tk	2.24	43	6.0	1.1 C	2,693	2-wh split	1.12	5,500	Pierced 74mm at 1,000yd
17pr QF gun	A/Tk	3.0	55	17	8.2 C	2,900	2-wh split	2.06	10,000	Pierced 109mm at 1,000yd

Then and Now

Right:
Reconnaissance patrol, 1894; the 2nd Middlesex Volunteers bicycle platoon.

Below right:
Reconnaissance patrol, 1984; the 7th Battalion Royal Anglian Regiment (TA) with their camouflaged Land Rovers.

Below:
Bridgebuilding in 1894; constructing a Berthon Boat pontoon bridge in camp.

Bottom:
Bridgebuilding, 1976. An M2 mechanised bridge over the River Weser, Germany, during Exercise 'Spearpoint'.

Above:
The ammunition mule of the 2nd Battalion, East Lancashire Regiment, 1896. He carried 2,200 rounds of .303in rifle ammunition.

Left:
The 'ammunition mule' of 32nd Field Regiment RA, 1970; an Alvis Stalwart load carrier with 5,000kg of 175mm shells aboard.

Below left:
Artillery then: a 12pdr breech-loading gun during the New Forest manoeuvres, August 1895.

Below:
Artillery now: a 155mm FH70 howitzer firing during NATO trials in Sardinia.

7 An Uneasy Peace

In 1943 the British had been persuaded to adopt the American M4 Sherman tank as their principal battle tank, largely because their own designs were so unreliable and their factories incapable of producing tanks in the volume required in time for the planned invasion of Europe. When the war ended there were, in fact, some good British tanks in service, notably the Churchill, Cromwell and Comet, but these marked the end of the infantry and cruiser concept. The Sherman fitted neither of these classifications, being an all-rounder or a tank for all seasons as it were. This seems to have finally caused the scales to fall from British eyes, aided by General Montgomery who, as early as 1942, had demanded a 'universal' tank to fill both roles and, into the bargain, provide a chassis for self propelled guns or specialised armoured vehicles. Montgomery being an infantryman, it is hardly surprising that he ran into considerable opposition from tank experts who maintained that such a device was impossible. But he continued to press his idea and, as the war went on and he became a more important figure, so his opinions began to carry more weight. At last, in 1944, a design contract was given for a new 'heavy cruiser' to carry a 17pdr gun, be well armoured, and have a new type of suspension which used less interior space than previous systems. The result was the Centurion, which appeared too late for action in Europe. Even without the test of combat it looked as if British designers had managed to get it right at last, and with subsequent refinement the Centurion turned out to be a very good tank indeed.

Another piece of 'unfinished business' from the war

Below:
Training; a soldier of 1st Battalion, 2nd King Edward's Own Gurkha Rifles practising an assault river crossing in Brunei, 1975.

Bottom:
Traditions continue. 74th 'Battleaxe Company' Royal Artillery parade a French axe, captured at Fort Desaix in Martinique in 1809, on the anniversary of the battle every year. By custom the axe is carried by 'the tallest man with a moustache' in the battery, irrespective of rank.

Below right:
Training; a soldier using an FN-FAL 7.62mm rifle fitted with a Centronic laser projector in its sight unit. He has detectors mounted on his body harness. When 'shot' with a laser beam the detectors cause an alarm to sound, which can only be silenced by an umpire.

years was the development of recoilless guns. These had first been suggested by a company called the Broadway Trust, part of the Beardmore organisation which was experienced in gun manufacture, and was the invention of Sir Dennis Burney. The principle of operation was that a perforated cartridge case allowed four-fifths of the propellant gas to be directed backwards through jet nozzles so as to develop thrust and thus counteract the recoiling movement of the gun due to the forward ejection of the shell. A number of experimental guns were built and tested but the war ended before any firm conclusions could be drawn. With the war over the existing designs were 'frozen' and the whole principle re-examined by the Royal Armaments Research & Development Establishment (RARDE). Its deliberations took several years but eventually led to the manufacture and issue of a potent 120mm recoilless gun known as the BAT (for Battalion Anti-Tank weapon) which became the principal infantry anti-tank armament in the middle 1950s.

As discussed previously, conventional anti-tank guns had reached monster proportions by 1945 and there was a sense of dismay among the infantry, since it seemed that nothing capable of being manhandled would be up to dealing with modern tanks. The BAT changed this; being a recoilless gun it was extremely light (since there was no heavy recoil mechanism, no need for a heavy carriage and no need for a heavy barrel) and due to a new type of projectile, also pioneered by Burney, it could destroy the heaviest tank with a single shot. The new shell was called the 'squash-head' shell, since it was filled with plastic explosive and had its fuze in the base. When it struck a hard target the nose would collapse and allow the soft explosive to spread on to the target material like a poultice, after which the base fuze would detonate it. This caused a violent shock wave to pass into the material of the target and, by complex reflections and interactions, shake free a slab of material from the inner surface. In the case of a tank this could be a slab of steel weighing perhaps 20lb, driven off at several hundred feet per second, spinning into the tank and creating immense damage.

The Centurion and the BAT were virtually the only major pieces of new equipment to be issued to the army in the 10 years following the end of the war. The war years had seen massive production, the store depots were full, and the Treasury was reluctant to see money spent when all that wartime equipment was there to be used up. The Korean War, so far as the British were concerned, was fought almost entirely with wartime equipment, the sole

Top left:
Infantrymen negotiating a barbed wire obstacle during exercise 'Avon Express', 1977.

Above left:
Wherever the Army went, its traditions and ceremonials went with it. Here is the Corps of Drums of the Leicestershire Regiment beating Retreat on a Korean hillside in 1952, well within mortar and artillery range of the enemy.

Left:
'Keeping the Army in the Public Eye' is a continuing endeavour. This is Artillery Day at the Royal School of Artillery, held every two years and attended by the public in their thousands.

exception being the first combat use of the Centurion tank. The Malayan Emergency was fought with wartime equipment, as was the Suez Invasion. Financial restraints were not the only reason for this; in 1949 the setting up of NATO and various heady concepts of standardisation had caused a general slowing of development ideas until such times as the NATO idea was better understood, and by the middle of the 1950s sufficient areas of agreement had been blocked out to make it obvious that much of the current development programme could be abandoned, since none of it was likely to appeal to the other members of NATO.

The first, and highly significant, disagreement had arisen in 1949 over the selection of new infantry weapons, and it was an unseemly wrangle which soured relationships for quite some time and which gave designers and soldiers a preview of the problems they were likely to face in the future.

In brief, during the war the Germans had developed an 'assault rifle' using a shorter-than-usual cartridge. This had sufficient performance for something like 95% of normal battle requirements, since analysis had shown that few soldiers ever fired their weapons at ranges greater than 300-400yd. The idea, and the underlying philosophy, appealed to the British and the RSAF designed a revolutionary rifle, the EM2, chambered for a new 7mm short cartridge. It was thoroughly tried and tested and approved for issue in 1949. But with the setting-up of NATO it was thought advisable for all members to use the same basic rifle and machine gun cartridge, even if they didn't use the same rifle, so the British 7mm came under examination by other armies. The Canadian and Belgian armies, and the other continentals, saw the sense of the 7mm round and would probably have been happy to adopt it, but the major partner in NATO was the American contingent, which was also the principal source of finance, and was out to standardise NATO on American equipment wherever possible. The Americans objected to the 7mm cartridge on the grounds that it lacked range, the very characteristic which had been designed out of it, and after a long and bitter wrangle forced NATO to adopt a 7.62mm cartridge which was, in fact, no more than the current 0.30 American bullet in a slightly shorter cartridge case.

This wrangle lasted until 1957, and at the end of it the British Army was in need of a rifle; the EM2 could not be converted to use the 7.62mm cartridge and there was nothing else suitable in the design archives. The Belgians, in their usual practical way, had seen which way the wind was blowing much earlier than anyone else and had taken the trouble to design and perfect an automatic rifle in 7.62mm calibre, so that now they were able to offer it to Britain which, having nothing else, had to accept it. The FN (Fabrique Nationale d'Armes de Guerre) self-loading rifle, which became universally known in British service as the SLR, was, fortunately, a very good weapon and the Army had no grounds for complaint on that score, but it was something of a shock to have to adopt a foreign weapon as the basic soldier's tool.

It was the Royal Artillery's turn to suffer a culture shock next. At the close of the war it had been discussing the replacement of the 25pdr gun-howitzer at some length. The principal defect lay not so much in the gun as in the shell; it had been designed from low-grade steel,

Above:
An infantry patrol passing through a village in the Gambia, 1977.

Below:
A military policewoman, in fragmentation jacket, searching shopping bags in Belfast.

Bottom left:
A British infantryman in full winter warfare equipment, and with his day's ration laid out before him, during an exercise in Norway, 1980.

Bottom right:
A soldier of the 1980s in full NBC protective clothing.

with an eye on possible wartime production problems, and consequently a low proportion of its 25lb weight was high explosive — about 7%. This meant a poor lethal radius, especially when compared with the 35lb shells, of better grade steel and consequently higher explosive loading, used in the American and German 105mm howitzers. A more lethal shell was therefore of first priority. This was designed, but was slightly longer and heavier than the standard 25lb shell and demanded, for best performance (the magic 15,000yd returned at this point) a new gun. Two or three designs were studied, but the most unusual and attractive came from a company which had never previously figured in the gun business. Guest, Keen & Knettlefold was the maker of screws and fastenings, and yet it came up with a gun design which came within a hairsbreadth of being adopted for service. The 'GKN Gun' was an 88mm weapon (the 25pdr had been 87mm) of fairly conventional form, but the unusual feature was an overhead shield of glass-fibre which acted both as a splinter protection and also, with the aid of special side-curtains, to protect the crew from nuclear flash effects.

At this point agreement was reached among NATO countries to adopt certain artillery calibres as standard; close support weapons (ie the old 'field gun' class) would be 105mm, and medium or general support weapons (the old 'medium guns') would be of 155mm calibre. Since neither of these were common in European NATO countries, this can be seen as another example of American pressure. What it meant to the British was that, once again, their chosen calibre was non-standard, nothing of the right calibre was available at home, and they must go out into the world markets to find suitable weapons.

Doubtless the Americans were hoping to unload stocks of their wartime M1 105mm howitzers, but the British went instead to Italy and bought a short-barrelled pack howitzer instead. This had some virtues; it could be dismantled for mule or helicopter carriage, could be adapted to high or low positions for general or anti-tank firing, and had an ingenious triple-expansion recoil system which made the weapon very compact. On the debit side it was chambered for the standard American M1 ammunition, which was deficient in range, had a rise-to-open breechblock which would remove a careless man's fingers at the drop of a hat, and had a distressing tendency to fall to pieces after being towed for more than 30 or so miles.

Once this 'interim' equipment was in service, work at high priority began to develop a purely British 105mm design of self-propelled gun, principally to outfit the armoured divisions in Germany. The chassis, developed by Vickers, had some commonality of parts with the FV432 armoured personnel carrier which was being developed at the same time, while the gun was a completely new design from RARDE which although of the standard 105mm calibre fired ammunition quite different to any other NATO weapon and produced a maximum range of 17,000m, also far better than any other 105mm gun. The resulting equipment was called Abbot (there is an ecclesiastical tradition in the naming of self-propelled guns) and was a turreted tracked vehicle with the gun capable of being elevated to 70deg and capable of all-round fire. It entered service in 1965 and is still in use.

In the matter of the satisfying the 155mm requirement the choice was simple: buy American. Developing a totally new calibre of gun would have been too demanding in research and design facilities and money. A small number of 155mm Howitzer M44 were bought from the USA in 1956 to fill the most urgent requirements, after which Britain waited for the Americans to perfect their improved model, the M109, which was purchased in 1965. This was a turreted equipment, a considerably better weapon than the M44 which was an open-topped machine.

Finally, with the NATO requirement satisfied, it was time to turn to developing a towed gun to replace the Italian pack howitzer. The requirement was stringent, since it was vital to have a weapon which could be helicopter-lifted, and yet be able to fire the same 105mm ammunition as Abbot to the same range. The result was the 105mm Light Gun, which was first issued in 1974.

Below:
An artillery forward observer, with radio, carries an FN-FAL rifle for personal protection.

Bottom:
Design staff of the Royal Small Arms Factory, Enfield, on the occasion of the first public showing of the 4.85mm Enfield rifle system in 1976. The rifle is on the left, the light machine gun on the right.

Top:
The Swedish 84mm Carl Gustav recoilless gun, now the standard infantry anti-tank weapon in the British and many other armies. Though shown here on a tripod, it is normally fired from the man's shoulder. *FFV Ordnance Division*

Above centre:
The experimental 7mm EM2 rifle of 1949, showing its unconventional shape.

Above:
A 7.62mm General Purpose Machine Gun (GPMG) of the 1st Battalion, the Royal Anglian Regiment being used in the sustained fire role from a tripod.

Extensive use of light alloys and other weight-saving techniques produced the desired answer, and the weapon can be lifted under a Puma helicopter to permit rapid deployment. A replacement barrel was also designed for the gun, chambered for the American M1 ammunition, so that if the gun is required to serve where American ammunition is more easily available, then this barrel can be substituted for the standard one.

While all this re-equipping had been going on the army had been undergoing a considerable change. When the war ended in 1945 compulsory military service had not automatically ended with it, as most people had expected when it was first introduced. One reason was a matter of simple equity; when the war ended there were several thousand young men just getting used to the feel and fit of military uniform, and a general demobilisation which included them would have been unjust to those who had put in five or six years of service. Moreover while the vast numbers of wartime conscripts were being processed out of the army, hands were still needed to keep the system running. And well before these last wartime inductees were thinking of leaving the political picture had changed and it became apparent that the army had to be kept on at a greater strength than could be obtained by voluntary enlistment. So National Service continued, with 18-year olds serving for two years. Even so, when the Korean War broke out in 1950 it was necessary to activate reserve forces, since the army was thinly-stretched across the world. At that time garrisons were still in various African colonies, in Malaya (fighting the Communist insurgents), in Egypt and North Africa, occupying Germany, reinforcing Hong Kong against the possible threat of the Chinese Communists who had now gained their country, in Italy and Trieste, in the Caribbean and in a score of other tiny locations.

Although there has since been a certain amount of refined complaint from some of the more literate conscripts, on the whole the average draftee took his service in good part and many took a considerable interest in what they were doing. The proof of this contention can be seen in the numbers who, close to the end of their compulsory period, volunteered to serve an extra year when their regiments were ordered to Korea in 1951-53. Their explanation was simple: they had been extensively trained for almost two years to perform a warlike task, and now that there was a real war they wanted to see whether they could actually do it. This may sound unbelievable, but the author was a senior NCO in an artillery regiment ordered to Korea in 1951 and can name a dozen men who signed on to prove their point. And very good soldiers they made, when the shooting was for real.

Until about 1956 there was little in the Army which would have baffled a soldier of 1936; some of the equipment was better, but it worked the same as it had always done, and except for improvements in degree there had been very little change. But in the mid-1950s the big changes began.

When the British (and other Allied) technical intelligence staffs sifted through the documentation uncovered in Germany, several prospective air defence guided missiles came to light, some of which had actually got as far as prototypes and test firings. Similar work, though at extremely low priority, had been done in Britain and the USA, and in about 1949 the first British contracts to develop missiles were given out. The other German development which moved researchers was, of course, their A-4 rocket, and work on this type of weapon began in the USA as soon as the war ended. In 1956 British troops were sent to the USA to train on the Corporal tactical missile and in the following year it was brought into the British Army. In 1959 the Thunderbird air defence missile went into service and the medium and heavy anti-aircraft guns were retired. In 1956 too the coast defences were dismantled — there seemed little point in defending the shore with a cannon when a missile could pass over your head unscathed. Between 1959 and 1965 ground surveillance radar, electronic warfare equipment, new communciations equipment, pilotless observation drones, infra-red scanning, computers and many other examples of advanced technology made their appearance. The army was about to become a highly specialised force in which technology would replace manpower as far as possible.

In addition, the list of garrisons of the early 1950s had been ruthlessly cut; colonies had been handed over to self-government, postwar occupation of many countries had stopped, and the call on manpower had been almost halved. There was no longer any good justification, so far as the army was concerned, for keeping conscription, and since it had become something of a political football, it was ended in 1960. From that time forward the army became an all-volunteer professional force.

At the same time, because of the shedding of Empire, it became, for the first time in its history, an army primarily aimed at fighting a continental war in company with its NATO allies rather than a supply organisation for Empire garrisons with a small home defence appendage. This led to a massive reorganisation. The rundown in manpower led to amalgamation of infantry regiments and the disbandment of many, until the very regimental system itself appeared to be in danger of vanishing. Most analysts will say that the regimental system, as applied to infantry, is outmoded and inefficient; it probably is, but what is lost in sheer managerial aspects is more than regained by the *esprit de corps* and family pride which is engendered. Eventually the infantry organisation settled into five administrative divisions, with the Brigade of Guards and the Parachute Regiment as independent organisations.

The other significant change in the army lay in its social make-up. For the first time it was predominantly a married army. As we have seen, throughout the years prior to 1939 marriage was restricted to a small proportion of the rank and file, but the changing social climate of the postwar years and the changing educational and technical standards of the men enlisting gradually altered this. This change meant changes in military organisation as the army gradually assumed more responsibility for the off-duty life of its men and their dependants. Shops, cinemas, schools, radio and television services, medical and social services were all required and had to be built up and, more important, manned. It was impossible to provide these services from the limited manpower in uniform, and so the army began to grow an enormous civilian 'tail'. Workshops were operated, under military command, by civilians; barrack stores, cookhouses, fuel supply points, ammunition depots, instructional establishments, administrative offices, all were gradually 'civilianised', to the point where some establishments now have perhaps no more than 10% of their staff in uniform.

While the personnel were undergoing reorganisation,

Below:
Loading the 51mm mortar, a new design which has replaced the 2in model used during World War 2.

Bottom left:
A British soldier with body armour and a rifle fitted with image-intensifying night sight, Belfast, 1981.

Bottom right:
British troops of the Parachute Regiment armed with 7.62mm self-loading rifles; the man in the foreground also carries a folded M72 anti-tank rocket launcher slung from his shoulder.

so the equipment was being brought under scrutiny. The shape of the next war appeared to be one of high mobility, with forces capable of moving and relocating at high speed in the face of a mobile threat. There was also the shadow of nuclear warfare, demanding dispersion, concealment and protection. All this pointed to units mounted on wheels or tracks, capable of rapid movement and capable of independent operation. The days of massing thousands of troops and hundreds of guns to crack open a defended line were gone, since a nuclear device could remove such a threat in one blow; dispersion was the order of the day.

The first step was the adoption of an armoured personnel carrier (APC) for the infantry, to give them protection while on the move and allow them, to reach the battle area unscathed. The FV432 (it was originally called 'Trojan' but the name was dropped when someone recalled a civilian car owning that trade name) became the basic APC and variant models proliferated; a carrier for the infantry mortar, in which the mortar was installed so that it could fire out through a hatch in the roof; an armoured ambulance; a workshop vehicle; a command post vehicle for artillery units; and many other sub-types. The APC version carries 10 infantrymen in addition to the vehicle driver and commander and usually has a machine gun mounted on the roof hatch, though some models were fitted with small turrets. Later the 120mm BAT was fitted into the roof hatch, and anti-tank launchers and missiles were mounted. All this led to an argument which, in some quarters, has continued to this day and will doubtless continue for some time to come; what is the basic function of a tracked infantry-carrying vehicle? Is it to act simply as a 'battle taxi' and deliver the troops to their operational area, where they then dismount and fight in the traditional way? Or is it to be a 'fighting vehicle' with heavy armament and provision for the occupants to fire their personal weapons from inside, so that the vehicle becomes an aggressive sub-unit capable of fighting its way to its objective without the men having to dismount?

Mention of anti-tank launchers and the 120mm BAT gun brings us to the principal perceived threat to the armies of Western Europe, which is the superabundance of tanks in the Soviet bloc. Over the past 20 years the imbalance has remained roughly the same; the Warsaw Pact armies have about five main battle tanks (MBTs) to the West's one. As a result, a great deal of development work has gone into the provision of anti-tank weapons on every level, from simple hand-held rocket launchers to sophisticated missiles. As we have seen, the infantry received the BAT in the early 1950s, but this was a company weapon and required transportation to move it any distance. A more portable weapon, to replace the wartime PIAT was needed, and due to the mingling of British and US forces in Korea, the British decided to adopt the American 3.5in 'Super Bazooka' rocket launcher. This was an efficient, if rather clumsy, weapon and it remained in use until the 1960s, when it was replaced by another American device, the M72 66mm launcher. This was a light, telescoped tube which had a pre-packed rocket with hollow charge warhead sealed inside. To use, the soldier merely threw off the end caps, extended the telescoping tube, placed the device on his shoulder, aimed and fired; he then threw the tube away and obtained a fresh one. It was the British army's introduction to 'expendable weaponry' and it made a generation of elderly storekeepers flinch.

The drawback to the M72 launcher was simply that it was not powerful enough to harm really heavy armour of the sort to be anticipated on the front of Warsaw Pact tanks; something still heavier was needed, though it had still to be capable of being man-carried. This time the purchasing agents went to Sweden and bought the Carl Gustav 84mm recoilless gun, which became the platoon anti-tank weapon.

Strangely, although it was known that the Germans had been testing a guided missile for use against tanks in 1944-45, no work on this aspect of missle technology was begun in Britain after the war, and it was left to the

Below right:
The Short Blowpipe shoulder-fired air defence missile; fired in the general direction of the target, an infra-red seeker homes it on to the aircraft. *Shorts*

Below left:
Preparing to fire an 81mm mortar.

Bottom:
Modern technology; burying a sensitive seismic detector which will sense any movement in the vicinity and automatically report it by radio to a central computer.

Top left:
The Milan anti-tank guided missile; the missile is inside the cylindrical storage/launch tube which clamps to the firing post. The large lens is the object lens of the MIRA night-firing sight.

Top right:
The Vickers Vigilant man-portable anti-tank missile is fired; this was the first anti-tank wire-guided missile adopted by the British Army and it has since been replaced by Milan. *BAC*

Above left:
A CL-89 reconnaissance drone about to be launched. This jet-propelled machine carries cameras and other sensors to detect targets for artillery engagement.

Above right:
The Multiple Launch Rocket System (MLRS) has been developed in the USA and is scheduled to enter service with the British Army in 1985.

Australian Army to initiate a programme. Once begun, the British Ministry of Supply joined in, and its chief contribution appears to have been insistence on a massive squash-head warhead. The result was an enormous weapon, called Malkara, a few of which were adopted by the British in the late 1950s. Two missiles were mounted on a small armoured car, and operated by the Royal Armoured Corps; it remained in use until the middle 1970s, though it was grossly oversized for the job it was expected to do.

In the 1950s a number of abortive missile programmes were started and, eventually, cancelled due to cutbacks in defence spending, leading to some commercial firms having idle design staffs. Vickers, in this situation, began its own development of an anti-tank missile and produced Vigilant, a neat and, for its time, extremely advanced design. As with Malkara, it was controlled by electrical signals passed down a wire which unreeled as the missile flew, the operator steering it to the target by using an optical sight and a 'joystick' control. It used a hollow-charge warhead weighing 13lb and could defeat any potential target. Next came a larger missile called Swingfire, developed by Vickers once more, and this was fitted into an armoured carrier based on a light tank chassis and issued to Royal Artillery anti-tank regiments.

While these missiles were effective, they had become specialist arm weapons, leaving the infantry with only its launchers and guns, but in the early 1960s international cooperation began to make itself felt in this and other fields. Weapon development was now becoming extremely expensive; moreover there seemed to be little point in every member of NATO developing their own weapon for some particular application and then squabbling over which was going to be adopted as standard, if any. As a result, first manufacturers and then governments began exploring the possibility of collaborating on some projects for which there was an obvious common need. If the collaborating countries' armies could be persuaded to agree upon their requirements, then the design work could be parcelled out among suitable firms — one to develop, say, a warhead, one a missile body, another the guidance system — and once the device was made to work it could become common issue in the participating countries and offered elsewhere in NATO.

In some instances this system has failed, generally where national preferences are so markedly different that compromise is impossible. MBTs are a prime example of this; the past 30 years have been littered with torn-up agreements as the various parties have failed to agree on the relative priorities of gunpower, protection and mobility. But in lesser weapons some extremely effective programmes have been highly successful, and one of the

Top:
Artillery practice; NCO students on No 11 Long Gunnery Staff Course firing a 25pdr gun at Blackball Firs anti-tank range, Salisbury Plain, 1953.

Above:
An experiment which was dropped; a 5.5in medium gun mounted in a Centurion tank chassis as a possible self-propelled general support gun. The NATO agreement on adoption of 155mm as the standard medium calibre ended this idea.

Above right:
Abbot, the 105mm self-propelled gun adopted in 1962. *Vickers*

Below:
The 105mm light gun fires the same ammunition as Abbot and outperforms every other gun of its class.

first was a cooperative venture between France and Germany (with Britain joining in at a later stage) to develop an infantry anti-tank missile. The result was Milan, technically known as a 'second-generation' missile and adopted in the late 1970s by Britain, France, Germany, Belgium and Greece in NATO and also sold to other countries. 'Second Generation' refers to the guidance method; Milan is wire-guided, but the operator merely has to keep his optical sight laid on the target. Inside the sight is an infra-red detector which reacts to a flare in the tail of the missile. After launching, the missile is pre-programmed to steer into the optical sight field of view; the detector spots the flare and measures its displacement from the axis of the sight, calculates corrections to bring the missile into the sight line, and automatically sends them down the connecting wire. The missile thus steers itself into alignment with the sight, and provided the operator keeps his sight steady on the target the missile is 95% certain to hit at ranges out to 3km. In 1983 Milan was further improved by the addition of an infra-red night sight which allows accurate firing to ranges of 2km in complete darkness.

Another international collaborative venture was to provide a standard 155mm towed howitzer. This began in 1968 when Britain, Germany and the USA all agreed to join in developing a new weapon. Once the preliminary specifications began to go down on paper it was obvious that the Americans saw things differently, and they withdrew, leaving Britain and Germany to go it alone. Italy, however, then joined in and the specification was

Top:
The Italian M56 105mm pack howitzer, demonstrating how the trail could be folded to reduce the length when towing.

Above:
The 5.5in medium gun entered service in 1942 and remained in use until 1980. The prominent 'horns' contain springs to balance the muzzle weight of the gun.

Above right:
'Longhand' was the last medium anti-aircraft gun to be approved for British service. It was a 3.7in gun with automatic ammunition feed, and could reach a rate of fire of some 60 rounds/minute. Within weeks of its formal approval the guided missile entered service and made it obsolete.

finally agreed in 1970. What was wanted was a 155mm howitzer capable of firing to a range of 24km and fitted with 'auxiliary propulsion'. By 1975 six guns had been built and a three-nation trials battery tested it in Germany, leading to some changes in design. Production began in 1978 and the FH70 howitzer is now in service with the three participating countries and has also been sold outside NATO.

'Auxiliary propulsion' means fitting the gun carriage with a motor unit which will drive the main wheels; the trail legs are supported on two smaller wheels which are steerable, so that the gun, in the absence of its normal towing vehicle, can be driven fairly rapidly across country. This requirement stemmed from improvements in target detection methods and from the need for dispersion. As pointed out previously, there is no place today for massed ranks of guns or for weapons which cannot be moved quickly. After an artillery piece has fired there is a high probability that within minutes it will find itself under retaliatory fine, and so the ability to displace rapidly is essential. If the gun has to be emplaced and concealed the job is made far more difficult if a large and powerful towing vehicle also has to be concealed, so it is normal for the towing vehicle to leave the gun position and conceal itself some miles behind, being called forward when required. But this delay, while the tractor comes forward, could be fatal, and thus the auxiliary propulsion system allows the gun to make an immediate move once it has completed firing.

The other technical requirement arising from this situation is for the gun to be able to fire a 'burst' of shots very rapidly, so as to put effective fire down on the enemy in the shortest possible time. Operational research during the latter part of World War 2 showed that the effect of artillery fire is greatest when a given number of shells fall in a short space of time; they have a greater psychological effect on the victims than the same number spread over a longer period, even though the actual damage done may be the same. So the FH70 howitzer is fitted with mechanical ammunition handling devices which allow it to fire a burst of six shots in less than one minute.

As might be imagined, the success of FH70 led to a demand for the same weapon to be installed in a self-propelled carriage to replace the American M109 weapons in NATO service. This collaboration, however, appears to have run into difficulties. Development began in 1973, under the title SP70; two prototypes were built by 1979 and tested, leading to considerable redesign. Trials of further prototypes are continuing, with the hope of getting the weapon into service by 1986 but, frankly, few soldiers have any faith in this and the weapon is now being openly called SP90 by most NATO artillerymen.

One other aspect of the escalating expense of defence materiel is the pressure it puts on designers to develop equipment which will not only satisfy their own army (or navy or air force) but which will be equally attractive to foreign buyers. The enormous expenditure necessary to get a weapon into production has to be amortised over the production run of the weapon; thus if the army requires 1,000 tanks, then the cost of research, development, design, tooling and setting up for manufacture must all be spread across the 1,000, in addition to the basic price of the materials and workforce which actually go into their construction. If this capital figure can be spread more thinly by building 2,000, the second thousand being for sale overseas, then the unit price per tank comes down considerably, making it cheaper for army and, *inter alia*, cheaper for the overseas customer. This is, of course, another aspect in the co-production idea, since building enough equipments for three countries again helps to bring the unit price down to an affordable level.

However, there are some areas in which armies will refuse to compromise in order to make a weapon more attractive to the export market; so far as the British army is concerned, tanks fall into this area. Its experience during 1935-45, when rival design agencies argued and pulled this way and that, modifying designs to suit their own ideas and virtually designing by committee, was so traumatic that once a specification has been decided upon the British Army will bitterly resist any attempt to modify it to suit the needs, real or imagined, of a third party. Once the design has been built and adopted, however, then flexibility is permitted to come into the arena, and if a foreign country wishes to make changes (at its own expense) then it is permitted to do so. Occasionally this post-design modification works for the army's benefit, particularly where the purchaser is sufficiently rich to demand something the British Army would otherwise not be able to afford. In such cases the buyer amortises the development and the army, on its second purchasing trip, benefits.

The Centurion tank had seen several stages of improvement since its introduction. It was originally fitted with the 17pdr gun but which was soon discarded for a better weapon, a 20pdr with which the tank saw service in Korea. In 1959 a high-velocity 105mm gun was fitted, and this later became the standard tank gun throughout NATO. In the 1950s too there was development and limited production of a heavy tank, the Conqueror, armed with a 120mm gun, but this was an unsatisfactory design, and in the late 1950s a design was drawn up for a tank to replace both the Centurion and the Conqueror, a tank nimble enough to be a medium but with the firepower of a heavy. The result was Chieftain.

Chieftain appeared in 1961 in prototype form, and the first production models reached regiments in 1964. It was an excellent design and the main armament was a 120mm gun firing a powerful squash-head shell and an equally devastating piercing shot, using a bagged charge as the propellant. This was a novelty in itself, since tank

Below left:
The Challenger main battle tank, introduced into service in 1983, is an uprated Chieftain with laminated armour and a 120mm high-velocity gun using electronic fire control methods.

Bottom left:
Royal Irish Rangers leave their FV432 armoured personnel carrier during a reconnaissance patrol.

Below right:
Cymbeline, a radar which can spot mortar bombs in flight and, by deducing their trajectory, calculate the position of the mortar which fired them. This data can then be transmitted to an artillery battery for retaliatory fire.

ammunition was invariably a fixed, brass-cased round which could be loaded in one movement. But the Chieftain round was in two units — shot and cartridge — and the idea took some getting used to. Some 900 were built for the British Army and then about 700 were bought by Iran (in the days of the Shah). At this point we begin to see the application of the 'foreign customer improvement factor'. After the 700 Chieftains had been delivered to Iran, the Shah, who was well able to afford it, asked for an improved version, to be known as Shir 1, with a new Rolls-Royce engine, a new transmission (giving it better mobility) and improved electronic fire control equipment. 125 of these were ordered in 1974, and at just about the same time a new form of protection was announced, called Chobham Armour.

Chobham Armour (named after the location of the Fighting Vehicles Establishment which had developed it) is still secret, but it is known to be a 'sandwich' of various materials — ceramics, tungsten and other exotic materials have all been mentioned — built into an armour plate so as to afford specific resistances to different types of attack. It was expensive; there was no way in which the British Army could have it retrospectively fitted to its existing tanks, and there was no money available to allow new tanks, incorporating Chobham Armour, to be built for several years. But it was within the purse of the Shah of Iran, who promptly ordered 1,225 Shir 2 tanks, even more advanced models incorporating Chobham Armour, to be built.

However, as is well known, events overtook the Shah; he was deposed in 1979, Iran passed into other hands, and as a natural result the Shir 1 and Shir 2 orders collapsed before any deliveries could be made.

The British Army now had a problem on its hands; at that time plans were slowly going forward on the design of a next-generation MBT, loosely called MBT-80 and roughly scheduled to reach service some time towards the end of the 1980s. But if no tank production took place until the mid 1980s, the work force at the Royal Ordnance Factory at Leeds, which built the army's tanks, would be either standing idle or, out of boredom, would have all left to find other work with the result that when the new tank was ready to go into production there would be no skilled engineers available to build it.

Alternatively, it could forget MBT-80 and cash in on the development work which had been done (and mostly paid for) on behalf of the Shah of Iran. By making some small modifications to Shir 2, to bring it into line with British Army practice, it could become the next British MBT, would keep the Leeds workforce occupied until the next generation appeared, and, into the bargain, would

Below left:
The 155mm M109 self-propelled howitzer, an American design which has been adopted throughout the NATO armies for the sake of standardisation.

Below:
A Swingfire anti-tank wire-guided missile is launched from an Alvis Striker launch vehicle. Previously operated by Royal Artillery batteries, these equipments are now in the hands of the Royal Armoured Corps.

Bottom left:
Ferret armoured cars used by the British element of the UN peacekeeping force in Cyprus.

Bottom:
A Fox armoured car with a 30mm Rarden semi-automatic cannon.

Top left:
The Centurion AVRE (Armoured Vehicle, Royal Engineers) mounts a bulldozer blade and a 165mm 'demolition gun'.

Top:
The Centurion Mk 7 battle tank. Developed in 1945, the Centurion was the first 'universal tank' putting an end to the artificial distinction of 'infantry' and 'cruiser' types.

Above left:
The MCV-80 (Mechanised Combat Vehicle of the 1980s) is the latest infantry vehicle, due in service in 1986. It can carry a fully equipped infantry squad and is armed with a 30mm Rarden cannon and a 7.62mm machine gun.

Above right:
A highly specialised vehicle is this Centurion BARV (Beach Armoured Recovery Vehicle). Amphibious, it is based on a Centurion chassis and can rescue tanks and small craft which have come to grief during a landing operation.

provide a good modern tank at considerably less than the army would have to pay for developing it themselves.

This was the course taken; the MBT-80 programme was abandoned, though much of the basic work has actually been carried over to a new programme tentatively called MBT-95, and the Shir 2, slightly modified and re-christened Challenger, was put into production. It went into service with armoured regiments in Germany in 1984 and its initial 'outing', during the major NATO exercises in that year, indicate that it is a powerful and efficient vehicle.

Parallel with the development of Challenger, and to complement it in the armoured divisions in Germany, is a new vehicle for the infantry. The argument of 'battle taxi' versus 'fighting vehicle' has been resolved in the British Army by the usual British compromise; troops in armoured divisions will receive a tracked fighting vehicle, known as MCV-80 (Mechanised Combat Vehicle 80) while those in 'marching' divisions will be equipped with Saxon, a wheeled APC. MCV-80 is a turretted vehicle mounting a 30mm semi-automatic cannon and capable of carrying eight infantrymen and their equipment. The first four pilot models were seen in operation during the 1984 exercises and the troops operating them (the Irish Guards) appeared to be impressed with their capabilities.

One more new weapon awaits in the wings, an infantry rifle. The 7.62mm SLR rifle adopted in the 1950s, after the fiasco over the 7mm cartridge, is reaching the end of its economic life, the point where it costs more to repair weapons that it would to purchase a new design. Moreover, in the middle 1960s the American Army had adopted a totally new calibre, 5.56mm, for their service rifle — this without consulting NATO — giving them a cartridge which in every respect was less potent than the 7mm they had refused 10 years earlier. And so in the late 1970s the European NATO armies, all faced with the question of replacing their ageing infantry rifles, began a long series of trials to settle, once and for all, what the next NATO small arms cartridge would be. Provided all could agree on the cartridge, the choice of rifle was left to the individual countries, and the RSAF Enfield developed a new rifle, known as SA80 (Small Arm of the 80s), and a new cartridge in 4.85mm calibre.

There were good ballistic reasons for selecting this

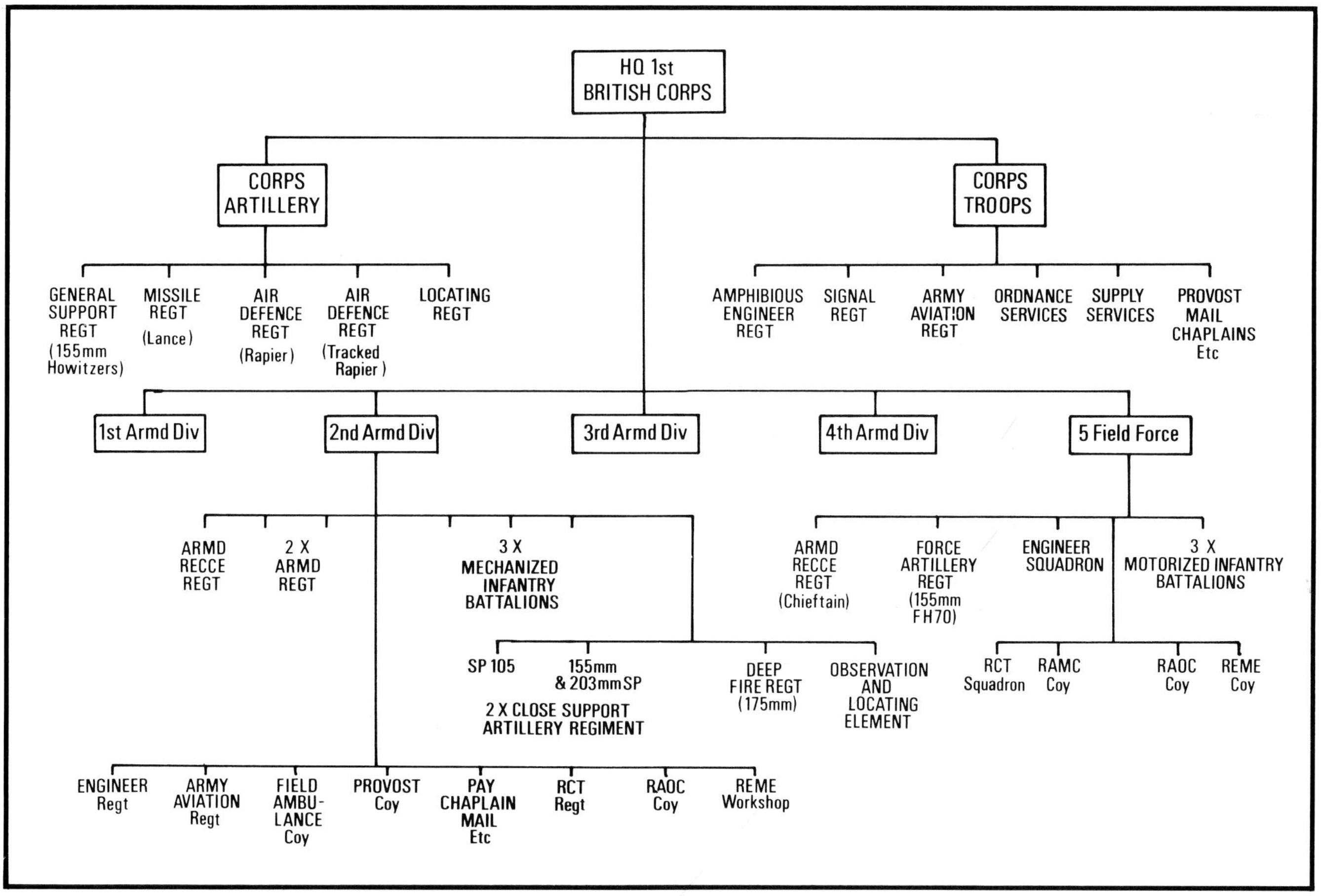

- HQ 1st BRITISH CORPS
  - CORPS ARTILLERY
    - GENERAL SUPPORT REGT (155mm Howitzers)
    - MISSILE REGT (Lance)
    - AIR DEFENCE REGT (Rapier)
    - AIR DEFENCE REGT (Tracked Rapier)
    - LOCATING REGT
  - CORPS TROOPS
    - AMPHIBIOUS ENGINEER REGT
    - SIGNAL REGT
    - ARMY AVIATION REGT
    - ORDNANCE SERVICES
    - SUPPLY SERVICES
    - PROVOST MAIL CHAPLAINS Etc
  - 1st Armd Div
  - 2nd Armd Div
    - ARMD RECCE REGT
    - 2 X ARMD REGT
    - 3 X MECHANIZED INFANTRY BATTALIONS
    - 2 X CLOSE SUPPORT ARTILLERY REGIMENT
      - SP 105
      - 155mm & 203mm SP
    - ENGINEER Regt
    - ARMY AVIATION Regt
    - FIELD AMBU-LANCE Coy
    - PROVOST Coy
    - PAY CHAPLAIN MAIL Etc
    - RCT Regt
    - RAOC Coy
    - REME Workshop
  - 3rd Armd Div
  - 4th Armd Div
  - 5 Field Force
    - ARMD RECCE REGT (Chieftain)
    - FORCE ARTILLERY REGT (155mm FH70)
      - DEEP FIRE REGT (175mm)
      - OBSERVATION AND LOCATING ELEMENT
    - ENGINEER SQUADRON
      - RCT Squadron
      - RAMC Coy
    - 3 X MOTORIZED INFANTRY BATTALIONS
      - RAOC Coy
      - REME Coy

Above:
Organisation of 1 Brit Corps in Germany in 1985.

Left:
The latest addition to the air defence armoury is Tracked Rapier, a combination of an American tracked chassis and the British Rapier guided missile launcher. It is seen here during its first deployment in Germany in 1984.

calibre, but there were also good political and common-sense reasons for suspecting that, after all the testing died away, the 5.56mm cartridge would be adopted; for one thing several NATO countries had invested large sums of money in 5.56mm cartridge-manufacturing machinery, since many of them had adopted the calibre as an auxiliary to their standard. So the Enfield designers, remembering their lesson of the EM2 rifle, made sure that SA80 would be capable of being redesigned, with minimum changes, to suit the 5.56mm cartridge.

And, sure enough, the 5.56mm cartridge became the new NATO standard in 1981, though with a new Belgian bullet which was more effective than the original American pattern. SA80 was duly rejigged to suit, and it is entering production in 1985, with issues to the army beginning in 1986. The rifle is a totally new departure, being what the experts call a 'bullpup', a word of dubious origin which signifies that the breech and magazine are inside the butt, close to the firer's cheek, so giving the greatest possible length of barrel within a short overall length of the rifle. Made of stamped and pressed metal and with a low-power optical sight as standard, it is a far cry from the carefully-machined and 'gunsmithed' rifles of yesteryear, but it is just as effective.

The proof of the pudding is in the eating; the proof of an army's equipment and training is in war. The British Army has rarely been completely at peace since 1945, with intermittent minor wars and uprisings to be dealt with and, of course, with the running sore of internal security duties in Northern Ireland. But nothing in the past 20 years had demanded the fielding of any of the more sophisticated equipment, which therefore remained a largely unknown quantity. The brief Falklands Campaign of 1982 remedied this, however, and permitted the army to bring much of its latest equipment into use. The Light

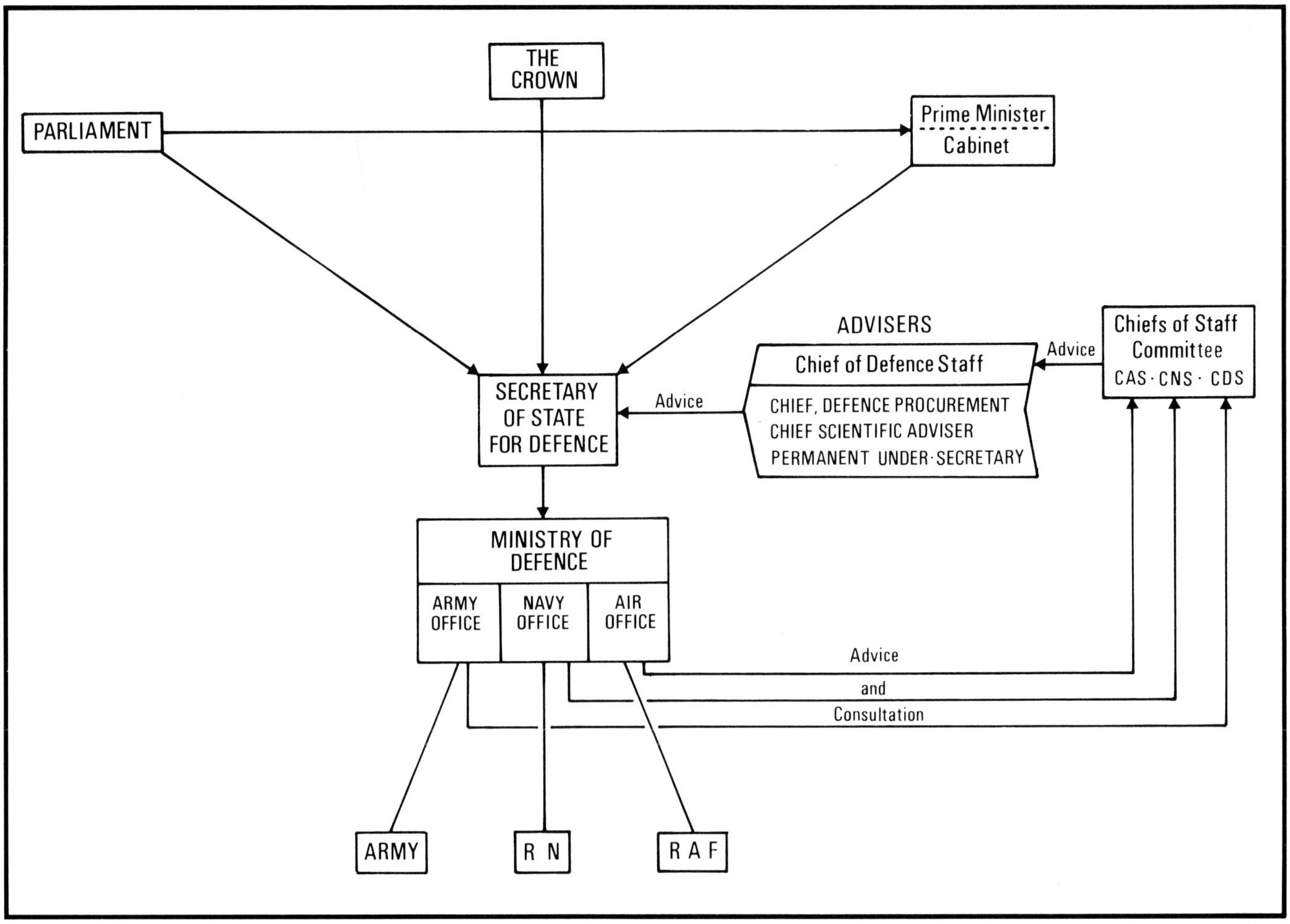

THE CROWN
PARLIAMENT
Prime Minister
Cabinet
ADVISERS
Chief of Defence Staff
CHIEF, DEFENCE PROCUREMENT
CHIEF SCIENTIFIC ADVISER
PERMANENT UNDER-SECRETARY
Advice
Chiefs of Staff Committee
CAS · CNS · CDS
Advice
SECRETARY OF STATE FOR DEFENCE
MINISTRY OF DEFENCE
ARMY OFFICE
NAVY OFFICE
AIR OFFICE
Advice and Consultation
ARMY
R N
R A F

Above:
UK defence organisation in the 1980s.

Right:
The Saxon wheeled armoured personnel carrier is intended to equip infantry units in non-armoured divisions, and particularly those units in Britain which are earmarked to reinforce NATO in Germany.

Below right:
A Chieftain tank of the Blues and Royals moving across a training ground in Germany.

Gun, the Rapier air defence missile, the Blowpipe shoulder-fired air defence missile, the Scorpion and Scimitar light tanks, night vision equipment, high-frequent radio equipment, laser rangefinders, position-finding equipment, artillery fire control computers, all these items and many more were put to operational test in an extremely harsh environment, one which was much more testing than Northwest Europe. Most came through with flying colours, to prove that the design and development system and the training of the modern soldier to operate complex equipment have no serious flaws. It would be foolish to say that the system is perfect; mistakes and mis-estimates are still made, but, bearing in mind that the military designers are now working at the front edge of technology, it is gratifying to find that the mistakes are relatively few.

Speaking generally, the final lesson we can extract from this brief overview of the past century and a half of military development is that whenever the army has known what it wanted and been specific about demanding it, then it has usually received a successful weapon. Where it has not been clear as to what it wanted — as, for the prime example, in the case of tank design in the 1935-40 period — then the result has been equally uncertain. This is less likely to occur today since today's soldier is a far more professional man than his father or his grandfather. Although there is still hunting and shooting, balls and soirees, officers and other ranks, the officer who hunted three days a week has long since departed, as has the 'professional private' who served his 21 years without seeking or meriting advancement. There is no room for passengers in the British Army of the 1980s, and scant respect for the man who is anything less than a dedicated professional. The army, like the men in it, is lean and fit and without superfluous fat, the result if you like, of a programme of selective breeding which began in the 1850s.

Above left:
The Combat Engineer Tractor emerges from a pond with a load of stores in its shovel. This unique machine can dig, bulldoze, and perform many other engineer and pioneer tasks with armoured protection.

Left:
An early experiment in the evolution of an infantry fighting vehicle was this FV432 fitted with an armoured car turret and 30mm Rarden gun in 1975. An example is seen here manned by the Royal Irish Rangers during an exercise.

Table 6: Arms of the NATO Era

Small Arms	Title	Calibre	Length (in)	Weight (lb/oz)	Magazine Capacity	Bullet Weight (gr)	Muzzle Velocity (ft/sec)	Muzzle Energy (ft/lb)	Effective Range (yd)	Remarks
1949	Rifle, Automatic, No 9	.280	39.0in	8/9	20	140	2,528	1,998	900	Adopted, but not introduced
1953	Rifle, Self-loading, L1A1	7.62mm	45.0in	9/7	20	144	2,750	2,682	600	First automatic rifle used
1960	Rifle, L42A1	7.62mm	46.5in	9/12	10	144	2,750	2,682	800	Bolt action sniping rifle
1985	Individual Weapon L85	5.56mm	30.3in	8/8	30	61	3,024	1,242	400	New NATO standard
1960	GPMG L7A3	7.62mm	48.5in	24.0	belt	144	2,750	2,682	600	900rd/min
1985	Light Support Wpn L86	5.56mm	35.4in	10.0	30 box	61	2,950	1,184	400	800rd/min
1957	Sterling SMG L2	9mm	27.0in	5.9	34 box	115	1,250	400	50	550rd/min

Note that 'Individual Weapon' is the new euphemism for 'rifle' and 'Light Support Weapon' replaces 'Light Machine Gun'

Title **Artillery**	Class	Calibre (in)	Barrel Length (calibres)	Shell Weight (lb)	Charge Weight (lb)	Muzzle Velocity (ft/sec)	Mounting	Weight in Action (tons)	Maximum Range (yd)	Remarks
105mm Pack How	CS	4.13	14	32.8	3.66 C	1,378	2-wh split	1.25	11,560	Ex-Italy
105mm Light Gun	CS	4.13	30	35.3		2,323	2-wheel	1.79	18,585	
105mm Abbot	CS	4.13	30	35.3		2,312	SP	17.18	18,915	
155mm How M109A2	GS	6.1		94.55	13.8C	2,246	SP	24.54	19,790	Ex-USA; nuclear shell
155mm How FH70	GS	6.1	39	95.87		2,885	SP: Aux prop	7.67	26,240	
175mm Gun M107	GS	6.89	60	147	55.1 C	3,025	SP	27.71	35,750	Ex-USA
203mm How M110A1	GS	8.0	25	200	29.75 C	1,950	SP	25.93	18,370	Ex-USA; nuclear shell
Missiles										
Lance	Tac	557mm	—	Nuc/HE	Solid	Mach 3	Rail launch	1.5	75 miles	Inertial guidance
Rapier	AA	127mm	—	HE	Solid	Mach 2+	Rail launch	94lb	7,650	Radar guidance
Blowpipe	AA	76mm	—	HE	Solid	Mach 1.5	Shoulder	24lb	3,280	Infra-red homing
Milan	A/Tk	115mm	—	HEAT	Solid	660	Tripod	15lb	2,185	Wire guidance
Swingfire	A/Tk	170mm	—	HEAT	Solid	600	Box launch	62lb	4,375	Wire guidance

Chronology 1854-1985

Year	Campaigns	Battles	New Equipment	Army Strength	Notable Events
1854	Crimea	Inkerman		140,000	Aldershot camp established. DCM introduced
1855	Crimea	Sebastopol			
1856	Crimea		Enfield .577 Short Rifle		Victoria Cross instituted
1857	Indian Mutiny	Lucknow			Army Hospital Service founded
1858	Indian Mutiny			230,000	
1859	3rd China War		12pdr Armstrong gun	204,000	Duke of Cambridge appointed C-in-C. La Gloire launched
1860	Maori War	Sack of Peking			Quebec garrison withdrawn. Royal Commission on Defence of UK
1861	Maori War		6pdr RBL; 7in RBL guns. Westley Richards cavalry carbine	227,168. Horse strength, 13,604	Educational qualification for promotion instituted
1862			9pdr and 40pdr RBL guns	215,872	
1863	1st Ashanti War			222,781	First Soldier's Institute in Aldershot
1864	2nd Maori War		64pdr RML Coast gun	216,791	
1865	2nd Maori War		7in and 9in RML Coast guns	213,968	Strength: 10,807 officers; 13,431 Sergeants and Farriers; 4,592 trumpeters and drummers; 185,147 rank and file.
1866	Fenian Raids			205,356	
1867	Abyssinia		Snider-Enfield rifle	200,281	Army Reserve Act
1868	Abyssinia	Magdala	10in RML Coast gun	200,015	
1869	3rd Maori War			195,606	Reduction of Colonial Garrisons begins
1870	Red River			184,314	Australia, New Zealand, Canada except Halifax and Esquimault, all turned over to local forces. Cardwell reforms begin. Short Service Enlistment Act. Colonial Garrisons reduced from 50,000 to 26,000.
1871			Gatling Gun; Martini-Henry rifle; 9pdr RML field, 11in, 12in RML Coast guns	187,746	Abolition of Purchase. First large-scale peacetime exercises held in Britain.
1872			16pdr RML Heavy Field gun	192,672	141 Infantry Battalions. Military Localisation Act passed.
1873	2nd Ashanti War		25pdr RML Siege gun	191,415	Horses, 14,924
1874	2nd Ashanti War		40pdr RML Coast gun	185,635	Soldiers' Institute, Portsmouth
1875	Naga Hills Expedition		12.5in RML Coast gun	186,432	
1876				183,949	
1877	Kaffir War			190,015	William Robertson enlists
1878	2nd Afghan War		6.3in RML howitzer	190,243	First military balloons at Woolwich
1879	Zulu War	Isandlwhana, Rorke's Drift		191,933	Last flogging on active service. 11 VCs won at Rorke's Drift, the greatest number ever awarded for a single engagement.
1880	Mohmand Expedition	Kabul-Kandahar	Enfield .476 revolver	191,804	Horses, 15,388
1881	Transvaal War	Laing's Nek; Majuba		188,958	Numbered regiments replaced by County titles. Warrant rank created. Northamptonshire Regiment carried colours in battle for the last time at Laing's Nek.
1882	Egypt	Tel-el-Kebir	13pdr RML Field Gun; 6in BL Coast gun	189,133	Garrison in Egypt first formed. Robertson promoted sergeant.
1883	Sudan	Kashgil	100ton RML Coast gun	193,397	
1884	Sudan	Gordon Relief	Gardner & Nordenfelt machine guns. 12in BL Coast gun	181,227	Dervishes broke British square to Tamai
1885	Sudan	Abu Klea		188,657	Khaki dress adopted in India. Robertson becomes Sergeant-Major.

Year	Campaigns	Battles	New Equipment	Army Strength	Notable Events
1886	3rd Burma War		Very's signal pistol	200,785	DSO instituted
1887	3rd Burma War		Webley revolver	208,357	
1888	Hazara Expedition		Lee-Metford rifle	211,021	Robertson promoted to Second Lieutenant.
1889	Sierra Leone		Maxim machine gun	211,030	
1890	Mashonaland		9.2in Coast gun; Pom-Pom. Cordite propellant	210,218	Barracks Act; £3 million for home and overseas
1891	Hunza; Naga			210,499	
1892	Gambia: Chin Hills		13.5in BL Coast	211,590	
1893	1st Matabele War		12pdr BL Field gun	217,789	Army Pay Corps established
1894	3rd Ashanti War		12pdr QF Coast gun	219,400	Horses: 14,685
1895	Waziristan	Siege of Chitral	Long Lee-Enfield rifle	222,151	.303 calibre introduced for small arms
1896	2nd Matabele; 4th Ashanti	Jameson Raid	15pdr BL Field gun; 6in 30cwt howitzer	222,194	Khaki adopted for all foreign service. Robertson goes to Staff College.
1897	Sudan	Dargai		220,869	Purchase of land on Salisbury Plain begins
1898	Tirah	Omdurman		221,003	RAMC formed
1899	Boer War	Modder River; Colenso; Magersfontein		231,851	Royal Artillery split into Field, Horse and Garrison branches
1900	Boxer Rebellion	Spion Kop; Ladysmith Mafeking		421,173	Irish Guards formed
1901	5th Ashanti		10pdr BL jointed gun; 15pdr QF Erhardt gun	397,682	Military Prison Staff Corps established
1902	Boer War			324,653	Khaki service dress adopted for general wear.
1903				292,411	Horses, 46,204
1904	Lhasa Expedition		60pdr BL Gun; 13pdr and 18pdr QF Field guns	287,240	Army Council created; Committee of Imperial Defence created.
1905			7.5in BL and 9.2in High Angle coast guns	272,133	Halifax Nova Scotia garrison withdrawn
1906				263,117	156 infantry battalions; Esquimault garrison withdrawn
1907			Short Lee-Enfield rifle	248,487	Haldane reforms; 6 infantry divisions and 2 cavalry divisions formed
1908	Mohmand Expedition			251,324	Territorial Army replaces Volunteers. Robertson becomes Chief of Staff, Aldershot.
1909			4.5in QF howitzer	253,405	Horses: 29,781
1910				252,686	Robertson Major-General, Commandant of Staff College
1911				254,309	Air Battalion R.E. established
1912			Vickers machine gun	253,762	Royal Flying Corps founded
1913				253,540	Strength: 31 regiments Cavalry, 157 infantry battalions; 169 field artillery batteries, 98 Garrison Artillery companies. Army estimates: £28,220,000, of which £8,683,000 pay and allowances. Robertson knighted and becomes Director of Military Training
1914	World War 1	Mons, Le Cateau	Lewis Gun; Rolls-Royce armoured car; 13pdr AA gun; Trench mortars	1,327,372	Robertson Quartermaster-General in France

Below:
A defensive position, 1896. 1st Battalion, Prince of Wales' Own Yorkshire Light Infantry in training at the Curragh, Ireland.

Above:
Scimitar CVR(T) — Combat Vehicle, Reconnaissance (Tracked) — armed with a 30mm Rarden gun, during Exercise 'Bold Guard'.

Year	*Campaigns*	*Battles*	*New Equipment*	*Army Strength*	*Notable Events*
1915	World War 1	Neuve Chapelle; Loos; Gallipoli; 2nd Ypres	Poison Gas; railway guns; Stokes mortar	2,475,764	WOI and WOII grades introduced. Welsh Guards formed. Robertson Lt-General and CIGS.
1916	World War 1	Somme	Enfield P'14 rifle; Tanks	3,343,797	Machine Gun Corps formed; conscription introduced. Steel helmet adopted
1917	World War 1	3rd Ypres; Messines; Cambrai		3,833,017	Tank corps formed; Women's Auxiliary Army Corps formed.
1918	World War 1	2nd Somme	Whippet tank	3,838,265	Robertson resigns CIGS, commands Eastern Cmd.
1919	Russia			1,064,743	'Ten Year Rule' adopted
1920			18in railway howitzer	434,725	Women's Corps disbanded. Robertson becomes Field Marshal, retires.
1921				217,477	Machine Gun Corps disbanded. Southern Irish regiments disbanded.
1922				296,948	Dental Corps created
1923				205,095	Royal Tank Corps formed
1924				207,152	Royal Artillery reformed into one regiment.
1925				209,391	
1926			Vickers Medium tank	205,758	Corps of Military Police founded
1927			Birch SP gun	205,196	Experimental Mechanised Force formed
1928				197,818	
1929	North-West Frontier			194,026	
1930				188,460	
1931				192,939	Tank brigade manoeuvred by radio command.
1932			.38 Enfield revolver	192,677	
1933				195,256	Hitler assumed power in Germany. 'Ten Year Rule' abrogated.
1934				195,845	
1935				196,137	First Panzer Divisions formed
1936			3in Mortar; Vickers light tank	192,325	Hitler marches into Rhineland
1937	Waziristan		Bren gun; Boys A/tk rifle		Rearmament begins
1938			Matilda 1; Crusader 4 tanks		Battledress adopted
1939	World War 2		No 4 rifle; Matilda 2 tank		Conscription introduced before war. Army now completely mechanised.
1940	World War 2	Dunkirk; Keren Sidi Barrani	Sten gun; Valentine tank	2,075,000	Paratroops and Commandos formed

Year	Campaigns	Battles	New Equipment	Army Strength	Notable Events
1941	World War 2	Crusader; Hong Kong	Churchill, Grant, Stuart tanks.	2,340,000	26 infantry divisions, 10 armoured divisions
1942	World War 2	Alamein; Singapore; Gazala; Tobruk	Cromwell tank	2,566,000	REME created; Air OPs introduced. Parachute Regiment and Glider Pilot Regiment formed.
1943	World War 2	Sicily; Italy	PIAT	2,680,000	Special Air Service and Air-Landing regiments formed
1944	World War 2	Gothic Line; Cassino Imphal; Kohima; D-Day; Falaise; Arnhem	No 5 rifle; APCs; Sherman and Comet tanks	2,760,000	
1945	World War 2	Rhine; Reichswald; Meiktila-Mandalay	Centurion tank; recoilless guns	2,920,000	14 Armoured divisions, 64 regiments of infantry
1946	Greece				
1947	Greece				Indian garrisons withdrawn
1948	Brit Honduras				Palestine garrisons withdrawn. Brigade of Gurkhas incorporated into British Army.
1949	Eritrea				NATO formed
1950	Malaya				
1951	Korean War	Solma-Ri			First issues of combat dress in Korea.
1952	Korean War	The Hook			
1953	Kenya		Self-loading rifle		7.62mm NATO calibre for small arms
1954	Kenya				Egyptian garrisons withdrawn
1955	Kenya				
1956	Suez		Conqueror tank		Coast artillery disbanded. Brigade Group organisation adopted.
1957	Bahrein		Sterling submachine gun		Glider Pilot Regt disbanded
1958	Jordan				Amalgamation of infantry regiments begins
1959			Saladin armoured car		Cyprus garrison withdrawn
1960			General purpose machine gun		Conscription ended; battle-dress abolished
1961	Kuwait				
1962	Belize			185,000	Ministry of Defence formed. War Office abolished.
1963	Borneo				
1964	Borneo				
1965	Radfan			229,000	Strength includes 4,911 WRAC, 1,619 QARANC
1966	Radfan				Volunteers re-created
1967	Oman		Chieftain tank	237,000	Aden garrison withdrawn. Royal Corps of Transport formed
1968	Oman			224,500	All Imperial roles abandoned. Yorks & Lancs and Cameronian Regiments disband rather than amalgamate. Divisional organisation re-adopted.
1969	Anguilla			210,000	Northern Ireland emergency begins. Army Strategic Command formed
1970	Oman				Camouflage pattern combat suits adopted. 2 Cavalry regiments, 5 Guards regiments, 14 Armoured regiments, 33 infantry regiments, Brigade of Gurkhas.
1971	Anguilla				
1972	Dhofar			177,700	Strength includes 5,600 women
1973	Dhofar		Scorpion tank, Fox armoured car		
1974	Oman				
1975	Oman			166,500	
1976	Oman			167,500	
1977	Belize			164,600	
1978	Belize			168,600	
1979	Belize			165,700	
1980	Belize				
1981	Belize			167,250	With 6,250 women, 7,100 Gurkhas and 1,100 locally enlisted
1982	Falklands	Goose Green; Stanley			
1983	Belize				
1984			Challenger tank		
1985			5.56mm rifle and machine gun		

Specifications

Small Arms

Year	Title	Calibre	Length (in)	Weight (lb/oz)	Magazine Capacity	Bullet Weight (gr)	Muzzle Velocity (ft/sec)	Muzzle Energy (ft/lb)	Effective Range (yd)	Remarks
Rifles										
1852	Enfield Musket P'52	.577	55	8/14	—	530	1,200	1,690	200	
1867	Snider-Enfield	.577	55	8/14	—	480	1,240	1,645	300	First breech-loader
1871	Martini-Henry	.45	49.5	8/10	—	480	1,350	1,948	400	
1888	Lee-Metford Mk I	.303	49.5	9/8	8	215	2,200	2,308	600	First magazine rifle
1895	Lee-Enfield Mk I	.303	49.5	9/4	10	215	2,200	2,308	600	Cordite adopted
1907	Lee-Enfield Mk III	.303	44.5	8/10	10	215	2,060	2,028	600	Short Lee-Enfield
1916	Enfield Pattern '14	.303	46.3	8/11	5	174	2,785	3,005	600	Made in USA on contract
1939	Enfield No 4 Mk I	.303	44.5	9/1	10	174	2,400	2,228	600	
1944	Enfield No 5 Mk I	.303	39.5	7/2	10	174	2,000	1,551	400	'Jungle Carbine'
1949	Rifle, Automatic, No 9	.280	39.0	8/9	20	140	2,528	1,998	900	Adopted, but not introduced
1953	Rifle, Self-loading, L1A1	7.62mm	45.0	9/7	20	144	2,750	2,682	600	First automatic rifle used
1960	Rifle, L42A1	7.62mm	46.5	9/12	10	144	2,750	2,682	800	Bolt action sniping rifle
1985	Individual Weapon L85	5.56mm	30.3	8/8	30	61	3,024	1,242	400	New NATO standard
Machine Guns										
1871	Gatling 10-barrel	.45	59.4	360	240 drum	480	1,350	1,954	1,000	800rd/min On wheeled mounting
1884	Gardner 2-barrel	.45	53.5	290	100	480	1,350	1,954	1,000	650rd/min First 'Machine Gun'
1884	Nordenfeldt 5-barrel	.45	46.0	154	Hopper	480	1,350	1,954	1,000	400rd/min
1889	Maxim Automatic	.45	43.5	60	250 belt	480	1,350	1,954	1,000	600rd/min First automatic gun
1912	Vickers Mark 1	.303	45.5	39.9	250 belt	215	2,444	2,855	2,000	450rd/min
1914	Lewis Mk I	.303	50.5	26.0	47 drum	215	2,444	2,855	600	550rd/min
1916	Hotchkiss Mk I	.303	46.7	27.0	30 strip	215	2,424	2,808	600	500rd/min
1937	Bren Mk I	.303	45.3	22.4	30 box	174	2,400	2,400	600	500rd/min
1960	GPMG L7A3	7.62mm	48.5	24.0	belt	144	2,750	2,682	600	900rd/min
1985	Light Support Wpn L86	5.56mm	35.4	10.0	30 box	61	2,950	1,184	400	800rd/min
Pistols										
1880	Enfield Mk I	.476	11.5	2.5	6-cyl	272	670	272	15	First cartridge revolver
1887	Webley Mk I	.442	10.2	2.1	6-cyl	265	600	212	15	
1915	Webley Mk 6	.455	11.2	2.4	6-cyl	265	655	252	15	
1932	Enfield No 2	.38	10.2	1.7	6-cyl	178	650	166	15	
1944	Browning GP35	9mm	7.8	2.1	13 box	115	1,100	309	20	
Submachine Guns										
1940	Thompson M1928	.45	33.7	10.8	20 box	230	910	423	50	800rd/min
1941	Sten Mk 2	9mm	35.7	7.7	32 box	115	1,000	256	30	450rd/min
1957	Sterling L2	9mm	27.0	5.9	34 box	115	1,250	400	50	550rd/min
Anti-Tank Rifle										
1937	Boys Mk I	.55	63.5	35.9	5 box	735	3,250	17,261	300	Pierced 21mm of armour at 300yd

Below:
The Rifle, Short, Magazine, Lee-Enfield Mk 3. Introduced in 1903 the 'SMLE' served the armies of the Empire until the 1950s and is still used in some countries.

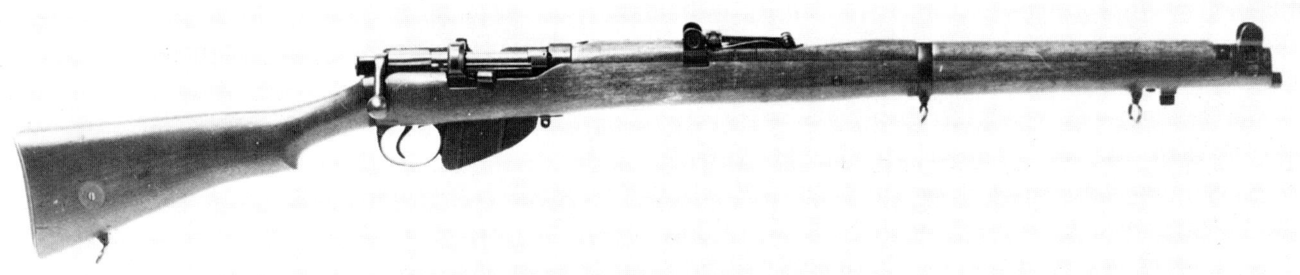

Above:
The prototype Crusader tank of 1940; production models were slightly different. 5,300 were built and it was the principal British tank in the Western Desert in 1941-42.

Armoured Vehicles

Date	Name	Weight (tons)	Crew	Power Output (hp)	Road Speed (mph)	Operating Range (miles)	Main Armament	Secondary Armament	Armour Thickness (mm)	Power/ Weight Ratio	Remarks
Tanks											
1916	Mark 1 Male	28	8	105	3.5	24	2×6pdr	4×MG	12	3.75	
1918	Mark 5 Male	29	8	150	4.5	35	2×6pdr	4×MG	12	5.17	
1918	Medium A Whippet	14	4	90	8	40	—	4×MG	14	6.42	
1918	Medium C Hornet	19.5	4	150	8	75	—	4×MG	14	7.69	
1919	Mark 8	37	12	300	6.5	—	2×6pdr	7×MG	16	8.11	
1926	Vickers Mark 2 Medium	13.5	5	90	16	120	1×3pdr	3×MG	12	6.66	
1936	Vickers Mark 6 Light	5.2	3	88	35	130	1×.5in MG	1×MG	14	16.9	
1938	Matilda 1	11	2	70	8	80	1×.5in MG	—	60	6.36	
1938	Cruiser Mk 4	14.75	4	340	30	90	1×2pdr	1×MG	38	23.05	
1938	Cruiser A9 Mk I	12.8	6	150	25	150	1×2pdr	3×MG	14	11.7	
1939	Matilda 2	26.5	4	190	15	160	1×2pdr	1×MG	78	7.16	
1939	Crusader 2	19	4/5	340	27	100	1×2pdr	2×MG	49	17.89	
1940	Valentine 3	16	4	130	15	90	1×2pdr	1×MG	65	8.12	
1941	Churchill 3	39	5	350	15	90	1×6pdr	2×MG	102	8.97	
1941	General Grant	27.7	6/7	340	24	120	1×75mm	1×37mm	51	12.28	Ex-USA M3 Medium
1941	General Stuart 1	12.23	4	250	36	70	1×37mm	4×MG	45	20.44	Ex-USA M3 Light
1942	General Stuart 6	14.73	4	220	36	100	1×37mm	3×MG	64	14.93	Ex-USA M5 Light
1942	Cromwell	27.5	5	600	40	173	1×6pr	2×MG	102	21.82	
1944	Comet	35.2	5	600	32	124	1×77mm	2×MG	102	17.04	
1944	Sherman 5C (Firefly)	32.18	4	370	25	100	1×17pdr	2×MG	51	12.28	Ex-USA M4A4 re-gunned
1945	Centurion 1	49	4	620	21	65	1×17pdr	1×20mm	152	12.65	
	Centurion 13	51	4	650	21	118	1×105mm	2×MG	152	12.74	
1956	Conqueror	65	4	810	21	95	1×120mm	2×MG	178	12.46	
1967	Chieftain	54	4	750	30	280	1×120mm	2×MG	classified	13.85	
1973	Scorpion	7.8	3	195	55	400	1×76mm	1×MG	classified	25.0	
1984	Challenger	59	4	1,200	35	classified	1×120mm	2×MG	classified	20.32	
Armoured Cars											
1914	Rolls-Royce	3.5	3	50	45	180	1×MG	—	9	14.3	
1928	Lanchester	5.8	4	88	45	200	1×.5in MG	2×MG	10	15.17	
1941	Daimler	7.5	3	95	50	205	1×2pdr	1×MG	16	12.66	
1941	Humber	6.74	3	90	45	250	1×15mm MG	1×MG	15	13.35	
1942	AEC	11	3	105	35	250	1×2pdr	2×MG	57	9.54	
1953	Ferret	3.42	2	129	58	186	1×MG	—	16	37.72	
1959	Saladin	11.4	3	160	45	250	1×76mm	2×MG	32	14.03	
1973	Fox	6.28	3	190	65	270	1×30mm	1×MG	classified	30.2	

Note: Where 'MG' is specified without indicating calibre, it means a rifle-calibre machine gun.

Artillery

Title	Class	Calibre (in)	Barrel Length (calibres)	Shell Weight (lb)	Charge Weight (lb)	Muzzle Velocity (ft/sec)	Mounting	Weight in Action (tons)	Maximum Range (yd)	Remarks
1855 Smoothbore Artillery in Service										
68pdr of 95cwt	Coast	8	15	68	22 P	1,579	Garrison	6.2	3,170	
10in Shell Gun	Siege	10	11.2	93	12 P	1,257	2-wheel	5.5	1,700	
8in Shell Gun	Siege	8	13.5	46	9.5 P	1,488	2-wheel	4.2	2,000	
32pdr of 58cwt	Siege	6.17	19.45	32	10.6 P	1,690	2-wheel	3.75	2,900	
24pdr of 52cwt	Siege	5.6	21.4	24	8 P	1,720	2-wheel	3.75	2,400	
18pdr of 42cwt	Field	5.09	22.4	18	8 P	1,690	2-wheel	2.8	2,300	
12pdr New Medium	Field	4.52	17.25	12	4 P	1,770	2-wheel	1.75	1,400	
6pdr Medium	Horse	3.57	23.5	6	1.5 P	1,485	2-wheel	1.15	1,400	
24pdr How	Siege	5.6	10	17.5	2.5 P	1,223	2-wheel	1.25	1,025	
1870 Rifled Breech Loaders (Armstrong)										
6pdr of 3cwt	Field	2.5	21.2	5.75	12oz P	1,046	2-wheel	0.75	3,235@11°	
9pdr of 6cwt	Horse	3.0	17.6	8.5	1.2 P	1,055	2-wheel	1.3	2,675@9°	
12pdr of 8cwt	Field	3.0	20.4	11.25	1.5 P	1,172	2-wheel	1.6	3,100@9°	
40pdr of 35cwt	Coast	4.75	22.4	41	5 P	1,180	Sliding	3.9	4,300@13°	
110pdr of 81cwt	Coast	7.0	14.2	90	11 P	1,165	Sliding	7.45	3,250@10°	
1880 Rifled Muzzle Loaders										
9pdr of 8cwt	Field	3.0	21	9	1.75 P	1,330	2-wheel	1.05	3,000@9°	
16pdr of 12cwt	Field	3.6	19	16	3.25 P	1,355	2-wheel	1.50	3,000@8°	
40pdr of 34cwt	Siege	4.75	22	38	7 P	1,380	2-wheel		3,655@9°	
7in of 7 tons	Coast	7.0	18	114	30 P	1,525	Casemate	12.4	4,600@10°	
9in of 12 tons	Coast	9.0	13.8	249	43 P	1,445	Casemate	27.3	4,500@10°	
12.5in of 38 tons	Coast	12.5	15.8	802	160 P	1,463	Casemate	52.35	3,850@7°	
16in of 80 tons	Coast	16.0	18	1,700	450 P	1,540	Turret	895	5,500@8°	Special to Dover
17.72in of 100 tons	Coast	17.72	20.5	2,000	450 P	1,548	Barbette			Special to Gibraltar & Malta
1914 Breech-Loaders and Quick-Firers										
12pdr BL	Horse	3.0	22	12.5	12oz C	1,585	2-wheel	0.75	6,000	
13pdr QF	Horse	3.0	23	12.5	1.25 C	1,675	2-wheel	0.95	5,900	
18pdr QF	Field	3.3	28	18.5	1.45 C	1,615	2-wheel	1.25	6,525	
4.5in QF How	Field	4.5	13.4	35	1.0 C	1,010	2-wheel	1.35	7,300	
60pdr BL Gun	Siege	5.0	32	60	9.75 C	2,080	2-wheel	4.4	12,300	
9.2in BL How I	Siege	9.2	13.2	290	10.9 C	1,187	Siege	13.35	10,060	
12pdr of 12cwt QF	Coast	3.0	40	12.5	2.0 C	2,258	Pedestal	4.1	8,000	
4.7in QF Mk 2	Coast	4.72	40	45	5.5 C	2,150	Pedestal	Various	11,800	
6in BL Mk 7	Coast	6.0	45	100	11.5 C	2,493	Barbette	16.1	12,000	
9.2in BL Mk I0	Coast	9.2	46.5	380	120 C	2,643	Barbette	157	29,200	
3in of 20cwt HA**	AA	3.0	45	16	2.5 C	2,500	Pedestal	5.9	23,500ft maximum ceiling	

Note that until the turn of the century, maximum range was of academic interest and was frequently never determined or recorded as such; the only significant maximum range was that at which shrapnel shell lost its lethality. The maximum ranges quoted for RBL and RML guns have been ascertained from trial reports which specified the angle of elevation at which this range was reached; absolute maximum would depend upon the mounting and the angle of elevation possible thereon. In the case of 'modern' BL guns of 1914 and onward, the maximum range is the maximum on the standard mounting.

Below:
The 4.7in quick-firing gun was a naval weapon pressed into army service in South Africa to fill the need for a long-ranging gun. It remained in use until after World War 1 but was unpopular as a field weapon, being too much gun for too little shell.

Above:
The 17pdr (3in) anti-tank gun, developed in 1942, became the undisputed master of any wartime tank. Its discarding sabot projectile could pierce over 10in of armour at 1,000yd range.

1942 Artillery's Zenith

25pdr Gun-Howitzer	Field	3.45	26.7	25	1.75 C	1,700	2-wheel	1.77	13,400	
3.7in Mountain How	Field	3.7	11.7	20	9oz C	973	2-wh split	0.82	6,000	
4.5in BL Gun	Medium	4.5	41	55	9 C	2,250	2-wh split	5.75	20,500	
5.5in BL Gun	Medium	5.5	30	100	9.2 C	1,675	2-wh split	6.09	16,200	
7.2in BL How Mk 4	Heavy	7.2	22.4	200	19.8 C	1,700	2-wheel	10.16	16,900	
9.2in BL How Mk I	S/Heavy	9.2	17.3	290	28 C	1,600	Siege	16.2	13,935	
12in BL How Mk 3	S/Heavy	12.0	17.3	750	48 C	1,468	Rail truck	76	14,350	
13.5in BL Gun	S/Heavy	13.5	45	1,250	293 C	2,550	Rail truck	240	40,000	
18in BL Howitzer	S/Heavy	18.0	35	2,500	282 C	1,880	Rail truck	250	22,300	
6in BL Mk 24	Coast	6.0	45	102	31 C	2,825	Pedestal		24,500	
9.2in BL Mk I0	Coast	9.2	46.7	380	53.5C	2,700	Barbette	125	36,700	
15in BL Mk 2	Coast	15.0	42.4	1,938	432 C	2,680	Barbette	373	42,000	Dover & Singapore only
40mm Bofors	AA	1.57	56.2	2.0	9oz C	2,700	4-wh pedestal	1.95	10,800 and 5,000ft ceiling	
3.7in QF Mk 3	AA	3.7	50	28	8.5 C	2,600	4-wh pedestal	9.2	20,600 and 32,000ft ceiling	
4.5in QF Mk 2	AA	4.5	45	54	14 C	2,400	4-wh pedestal	14.75	22,800 and 34,500ft ceiling	
6pdr of 7cwt	A/Tk	2.24	43	6.0	1.1 C	2,693	2-wh split	1.12	5,500 Pierced 74mm at 1,000yd	

1980 Artillery for Mobile War

105mm Pack How	CS	4.13	14	32.8	3.66 C	1,378	2-wh split	1.25	11,560	Ex-Italy
105mm Light Gun	CS	4.13	30	35.3		2,323	2-wheel	1.79	18,585	
105mm Abbot	CS	4.13	30	35.3		2,312	SP	17.18	18,915	
155mm How M109A2	GS	6.1		94.55	13.8 C	2,246	SP	24.54	19,790	Ex-USA; nuclear shell
155mm How FH70	GS	6.1	39	95.87		2,885	SP: Aux prop	7.67	26,240	
175mm Gun M107	GS	6.89	60	147	55.1 C	3,025	SP	27.71	35,750	Ex-USA
203mm How M110A1	GS	8.0	25	200	29.75 C	1,950	SP	25.93	18,370	Ex-USA; nuclear shell

1985 The Missile Armoury

Lance	Tac	557mm	—	Nuc/HE	Solid	Mach 3	Rail launch	1.5	75 miles	Inertial guidance
Rapier	AA	127mm	—	HE	Solid	Mach 2+	Rail launch	94lb	7,650	Radar guidance
Blowpipe	AA	76mm	—	HE	Solid	Mach 1.5	Shoulder	24lb	3,280	Infra-red homing
Milan	A/Tk	115mm	—	HEAT	Solid	660	Tripod	15lb	2,185	Wire guidance
Swingfire	A/Tk	170mm	—	HEAT	Solid	600	Box launch	62lb	4,375	Wire guidance

ABBREVIATIONS

Title column: cwt — hundredweight (112lb)
BL — breech loading – ie uses bagged charge
RBL — rifled breech loading (Armstrong)
QF — quick-firing – ie uses brass cartridge case
How — howitzer

Class column: CS — close support
GS — general support

Shell column: Missile warheads described as:
HE — high explosive
Nuc/HE — nuclear or high explosive alternatives
HEAT — High explosive, anti-tank – shaped charge

Charge column: P — black powder
C — Cordite

Mounting column: Split — split trail carriage
Siege — siege mounting on ground platform
Aux prop — auxiliary propulsion

Index

GREENLAND
NORTH AMERICA
Vancouver
Ottawa
St Johns
Halifax
Bermuda
Jamaica
West Indies
BELIZE
Georgetown
NORTHERN IRELAND
Gibraltar
Freetown
Accra
Ascension
St Helena
SOUTH AMERICA
FALKLAND IS
Stanley
CAMPAIGNS 1945-85
GARRISONS 1985
GARRISONS 1880-1920